# READING GANDHI

---

*About the Editor :*

**Dr. Surjit Kaur Jolly (b.1950)** started her career as a Lecturer of History and later became the Principal of Shyama Prasad Mukherji College, University of Delhi, Delhi. Her area of specialization includes Gender Issues, Ecology, Human Rights, Spiritualism, Comparative Religions and Gandhi.

An efficient administrator and scholar of repute, Dr. Jolly is actively associated with a number of professional organizations/ institutions in various capacities and visited USA, U.K., Germany, France, Russia, Japan and many other countries. For her outstanding contribution in the field of education and society, she received number of awards like—Eminent Personality Award (1997); Award for Contribution to Commonwealth Youth Programme; Ambassador for Peace Award; Best Administrator's Award; Bharat Jyoti Award; Award for Communal Harmony; Outstanding Achievements Award; Lifetime Achievement Award by 2004 Tertiary Education and Knowledge Summit and The Lions Club honoured her with Prashasti Patra.

Widely travelled women in India and abroad, she has presented a number of Research Papers on various contemporary themes at National and International forums. She has contributed more than fifty articles in reputed professional journals and edited volumes as also authored books.

# Reading Gandhi

*Edited by*

**Dr. S. K. Jolly**

**CONCEPT PUBLISHING COMPANY, NEW DELHI-110059**

**Cataloging in Publication Data—DK**
*Courtesy:* D.K. Agencies (P) Ltd. <docinfo@dkagencies.com>

**Reading Gandhi** / edited by S.K. Jolly.
p. cm.
Contributed articles.
Includes bibliographical references.
Includes index.
ISBN 8180693562

1. Gandhi, Mahatma, 1869-1948.—Political and social views. 2. India—Politics and government—1919-1947. I. Jolly, S. K.

DDC 954.035 22



ISBN: 81-8069-356-2 (HB)

First Published 2006



*Published and Printed by*
Ashok Kumar Mittal
**Concept Publishing Company**
A/15-16, Commercial Block, Mohan Garden
New Delhi-110059 (India)
*Phones:* 25351460, 25351794
*Fax:* 091-11-25357103
*E-mail:* publishing@conceptpub.com

## Dedicated

To

*The everlasting memory of my dear father most revered Shri Arjan Singh who has been a constant source of inspiration and energy behind all my achievements. I owe this life to him and this book is a humble step towards the service of humanity for which he always stood.*

# Preface

Humanity is undergoing almost a phase of moral collapse and ethical nihilism. Service is being given in quest of personal aggrandizement. In the era of mad rush for power and material gain, the significance of Gandhian principle lies in stressing the permanent value of self-abnegation and to enshrine the primacy of goodness and character in place of the skill of manipulation and self-assertion. The whole world is in search of an alternative. Gandhi provides an answer and an alternative, which is above all, a ray of hope, a vision for future and a blue print for individual, state and society. Gandhi's relevance is eternal. His political philosophy possesses a variety of meanings ranging from religious purity to political expediency. He sought to apply moral values to the difficult domain of politics. A *'Karma Yogi'* in the true sense of Indian tradition, his moral and political thought is intrinsically linked with his religious and ethical beliefs. Such a thought always needs serious study and more so when the world is growing more and more corrupt and inhuman everyday. The interpretations of Gandhian thought and perspective needs to be reiterated again and again till the masses learn to adopt and practice it in their thought and deed.

Since my childhood I was fascinated by Gandhi's thought and action. My family is one of those thousands of families who lived through the partition and suffered tremendous loss and dislocation. As a result, I always felt that had Gandhi fasted unto death he would have averted this tragedy. However as I grew older and read more on Gandhi, my knowledge deepened and my perspective towards Gandhi changed. I tried to live by his principles and was especially influenced by his work *My Experiment with Truth*. When UGC launched the Epoch Making Thinkers Programme, we at Shyama Prasad Mukherji College, Delhi University also submitted a proposal to establish a Gandhian Studies Centre in the college. Our proposal was accepted and we feel privileged to be given a chance to be able to spread the Gandhian message and philosophy amongst the youth and community of our nation.

As a good coincidence, Delhi University also introduced the paper 'Reading Gandhi' at the under graduate level. Both the students and the teachers were facing problems regarding study material on Gandhi. I decided to work and solve their problems at the earliest. It was not possible for me to do justice to the subject. So I decided to bring an edited volume strictly as per the syllabus. I spoke to Gandhian Scholars and explained them about the project. They responded positively. A meeting was organized and finally, it took the form of present volume.

This collective endeavour would not have been possible in the present form without the support and help from friends and well-wishers. There are a number of persons behind the scene whose ideas, comments and suggestions have been included in the present volume. I shall be failing in my duty if I do not record my appreciation to all of them.

First and foremost, I would like to express my sincere gratitude to UGC for providing Gandhi Study Centre to my college.

I am equally grateful to Prof. R.P. Misra, Prof. J. N. Sharma, Prof. R.S. Yadav, Prof. Sushma Yadav, Dr. Ashu Pasricha, Dr. Anju Jhamb, Dr. Sweta Mishra, Dr. Neeru Kapoor, Anuradha Sharma, Dr. Jita Mishra and Sunita Gulati for immediate response. Without their support this dream project could not have been achieved. No words can be adequate in acknowledging their contribution.

I express my heartfelt gratitude to Dr. Anil Dutta Mishra, Deputy Director, National Gandhi Museum, Rajghat, who helped me at every stage of this work and provided critical comments with valuable suggestions to bring this work to fruition.

As always I received full support and patience of my dear family when I was busy with completion of this volume. My special thanks are due to Shri U.S. Jolly my husband and little Amitoj S. my grandson. I appreciate and thank my children Amit, Sonali, Arshi and Prabhnoor for their patience and help.

The Librarian Ms. Bhawana and staffs of Shyama Prasad Mukherji College, Parliamentary Library, Indian Institute of Public Administration, and National Gandhi Museum and Library have rendered their valuable help and support in the completion of this book. I express my heartfelt thanks to all of them.

Last but not the least, I am grateful to Shri Ashok Kumar Mittal of Concept Publishing Company for bring out the book in nice form and that too within record time.

**S.K. Jolly**

# Contents

# List of the Contributors

**Dr. Anju Jhamb**, Reader, Department of Political Science, Shyama Prasad Mukherji College, University of Delhi, Punjabi Bagh (West), New Delhi.

**Dr. Anil Dutta Mishra**, Deputy Director, National Gandhi Museum, Rajghat, New Delhi.

**Dr. Anuradha Sharma**, Lecturer, Department of Sociology, Shyama Prasad Mukherji College, University of Delhi, Punjabi Bagh (West), New Delhi.

**Dr. Ashu Pasricha**, Department of Gandhian Studies, Panjab University, Chandigarh.

**Dr. Jai Narain Sharma**, Professor, Department of Gandhian Studies, Panjab University, Chandigarh.

**Dr. Jita Mishra**, Lecturer, Department of Political Science, Venkateshwara College, University of Delhi, Dhaula Kuan, New Delhi.

**Dr. Neeru Kapoor**, Reader, Department of Economics, Delhi College of Arts and Commerce, University of Delhi, Netaji Nagar, New Delhi.

**Dr. R.P. Misra,** Fromer Vice-Chancellor, University of Allahabad and Mahatma Gandhi National Fellow, Gandhi Smriti and Darshan Samiti, Rajghat, New Delhi.

**Dr. R.S. Yadav**, Professor, Department of Political Science, Kurukshetra University, Kurukshetra.

**Ms. Sunita Gulati,** Deputy Librarian, Indian Institute of Public Administration, I.P. Estate, New Delhi.

**Dr. Surjit Kaur Jolly,** Principal, Shyama Prasad Mukherji College, University of Delhi, Punjabi Bagh (West), New Delhi.

**Dr. Sushma Yadav**, Professor, Ambedkar Chair in Social Justice, Indian Institute of Public Administration, I.P. Estate, New Delhi.

**Dr. Sweta Mishra**, Lecturer, Department of Political Science, Shyama Prasad Mukherji College, University of Delhi, Punjabi Bagh (West), New Delhi.

# 1
# Terence Ball On Reappraising Political Theory*

*- Sushma Yadav*

## Introduction

A few years back, when I was teaching the course on western political thought, year after year, students would ask me why it was that scholars specializing in Political theory continue to write political theory continue to write about the "classics" or the "great thinkers" of the past. Why could no one had the last word on Plato, Aristotle, Kautilya, Rousseau, Mill, Marx or Gandhi? Why could we not have a definitive work about these "Classics" of politics? Why so much fuss about understanding and/or interpreting these great text in the right context? Why should we read or bother to devise this or the interpretation instead of going straight to the text and see what the number of articles and books about the great political thinkers in order to survive as academicians in the age of 'publish or perish'?

These were oft-repeated yet unsettling questions to which I would hardly provide satisfactory answers except that the eternal valve of the classic for understanding the most fundamental questions regarding the origin and nature of man, society and state. At times, I would also argue about the perennial fascination of classic works for succeeding generations of scholars, each of which reads them a new and from their own point and world-view.

Besides, it can be easily added that these classics comprise political and literary traditions, which we renew and enrich by reading, analyzing and criticizing textually and contextually.

However, these answers could neither fully satisfy my students nor me. I kept on thinking about these queries, especially

* Paraphrased version of work of Terence Ball's *Reappraising Political Theory.*

when hearing complaints about a 'canon' of works by 'dead white men' whose ideas are pickled and preserved. Such complaints continue to become more numerous as years roll down. And, surprisingly, they have a long ancestry and a fascinating familiarity.

Earlier such criticisms were heard from but rarely and mostly from 'scientifically' minded political scientists, who complained that the worship of long-dead thinkers was impeding the development of genuinely scientific theories of political behaviour. Now-a-days, however, such criticisms come more often from quarters that one would normally expect to be sympathetic to the historical study of political thought. Among them are advocates and practitioners of analytical political philosophy, some of whom see a sustained and systematic interest in the history of political thought as an antiquarian distraction and an obstacle to our thinking for ourselves in more modern and presumably more fruitful ways, about the pressing political concerns of our own time. They tend to favour, not the historical study and interpretation of old texts, but the application of economic, rational choice and game-theoretic models and theories to questions of freedom, justice, political participation, and other concerns. Or, if they do study classic works, it is to look for insights or for forerunners and ancestors who share their views. Thus (to mention merely two of the many examples) Hobbes becomes a proto-rational choice theorist and the Hobbesian state of nature a model of decision-making under conditions of perfect rationality and imperfect information; and Kautilya becomes guide to a perfect art of statesmanship and administration.

A second set of objections comes from proponents of 'multiculturalism' in the modern curriculum. We should not, they say, be in the thrall of old books by 'dead white men', since these 'canonical' texts tend to preserve and legitimize the power of living white males, and to 'marginalize' the views of women, blacks, gays, and other minorities[1]. The need imperative they feel and argue, first is to deconstruct this 'canon' in order to show how it functions to empower some while disempowering or oppressing others; and then to discard, or at least delegitimize and move to the margins, the very idea that there are 'classic' works in political theory that repay careful study by both sexes, regardless of race or nationality or sexual preference.

Such sweeping criticism has, usually, provoked protest from defenders of 'the great books' and the 'timeless truths' that they teach to the fortunate few. The disciples of the late Leo Strauss have been particularly vocal on this score and have, also, succeeded in conforming closely to the stereotype or caricature created by postmodern critics of the texts comprising the canon. Since this is a write up article about the problems and pleasures of interpreting such texts, I suppose I should begin by saying something in defence of such enterprise.

Consider first the matter of method. There is in modern academic discourse much ado about one's method or approach to the interpretation of texts. Being aware of, and attentive to, matters of method is no doubt necessary, and to proceed methodically is surely an admirable trait for a scholar (as indeed it could be for a motor mechanic or a carpenter or anyone who practices a skilled craft). The danger is that these means have a way of becoming, ends in themselves: method becomes 'methodology', and a driving force in its own right. And Terence Ball feels, but ours is for better or worse an age in which method precedes matter and sometimes pre-empts substance. If one's enquiries are to be both intelligible and legitimate, one must conform to the norms of one's own age and culture, and ours requires that one begin by describing and defending one's method or approach.[2]

Any reappraisal or interpretation of a text/theory/philosophy, textual or contextual has to begin with a belief that interpretation is both inescapable and necessary. Next, several strategies of interpretation competing for attention and even, one might say, allegiance have to be considered and even debated. One may find several of these strategies to be mutually compatible, in as much as each answers to quite different but entirely legitimate interests. Therefore, one may have to look for a problem-centred and multi-method approach to interpretation leading to reappraisals and at times revisionist critiques/interpretations.

## The Inescapability of Interpretation

Disputes over interpretation are almost certainly as old as the human species itself. Although unwritten, the first 'texts'—

omens and portents, animal bones and entrails had to be 'read' and their meaning made clear. Later still, the singers of tales told and retold stories whose meaning was interpreted and reinterpreted from one generation to another[3]. With the advent of the written word came new and even more intractable problems of interpretation, and along with it, there also emerged a written record of the sorts of difficulties faced by interpreters, commentators, and critics[4]. Aristotle's *Poetics* is perhaps the most famous, if not the earliest, example of the genre. It could not be said any more that questions of interpretation were merely pleasant pastimes enjoyed by the idle and affluent because lives were often at stake in the interpretation of legal and religious texts. What counts as a capital crime, or as heresy or blasphemy, is a matter of interpretation not only of legal or religious texts, but of the intent of the accused. Thus, questions of interpretation constitute what Terence Ball has called 'deadly hermeneutics'— deadly inasmuch as people's lives, liberties, and happiness hang in the balance.[5]

Another feature of this long history of ideas is the periodic and recurring call to 'get back to basics'— to the text, the author, the author's intention, or whatever—and eschew interpretation altogether. This is the call made with almost predictable regularity by fundamentalists in law and literature as well as in religion. The law or the scripture, they say, has become encrusted with interpretation, each successive layer of which skews or distorts the original or 'true' meaning of the text and/or its author and in the case of Holy Scripture, Author. The first task must accordingly be to undo the damage done by earlier commentators. It is in this context that Luther claims interpretation to be 'the scum of holy scripture' and calls for a return to the 'straight road' of scripture, unadorned and undistorted by commentary or interpretation. He explains in the preface to his translation of the New Testament that his own preface is necessary only because earlier interpreters 'have perverted the understanding of Christian people till they have no inkling of the meaning of the gospel.... This distressing state of affairs calls for some sort of guidance by way of preface, to free the ordinary man from his false though familiar notions [and] to lead him into the straight road.[6] The irony Ball feels is, that Luther's fulmination against interpretation is itself inescapably interpretive, inasmuch as it amounts to a defence of one kind of interpretive strategy against other alternatives.[7]

Even now, in one version or another, variations on Luther's complaint can be heard not only from religious fundamentalists, but from judges, lawyers, and literary critics. In the United States some conservative jurists have called even for a return to the 'original intent' of the Founders. And among literary critics some, such as Susan Sontag, take their stand 'against interpretation'.[8]

But surely it is as absurd to be 'against' as it is to be 'for' interpretation, much less to 'love' it, as Professor Fish professes to do.[9] Whether one likes or dislikes interpretations is quite beside the point, for one really has no choice in the matter. The decision to interpret or not to interpret is not an option open to human beings, but a requirement that comes, so to speak, with the territory of being human. For our language-using and meaning-seeking species, interpretation is inescapable. Heidegger put the point with absolute clarity when he said that for human beings interpretation is an ontological category. And Gadamer has underscored the point by saying that hermeneutics—the art and practice of interpretation—is a matter not of method but of ontological necessity.[10]

The world we inhabit and the texts we read, says Gadamer, are never raw sense-data or some ideal *objet **trouve*** but are 'always already' interpreted and invested with meaning. We are born and grow into a world made meaningful by the language we speak and the traditions we inherit. And these in turn supply us with our own culturally and historically specific standpoint or set of 'prejudices' acting as the vantage-point from which we make sense of our world and the creatures, texts, signs, and artifacts that comprise the world for us. But Gadamer also insists that this standpoint, far from being static and unchanging, is historically situated and subject to criticism and alteration. Indeed, the central thrust of Gadamer's hermeneutics is that, while we necessarily begin with our own present-day prejudices, we need not end with them unchanged and forever intact. We extend or expand our present horizon of understanding by encountering and attempting to understand prejudices and practices that at first sight seems strange or alien.

By encountering and trying to come to some understanding of the alien and unfamiliar, we gain a better sense of the historically specific limitations of our own parochial horizon. We attempt to make a distant horizon compatible with our own. In thus effecting, or at least attempting, a **'fusion of horizons'** (Horizont verschmelzung), we at once appreciate our distance from and kinship with those whose perspectives differ markedly from our own. And in so doing, we also come to appreciate our common, if differently expressed, humanity. Thus, the art of interpretation, according to Gadamer, is an essential part of the art of living the life of a human being.

This art, however, is not a luxury but a necessity. We cannot dispense with interpretation or get by without it. As communicating and interacting social agents, each of us must in our daily lives interpret the meaning of the actions, practices, and utterances of other people. Suppose, for instance, that I see coming towards me a large man, knife in hand and wearing a blood-smeared smock. How I respond depends on how I interpret the meaning of what I see. Placing that sight in a larger interpretive context constituted by certain customs, conventions, and social roles—this is a meat market, that man is the butcher, and I am a customer—permits me to arrive at a correct interpretation and to act accordingly. Instead of fleeing in terror, if engage in a series of socially appropriate and recognizable acts like placing an order, making a purchase, paying for it, things remain clearer. Of course, such aspects of the everyday taken-for-granted 'life-world' are ordinarily unproblematic in so far as they are pre-interpreted; that is, we do not see a situation and then interpret it, but see and interpret it as a single seamless activity.[11]

However, matters are much more difficult, if we find ourselves in an alien age or culture with whose concepts, categories, customs, and practices we are completely unfamiliar. In such situations we are often at a loss to know what is being done, why it is so or what its meaning may be. We, therefore, need a 'translation', which is neither more nor less than an interpretation and, moreover effected by fusing that culture's horizon of meaning, with ours. A good translation or interpretation is one that decreases the strangeness of the sight, making it more familiar and accessible to an otherwise puzzled or perplexed observer. To provide such cross-cultural translations is usually the aim of the anthropologist, among others.

The historian of political thought also finds him or herself in a situation analogous to that of the anthropologist studying an alien culture.[12] The artifacts or 'texts' produced in political cultures preceding and differing from our own do not readily reveal their meanings even to the most careful reader. To read a text 'over and over again', as some advise, is no doubt necessary.[13] But it is hardly sufficient to enable us to arrive at anything like an adequate understanding of what, say for example, Machiavelli meant by Virtue or what Rousseau was trying to do in devising his scheme for a religion civile or what Vico and Marx meant in saying that human beings 'make' their own history or what Gandhi wanted to convey in '*Hind Swaraj*'. To try to make sense of such terms and actions requires that we interpret their meaning. There is no understanding without interpretation, and no interpretation without the possibility of multiple understandings or/and misunderstandings.

There is hardly a neutral standpoint or Archimedean point from which to interpret and appraise any text, classic or otherwise. All interpretation implies, and originates in, some vantage-point or standpoint or to use Gadamer's **term** 'prejudice'. Every interpretation, in short, implies an interest not simply in the sense that one is 'interested; in an author of text, but rather in the deeper or the transcendental sense that an interest provides the ground for and possibility of an interpretation—a standpoint from which enquiry can begin and interpretation proceed. These interests are usually multiple and varied. One's interests can be contemporary: what (for example) can Gandhi teach us about liberty? Or they may be more historical: why did Koutilya argument in 'Arthashastra' take the form they did? Who were Gandhi's main targets, and who are his intended audience? Or one's interests may be more narrowly linguistic or literary: what tropes and rhetorical stratagems did Gandhi's employ, and with what effect? What oppositions and antinomies does Gandhi's set up ('liberty' *vs*. 'authority'; self *vs*. other-regarding acts) and what ones does he deny or explicitly eschew ('liberty' *vs*. 'necessity', modernity *vs*.

traditions)? Or one's interests may be logical or philosophical: is Gandhi's argument in '*Hindi Swaraj*' or the curse of untouchability internally coherent and logically consistent? Are there gaps or lacunae in the argument? Does Gandhi's construct a compelling case?

None of these interests necessarily excludes the others. But they do construct what will count as a problem, what constitutes an interesting or important question, and what method might be most appropriate and fruitful for dealing with these matters. One would not, for example, assess the logical adequacy of Gandhi's argument by examining his use of tropes. Nor would one be able to answer questions posed from a historical interest or vantage-point by looking only at the logical structure of his argument.

One's method, in short, is dictated by the problem at hand and the interest that one seeks to serve. Thus all interpretations are, in a word, interest-laden. And because they necessarily answer to some interest or other, they cannot be normatively neutral or value-free. Or, to put the point more plainly, all interpretation implies appraisal; and all reinterpretation implies reappraisal. What is in these instances reappraised is not merely the text and author in question, but the adequacy or inadequacy of other interpretations that seek to satisfy a similar interest. Indeed, one's own attempts at interpretation and reappraisal typically begin with some sort of confusion arising in one's reading the text or in going through various interpretations of it.

That much, at least, seems to be fairly obvious and unproblematic. But by what means are we, as students of political theory, to interpret, criticize, and perhaps even appropriate for our own use the texts that comprise our contested canon or 'currency' or 'tradition of discourse'?[14] These are contentious questions, and one has to accept that the terrain on which they are addressed is hotly contested. There are many contestants the wards of Ball, One part of the battlefield is occupied by neo-Marxists, an adjoining part by 'realists', another by 'assorted post-structuralists' and 'deconstructionists', yet another by 'Straussians', and still another by the 'new historians' of political thought.[15] Each takes a distinctive approach to the history of political thought, and each is highly critical of the others.

Marxists interpret all political theories, past and present — save their own, perhaps—as ideological masks concealing and/or justifying the domination of one class by another.[16] Realists, some of whom are Marxists of one or another sort, view political ideas and theories as playing a causal role in reproducing and legitimating the structures comprising the social world[17]. Poststructuralists would like to deconstruct works by this or that author in order to show how his search for 'foundations' was actually an arbitrary construct it is such construct, multiculturalists critics contend, that contributed to oppression of one or another sort (women by men, blacks by whites, etc.).

Straussians, however, claim that a canon of works by Plato and a handful of other authors contain the Whole Truth about politics, a Truth which is eternal, unchanging, and accessible only to the fortunate few.[18] The 'new historians' of the 'Cambridge School', on the contrary, tend to view texts in political theory as forms of political action, grasping the point or meaning of which requires that one recover the intentions of the actor/author as well as the linguistic resources and conventions available to him or her.[19]

These are just brief outlines of the different broad perspective available to interpret and reappraise political ideas. Such sketches do not do justice to the often-at rich and suggestive insights offered by proponents of these perspectives. But they do suggest something of the diversity of views and vantage-points from which we reinterpret the meaning and reappraise the value of a rich and varied heritage.

## Strategies of Interpretation

There are number of and fault-lines that separate the several modern theories of interpretation. One of the most obvious of these is concerning the question of authorial Intent. Some of the most perplexing and recurring questions in legal, literary, and other kinds of interpretation are these: Can we identify an author's intention in writing this or that work? If we can, should we? What weight, if any, is to be assigned to an author's intentions? Have we discovered the 'meaning' of a text or more typically a particular passage, once we discover what the author intended or meant to do in writing it? Or is the meaning to be found in (the reading of) the text itself? Or do we forget the author's intent altogether and look instead at the consequence—often unintended—of an utterance or argument or text?

These are not abstractly academic questions. For example, some American jurists and constitutional scholars contend that the discovery of the 'original intent' of the framers of the Constitution settles the matter of meaning, once and for all. And a similar argument is advanced, albeit in different ways and for different reasons, by Quentin Skinner and other Cambridge new historians. It can be argued that the proponents of 'original intent' are wrong about legal or constitutional interpretation, which differs in important respects from interpretation in the history of political thought.[20] Here, however, one can try to defend the new historians against an oft-heard criticism—criticisms to which they have not been able to offer a wholly satisfactory reply.

For instance, one criticism leveled repeatedly against Skinner and the new historians of political thought is that the recovery of an author's intention is unimportant or irrelevant, even if possible in principle. The argument of these critics is that even if we accept Skinner's claim that political writing is a species of action, the fact remains that these sorts of actions—like all human actions—produce consequences unintended, unforeseen, and perhaps even unforeseeable by the actor/author. Hence, to recover an author's aims or intentions, even if possible, is beside the point[21]. The history of political thought is, or at any rate should be, the story of the consequences of authorial actions. It should, also, be about the uses to which a writer's ideas were later put by actors whose interpretation of the meaning of a term be it some utterance, phrase, passage, or entire text may not and need not accord with the authors own intentions. Or, to put it in other words, the historian's task is to trace the unintended consequences of purposive political action, which in this instance is the action of writing a political tract or treatise.[22]

While it is true that actions, including the act of writing, often produce unintended consequences, the contention that intentions are irrelevant or do not matter simply does not follow.

It is so because logically one cannot validly contention that a certain consequence X was unintended unless one can do two things. One must first be able to show what the author did intend or could conceivably have intended; and then one must be able to demonstrate that X differs from the end(s) that the author intended or could conceivably have intended to bring about. In other words, the very identification of a consequence as 'unintended' requires that one be able to identify what the author's intentions actually are, or were. Hence, it cannot be presumed or concluded that reference to an author's intention(s) is irrelevant or beside the point—particularly for anyone wishing to write the history of political thought or problems or episodes therein as the story of 'unintended consequences'!

This does not, in any case, mean that the historian of political thought should cease enquiries once he/she has succeeded in identifying an author's ideological-linguistic context and the intention(s) that emerge as possible or likely. That may only be taken to show what a term or utterance, or even an entire text, 'meant' for its author, and perhaps for his or her audience; and so it may help to recover the 'historical identity' of the text;[23] but it can hardly be taken as sufficient to show how it was received and interpreted by subsequent reader-authors and their audiences. Here, the 'reception' or 'reader-response' theories of interpretation can become significant.[24]

One has to keep in mind that text is not merely an artefact produced by an author; it is also a communication received by a reader. Its meaning at least in some part has to be the product of this process–the 'fusion of horizons' which can, at once be illumination and confusing for readers, interpreters and commentators. It is illuminating, inasmuch as it suggests that there is a vast distance to be bridged. But the metaphor is also confusing, in that a 'horizon' in the visual-perspective sense is one thing, not two, and therefore, not the sort of thing that could be joined or 'fused'.[25]

However, Alan Ryan seems to offer a more prosaic, and perhaps better, way of putting the matter. He says that in reading an earlier work of political theory we are usually tugged in two different directions at once. On the one hand, we want to know what the author was up to and what he or she meant in saying something. But, on the other hand, we also have to recognize that:

> "Once the essay or book in which we are interested has been put before the public, it takes on a life of its own. Whatever the copyright laws, an author has only a limited control over his own writings. What he writes will have implications which he did not see—implications in the narrow sense of more or less logical inferences from what he says to the consequences of what he says.... Works outlive their authors, and take on lives their writers might be perturbed to see."

As 'the most obvious instance' of this process, Ryan cites 'the history of how Machiavelli's major works were read, from 1520 to the 1980s with a sidelong glance at marx's (mis) reading of Hegel.[26]

Infact, what Ryan seems to refer to above are some of the manifold ways in which purposive political actions can and typically do, produce unintended consequences. And certainly these do present problems for the historian who takes an internationalist tack towards textual interpretation. These problems are not, however, insoluble or insurmountable, and need not pose any grave difficulty for an approach to interpretation via authorial intention. To appreciate just how and why this might be so, may be, one has to let us look outside the immediate purview of political theory.

'Suppose I arrive home late one evening. Entering my house, I flip the light switch and several things happen. The light comes on, as I intended that it should. But the light's coming on also wakes the cat, alerts a burglar in the adjoining room, annoys a neighbour, causes the dial in the electric meter to rotate, and raises my electric bill. Flipping the switch is my 'basic action'.[27] The light's coming on is my action under an internationalist description; that is what I was doing, or trying to do, when I flipped the switch. I did not intend, and could not have intended, to wake the cat or to frighten the burglar, since I was in no position to know that the cat was asleep or that the burglar was hiding in the adjoining room. And yet I did, i.e. brought about, all these things, not all of which were intended but all of which were made possible by my acting intentionally.

The above example beautiful and quite unambiguously depicts the difference between intended and unintended consequences of action.

The performance of a political action—including the act of writing— is not much unlike flipping the light switch. The basic action of putting pen to paper can be given an internationalist description: the author was doing, or attempting to do, a certain thing--to defend or to criticize royal absolutism, to justify or decry democracy/modernity to promote or oppose religious toleration, or any number of other things. But an author's action may well produce unintended consequences. His argument might, for example, later be used for purposes that the author did not address, and did not or perhaps could not have intended or even foreseen. The concepts used in constructing that argument, and the linguistic conventions according to which it was constructed, may well be misunderstood or deliberately ignored by later writers who wish to appropriate, extend, or perhaps amend what they understood/ took this earlier writer to have been doing. Some of these misunderstandings and/or rank misrepresentations may prove fruitful for other actors writers with their other, doubtless very different, aims and agendas. Two examples might serve to make this point clearer.

Some modern feminists have interpreted Locks as a proto-feminist, inasmuch as he was, as they are, critical of patriarchalism. Thus Melissa Butler, for one, contends that Locke's critique of Filmer's Patriarchia in the Two Treatises lays the groundwork, as it were, for modern feminist critiques of male dominion or 'patriarchy'.[28] Locke may himself be surprised to find himself enlisted as an early forerunner of feminism, and he might well be appalled at the prospect. But, while it would be mistake to claim that, in criticizing Filmer, Locke meant or even could conceivably have intended to add arguments to the arsenal of modern feminists, there is nothing necessarily wrong or illegitimate in taking the view that arguments constructed for one purpose may subsequently be put to some altogether different use. And this, most probably, has happened in the case of Locke's critique of patriarchalism. Locke has, as it were, no copyright or exclusive title to his ideas and arguments. They are part of the public domain, and may be interpreted, appropriated, and applied in almost any way by any political actor theorist/critic who finds them congenial or useful.

The second example comes from Margaret Leslie's critique of Gandhi and her defence of 'anachronistic' readings of earlier thinkers.[29] Strained analogies, and even anachronisms, may, in the hands of an ingenious writer such as Antonio Gramsci, prove to be politically persuasive when addressed to a certain sort of audience. In redescribing the Communist Party as the 'modern prince', Gramsci adapted and made creative use of what he took to be Machiavelli's notion of a ruthless and all powerful Principe. On Gramsci's reading, the Communist Party, like Machiavelli's prince, must be prepared to use guile, cunning, deceit, and violence to achieve worthy ends. By substituting 'Party' for 'prince', Gramsci was able to adapt Machiavelli's arguments to a more modern and distinctly different context. That Gramsci's use of Machiavelli's text was admittedly anachronistic is beside the point. As a political actor, Gramsci had, and used, the political equivalent of poetic licence.

Skinner's contention broadly, is that no such license is granted to historians of political thought. If we, as historians, are to understand the meaning that particular terms, utterances, claims, and arguments had for certain authors and their audiences, then surely we must, at a minimum, know something about the linguistic conventions of the day and the political concepts, languages, or idioms available to them. Thus it would be important to note, for example that the modern concept of the 'political party', as understood by Gramsci and his audience, was not available to Machiavelli and his contemporaries.[30] One might also note that certain key concepts in Machiavelli's vocabulary, such as fortuna, have no place in, and are arguably at odds with, Gramsci's own rather more deterministic Marxian framework.

To make these observations is of course to take nothing away from Gandhi, who wrote not as a scholar but as a practicing social reformer and activist who was in Skinner's sense an 'innovating ideologist'.[31] Gandhi, in other words, used an existing and already well-know stock of concepts and images to re describe and lend legitimacy to an institution widely regarded as suspect. An interpretation like Gandhi may be adjudged good (indigenous innovative, ingenious, path-breaking, persuasive, popular etc.) on political grounds even as it is adjudged deficient on scholarly grounds and *vice versa*.

We must remember that political actors, past and present, are most likely to fight conceptual ideological battles by at times even misrepresenting opponent's views, constructing arguments, and using almost any rhetorical weapon that comes to hand. And success in such endeavors depends, as often as not, upon one side's skill or sheer good luck in hitting upon an illuminating image or telling metaphor to make its case persuasive or at least palatable.[32] But it is also important to note that such arguments and appeals must be tailored to the tastes, standards, and outlook of the audience at which they are aimed. If one fails to take one's audience's standards into account, one runs the grave risk of having one's actions viewed as unintelligible and/or illegitimate. Both, intelligibility and legitimacy, are if for political agents, considerations of utmost importance. As skinner notes, the problem facing an agent who wishes to legitimise what he is doing at the same time as gaining what he wants cannot simply be the instrumental problem of tailoring his normative language in order to fit his projects. It must in part be the problem of tailoring his projects in order to fit the available normative language.'[33]

However revolutionary the ideologist... he will nevertheless be committed, once he has accepted the need to legitimate his behaviour, to attempting to show that some of the existing range of favourable evaluative-descriptive terms can somehow be applied as apt descriptions of his own apparently untoward actions. Every revolutionary is to this extent obliged to march backward into battle.[34]

At the same time, however, a political actor/author– Particularly one on whom we retrospectively bestow the honorific title of political theorist–does things not only with language, but to language in that his or her actions produce changes sometimes intended, sometimes not, in the vocabulary available to his or her audience and to subsequent speakers of the language.[35] Through the use of argument, analogy, metaphor, and other means, he or she may be able to alter the language of description and appraisal in certain ways, perhaps by extending the meaning of a term, or even by coining a new one. But any author daring to do so is likely to proceed cautiously and perhaps even apologetically, as Locke does, for example, in the Second Treatise, 'it may perhaps be censured as an impertinent criticism in a discourse of this nature', he writes, ' to find fault with words and names that have obtained in the World: And yet possibly it may not be amiss to offer new ones when the old are apt to lead Men into mistakes'....[36] The concept in question is 'paternal power', which in the political-linguistic context of late-seventeenth-century England was being put to a particular political use, namely justifying royal absolutism Locke's refutation of arguments in favour of royal absolutism relies rather less upon the coining of new terms than upon showing that 'paternal power', as used by Filmer and other apologists, was by the logical and linguistic standards of the day contradictory and incoherent, rested on misreading or misunderstandings of scripture.

Many other examples could be offered, but it seems quite clear that the history of political thought is in no small part the story of one theorist's commentary on, or criticisms of, a predecessor or a contemporary and among the most powerful weapons in any theorist's arsenal are argument, like Locke's against Filmer, whose objective is to show that an opponent has otherwise contradicted himself. Such Socratic questioning and criticism has been and remains, the political theorist's stock in trade.[37] In so far as its practitioners attend closely and critically to matters of logic and language, political theory is at once a form of political action and a species of philosophical enquiry. But the latter, far from being separate from the former, is an integral part of the enterprise. And both in turn play an integral role in the process of political innovation and conceptual change.[38] As Alasdair Macintyre aptly observes:

> 'Philosophical inquiry itself plays a part in changing moral [and political] concepts. It is not that we have a straightforward history of moral concepts and then a separate and secondary history of philosophical comment. For to analyze a concept philosophically may often be to assist in its transformation

by suggesting that it needs revision, or is discredited in some way. Philosophy leaves everything as it is–except concepts. And since to possess a concept involves behaving or being able to behave in certain ways in certain circumstances, to alter concepts, whether by modifying existing concepts or by making new concepts available or by destroying old ones, is to alter behaviour. A history, which takes this point seriously, which is concerned with the role of philosophy in relation to actual conduct, cannot be philosophically neutral.'[39]

It is in part the hybrid character of political theory that makes its history, or any particular episode therein, so difficult to interpret and so instructive to study and reflect upon.

There are many different ways of interpreting and understanding what earlier thinkers were doing, and why, and what consequences (intended and unintended) followed from their actions. Let us try to sketch the outlines of the pluralistic and problem-centered approach taken in the present volume.

In trying to understand any aspect of or episode in the history of political thought, one does not and cannot return to the scene directly. The way back has been illuminated–or littered–by an intervening history of commentary and interpretation of both the political and scholarly varieties. In reading Filmer, for example, one cannot but be aware of the uses to which Patriarcha (1680) was put some three decades after his death by defenders of royal absolutism, nor can one be blind to or uninterested in the criticisms that Locke levelled against these latter-day Filmerians. These subsequent uses, interpretations, and criticism have, for us, come to be part of what Patriarcha 'means' and the place it occupies in the history of political thought.[40] These are facts about an author named Filmer and a text bearing the title Patriarcha. That they emerged or developed only after the text's publication and well after its author's death does not detract from of impugn their status as facts: that, on the contrary, is the nature of historical fact.[41]

But no reading is innocent or naïve; it is not a direct return to the text and/or context but is filtered through, and coloured by, other readers' reading. The methodological moral to be drawn from this is that we need to be aware of the ways in which our own readings are apt to be beholden to someone else's–and not so that we can be grateful to them, but so that we can critically assess and perhaps disagree and differ with them, in the hope of overcoming the limitations that they impose upon our understanding of (say) Locke or Rousseau or Gandhi. We need; in short, periodically to reappraise the value and validity of the interpretations we have inherited from earlier writers.

Perhaps surprisingly, this task is in one crucial respect like that of the natural scientist. As Imre Lakatos noted, a scientific theory offers a framework for interpreting 'the data'. But these data do not exist wholly independently of the theory: which data are to count as (relevant) data are determined, in part, by the theory (or interpretive framework) itself. Even our most direct observations are impregnated with expectations generated by the theory we hold. Thus there is no neutral or natural dividing line between 'observational' and 'theoretical' statements. All observation is 'theory-laden' and involves interpretation of some kind. But if that is true, how can a scientist favour one theory or interpretation over another? Is no theory better or worse than any other? The answer, according to Lakatos is that science is a search for truth, and this search takes the form of a 'three-cornered fight' between the data and two (or more) competing interpretations of it. Competing theories are not redundancies or luxuries, but are necessary to the enterprise of science itself.[42] So, too, are competing interpretations of texts essential to the enterprise of political theory.

We approach a text, in part, by way of other readings or interpretations of it, against which we counterpoise our own or someone else's alternative reading. Out of these competing readings comes a new, and mostly better, interpretation. This process is sometimes aided by the appearance of better and more accurate versions of a particular text, and even by the discovery of new, non-textual 'data'–such as, for example, the fact that Marx did not try to dedicate Das Kapital to Darwin.[43] But, these exceptions aside, we more typically begin by puzzling over a text, aided–or, we may come to belive, hindered–by someone else's attempt to make sense of the same work. And we come to reinterpret the former by taking issue with the latter.

Lakatos's three cornered fight is characteristic of all interpretive enquiry and has indeed served as an implicit standard among political theorists for quite some time. We have alluded already to Locke's critique of Filmer–a critique necessitated by the use to which Filmer's text was then being put by proponents of royal absolutism. One could also add many other examples including Gandhi's critique to modern civilization Marx's critique of capitalism, which proceeded by way of a critique of political economy, inasmuch as Adam Smith, David Ricardo, and others had supplied some of the concepts and categories in which capitalist production and distribution was redescribed, defended–and, not least, legitimated–in supposedly scientific terms.

But such multi-cornered fights are fought not only by political theorists turned activists, but by academic political theorists as well: the form of the fight, remains the same, whether the subject be science, political action, or political theory. For scholars the fight must be fair and be conducted according to the academic equivalent of the Marquis of Queensbury rules. One may not, for example, deliberately misquote or misleadingly paraphrase an author; one must not conceal or suppress counter-evidence that might weigh against one's interpretation; and so on.

These rules for fighting fair do not always or necessarily apply to political actors and activists themselves. The hermeneutical battles waged by innovating ideologists are often far from fair, are rarely scholarly, and are typically conducted by almost any means available. All these were primarily political rather than scholarly works; none can be trusted as reliable guides to the thinkers about whose views they were writing. And that is simply because politics is not scholarship, neither is scholarship politics. It seems to me a mistake–and an inexcusable conceit–to say, as some now do, that all scholarship is somehow 'political' or is 'itself' politics practiced by other means. That view tends to demeans both politics and scholarship.

However, this is not to say that a scholar's motives must not be political, it is only to emphasize that the methods and results of his/her researches must be judged according to scholarly standards, not political ones. The aim of scholarship is to seek and to tell the truth, as best one can discern it, and not to promote any particular partisan cause. Of course, if telling the truth about (say) the sources of Mill's feminism should in some way promote (say) the cause of feminism, well and good: but, as a scholar, one should not suppress or fail to tell the truth simply because one's cause might somehow be sullied or undermined.

One may take up a topic or a thinker out of political interest or ideological preference without thereby forfeiting one's scholarly credentials, indeed, it is probably fair so say that most students of political theory, myself included, have been motivated by political concerns.[44] But the worth of one's work is to be judged, not according to its 'political correctness' (or lack thereof), but according to its scholarly (in)adequacy. One historian of political thought may agree with another about politics but disagree strongly about the other's use of evidence and argument.

It is here, and on these grounds, that the three-cornered fight is waged. It may be, and must often is, a friendly fight between cordial combatants. But, friendly or not, the form is always the same: one interpretation of 'the data' is challenged by another, and both are put to test according to the available evidence (textual, linguistic, historical, etc.). But, since such evidence is rarely, if ever, self-evident, it requires interpretation to decipher/uncover tease out its meaning and significance for and bearing on the problem at hand. And for this purpose a rival interpretation is indispensable. The second, or rival, account proceeds not only as reference to these data, but also by way of critique of the first's interpretation of it. This critique is not a distraction or an unfortunate necessity, but is instead an essential feature of the history of political thought.

This is exactly the form in which Macpherson, for example, makes his case against the interpretations supplied by commentators who sketch a Picture of the tolerant, democratic and 'liberal' Locke. And the critics who have tried to recover the historical identity of the **Two Treatises** have worked their way back to Locke's texts and context by way of a critique of Macpherson and other interpreters.[45] Although this is not a move supported in the abstract methodological manifestos of the new historians, it is nevertheless one made with thorough regularity in their actual practice. Their programme, in practice, is not a 'fundamentalist' one deliberately avoiding any reference to an intervening history of interpretation, but is, on the contrary, one which takes off from–by taking issue with—prevailing interpretations that they consider to be defective or deficient. We see this kind of three-cornered fight even in the earlier and more militant phase of the 'new history' of political thought.

Consider, for example, John Dunn's preface to the Political Thought of John Locke (1969). His is, he says, a 'historical... account, of what Locke was talking about, not a doctrine written (perhaps unconsciously) by him in a sort of invisible ink which becomes apparent only in the writings of a succession of determined philosophers.

Yet the interpretive principles prescribed in Dunn's highly puritanical preface actually make possible the richness, subtlety, and suggestiveness of the reading of the Two Treatises that follows– a reading motivated by, and mounted against, what he takes to be the misreadings offered by Macpherson and Strauss, amongst others.

Not that, Dunn is alone in following this route. Quentin Skinner's manifesto of 1969, prescribing what historians of political thought ought (not) to do, proceeds by way of a critique of the ways in which historians have heretofore carried their trade. And elsewhere–for example in his enquiry into the ideological context of Hobbes's theory of obligation skinner makes his case, not by discarding intervening interpretations altogether and somehow returning directly to the original text and its context, but by way of a critique of contemporary interpretations of Hobbes's account of obligation, such as those proposed by Taylor and Warrender, amongst others. Exactly the same sort of move is made in his other historical work, including his studies of Machiavelli, More and other seminal figures in early modern political thought.[46]

What are we to make of this? If, we are to understand the pronouncements and the practices of the new historians. We must, I think, view them in much the same way that they view the writings and actions of historical actors. Their methodological prescriptions must be understood, in part, as polemics directed against a certain sort of historian or commentator. On the one side those 'textualists' who read a piece of political theory as a timeless text of the sort imagined and idealized by New Critics who held that historical context and authorial intention are utterly irrelevant (indeed they claimed that to look for meaning in authorial intention is to commit something they called 'the intentional fallacy').[47] On the other side one finds 'contextualists' including conservative Namierites and radical Marxists who, despite their differences, are alike in agreeing that 'ideas' are epiphenomenal, mere flotsam floating on an eternal sea of self–or class or party or national interest.

The purpose here, however, is neither to expound nor to defend the views of the historians but to suggest several affinities between their approach and the tack taken in the present volume. Foremost among these are the following. We are alike in agreeing about the importance, indeed the indispensability, of the intellectual, political, and linguistic contexts in which political texts appear and do their work. These contexts, in which a text was composed, but also the successive contexts in which it was received, read, interpreted, criticized, reread, and reinterpreted. These we might call the context of a text's composition and the subsequent contexts of its reception, respectively.

From this more complex conception of context, several implications follow. For one, authorial intentions, although important, are not in all cases all-important. For certain purposes one may wish to discover, recover, and restate an author's intentions so as to show what he or she was trying to convey in using a certain word or phrase, or constructing a particular argument in a particular way, or even composing an entire treatise. This is especially important in those instances in which one seeks to understand an author as a political actor. But sometimes we are less interested in Locke, say, than in what subsequent author–actors made of Locke's text, and quite possibly in ways that Locke would not or even could not have intended, did not foresee, and almost certainly would not have approved of political actions–including the act of writing–often produce unintended consequences. And this again for the simple reason that the very identification of an outcome as unintended logically requires that we be able, first, to describe the original intention and, secondly, show that the outcome differs from the one initially intended.

More than that, we are less likely to be interested in authors, tests, and/or contexts per se than we are in particular problems that arise as we attempt to understand them. As a rule we do not come to Plato, Locke, Rousseau or even Gandhi wanting to know all about them or their texts or their times, but because we are puzzled or troubled about something on which a certain sort of enquiry might shed some light. Did Locke really mean to defend the property rights of a rising bourgeoisie? How are we to understand the role of religion civil in Rousseau's Contract social? What are the probable sources of John Stuart Mill's feminist sympathies? What was the nature of Marx's debt to Darwin and what are its implications for his view of science and social theory? Did Gandhi really think the Indian economy could be made heal their through rural and cottage industries?

Such problems can come from any source and be of almost any sort. One might be interested in Mill because one is sympathetic to or highly critical of the liberal tradition, or because one believes that liberty is under threat and that Mill might shed some light on our modern predicament. Or one might wish to assess the (in)adequacy of the Western and liberal conception of tolerance in the light of some contemporary question or issue, such as the Salman Rushdie affair, and find it both necessary and desirable to reread and reappraise Locke on toleration and Mill on liberty.[48] In short the problem-driven 'context of discovery' is wide open, and the 'context of justification' is comparatively restricted.[49] The problems can come from anywhere and be addressed via a variety of strategies; but the (in)adequacy of the solutions must be assessed according to more stringent scholarly criteria.

The historical study of political theory is, in sum, a problem-solving activity. It takes other interpretations as alternative solutions to some puzzle or problem, and then goes on to assess their adequacy *vis-à-vis* each other and in relation to one's own proposed solution. Interpretation is indeed a three cornered fight. Hence we cannot but take others' interpretations into account, reappraising their adequacy and value, as I attempt to do in the present volume.

This process of reappraisal is not incidental to the practice of political theory but is instead an indispensable, if not indeed defining, feature of theorizing. This craft is in an important sense backward looking. Political theory, more than any other vocation, takes its own past to be an essential part of its present. Its past includes a history not only of theorizing, of great (and not-so-great) books, but of commentary on and interpretation of those thinkers and tests.[50] It is through the latter that the former are reconsidered, criticized, and reevaluated–in short, reappraised. One might even put the point more strongly by saying that the seminal works of political theory are kept alive and vivid–keep their 'classic' status, not being worshipped at academic shrines but rather through carefully and critically reappraisal.[51]

It might, therefore, appear that political theory, at least as regards its reappraisive function, is a benign and harmless enterprise and the modern student of the subject a mildly curious creature in the academic zoo. Yet political theory is not without critics from various quarters, some of whom are occasionally quite vociferous. Some political scientists think of the political theorists in their midst as historians or, perhaps, philosophers. Historians, however, may not wish to claim them as colleagues, and philosophers might not understand political theorists' interest in history and, stranger still, in politics. All, moreover, are suspicious of the claim that thinkers long dead might somehow be connected with, and might in some respects illuminate, the darker recesses of our present condition.

Such suspicion sometimes erupts into open hostility. During the 'behavioural revolution of the 1950s and 1960s, many political scientists went on the offensive against the aliens in their midst. Political theory was charged with being antiquarian, non-empirical, and, worst of all normative'—that is concerned with the 'values' or subjective preferences of this or that long - dead thinker and/ or his or her present-day interpreter. This bill of indictment, as I attempt to show in Chapter 11, was predicated on the philosophy of sciences and a conception of cognitive meaningfulness that has long since been repudiated by philosophers of science. But academic political theorists were also attacked from the other side by critics who claimed that the 'classics' of political theory were the antiquated, sexist, racist, homophobic texts of dead white men; all sharing the aim of perpetuating and legitimating the dominance of themselves and their descendants. There was accordingly, a call to disavow, if not eliminate from the curriculum, the 'classics', the canon of 'Great books' that, when read and taken seriously by students, can only serve to justify the unjustifiable.

Since the present work is intended, in part, to be an answer to contextuailse, the classics and political theory therein, I would say that I do not think that the **charge** is merely ridiculous or entirely if founded. There are, if not texts, then certainly ways of reading or interpreting them, that give aid and comfort to those who wish the worst for some of their fellow human beings. One need only think, for example, of the ways in which Hitler and the Nazis used (and arguably abused) the works of Nietzsche, or Stalin the works of Marx, to justify genocidal policies. But it is no less important to note that the disclosure and criticism of such misunderstandings is itself an integral part of political theory. Far from being the sort of hagiographic exercise portrayed by some of its present-day detractors, the study of political theory is, above all, a relentlessly critical enterprise. As such, one of its essential features is its attention to the ways in which authors and texts are appropriated and used-or, as often as not, misappropriated and abused-by would-be defenders or disciples.

Five points merit particular mention in appreciating any perspective which can be adopted in reappraising political theory. The first and most important, as I have ncted already, is that of choosing a method. A method of interpretation varies with and is usually dictated by the particular interpretive problem being addressed, and not the other way round. A method is not like a stretch sock: one size does not fit all feet. Nor, by the same token, can any single method or approach-textual, contextual, Marxist, realist, Strauss Ian, or whatever–possibly illuminate, much less resolve, every conceivable problem of interpretation.

Second, these interpretive problems can come from any source, whether historical, contemporary, literary, political, or whatever. These problems provide the interest or vantage point from which interpretation proceeds.In the present volume my enquiries proceed not only from problems within the text, but, no less importantly, from questions raised, and interpretations advanced and defended, by subsequent commentators, often in idioms that were unavailable to the author. Charges that the theories of Plato or Rousseau were 'totalitarian' or that Bentham was a 'feminist' fall under this heading. Although anachronistic, these characterizations are not necessarily illegitimate. They may be useful and illuminating in some contexts but not in others, and a stimulus to the reinterpretation and reappraisal of a theorist and his or her work.

Third, it may be worth trying, in so far as possible and where appropriate, to place the text within two contexts, the first being the context of its composition which necessarily includes some reference to its author's intentions and the second being the various contexts of its reception which may or may not take account of authorial intent.

A fourth feature is that an attempt be made, wherever possible, to show how an earlier theorist, and/or a subsequent interpretation, casts light on contemporary problems. The light must of necessity be indirect or reflected–Machiavelli and Marx, for example, are not our contemporaries–but no less valuable for that. A particular way of reading Thucydides or Machiavelli for instance could conceivably illuminate the darker corners of our present condition as no reading of a modern self-styled 'realist' such as Henry Kissinger can.

Fifth, and finally, our aim should invariably be to try to show what a pluralist and problem-driven approach to the history of political thought can (and cannot) hope to achieve. If the proof of the pudding be in the eating, then nothing is to be gained by talking about pudding in the abstract, or various recipes for pudding, or what various culinary experts–imported from France or elsewhere–have to say about the matter. Nor will a General Theory of Pudding be of much use. One must sample for oneself and, in so far as possible, trust one's own taste-buds, whether the result be retching or, as I hope, the kind of curiosity that leads one to one's own, and doubtless better readings and reflections.

## Plan of the present work

This attempt to reassess the role and present predicament of political theory begins by looking at the 'behavioural revolution' in American political science and, more specifically, its animus against 'traditional' or 'normative' political theory. Its hostility towards political theory was driven by a particular philosophy of science–Logical Positivism–which has since been discredited and abandoned by philosophers and latterly by most political scientists. The recent revival of political theory owes a good deal to the demise of its philosophical nemesis. But before we congratulate ourselves on our ostensible victory, we had better take a careful look at our vacation's increasing withdrawal from the world and its tendency to turn in on itself and to concern itself with esoteric a spawned and nurtured within its own hermetically sealed hot-house. The result can only be increasing 'alienation of political theory'. I conclude by suggesting that we might resist these inward-turning tendencies and why and how we might do so.

The methodological moral of this tale is that we should be wary of some modern genealogists' claims about discursive discontinuities between discrete episteme or systems of thought.

But, by the same token, we should be no less suspicious of claims of intellectual ancestry and theoretical affinities across the centuries.

One can of course write the history of political thought in any number of ways and from any of several perspectives. In recent years feminism has proved to be among the most suggestive and fruitful of these theoretical vantage-points.

Feminist historians have, in their quest for forerunners, found a number of lesser known and largely unsung heroines and heroes, along with others of greater fame.

Many modern American and Asian students of political theory, it seems, are rather too eager to embrace European thinkers and theories as somehow superior to or more sophisticated than their own number and more prosaic ancestors and contemporaries. There is, of course, nothing wrong with looking abroad–quite the contrary–but there is something wrong with ignoring or dismissing out of hand what lies in one's own back yard. A modest effort to exhibit some of the things that one can discover by digging in one's own garden. Usually, while the topics may be more local and contextual but they do raise, I believe, questions of more universal interest and import.

Chapter 11 takes up the vexed and vexing question of legal, and more particularly constitutional, interpretation. How ought American citizens, and of course members of the Supreme Court to read and understand the Constitution? In the law, as in political theory, rival schools supply very different answers. But, I contend, lawyers and jurists do not, or ought not, to enjoy the hermeneutical leeway that political theorists enjoy. By taking a fresh look at one theory of interpretation–'originalism' or 'original intent'– I try to show some heretofore unsuspected pitfalls awaiting anyone who adopts such a strategy. Chief among these is that a thoroughgoing originalism would require one to accept the once–credible but now–discredited or defunct theories and vocabularies within whose terms the Founders thought about politics and framed the Constitution. And this, I argue, is a retrograde move for which there is no rational justification.

A fresh look at American individualism and national identity in the light of the contemporary 'communitarian/liberal' debate with special reference to three thinkers–John Rawls, Gerard O'Neill, and Richard Rorty–would show how a redescription in cultural or, even, 'mythic' terms may call attention to and illuminate certain aspects of their work in way that they might not recognize or agree with. No author is–or can be–aware of all possible sources of or influences on his or her thinking. Nor can one be aware of all the affinities that one's work might have with that of others, past and present. Nor, for that matter, can any author foresee all possible implications of any line of argument. Therefore, reappraising, reinterpreting and reinventing political theory has to be a continuous process to expand the horizon of knowledge and wisdom.

## Notes

1 Terence Ball, *Reappraising Political Theory*, OUP, 1995, p.4.

2 *Ibid.*, p.5.

3 See A.B. Lord, *The Singer of Tales,* (Cambridge, Mass, 1960).

4 R. Thomas, *Literacy and Orality in Ancient Greece* (Cambridge, 1993).

5 See for details, T. Ball 'Deadly Hermeneutics' in Ball (Ed.), *Idioms of Inquiry*, Albany, NY, 1987.

6 Luther, *Selections*, ed., J. Dillenberger, Garden City, N.Y., 1961,14.

7 T. Ball, *Reappraising Political Theory*, op.cit., p. 7.

8 S. Sontag, *Against Interpretation*, New York, 1966.

9 S. Fish, *Is there a Text in this class*? The Authority of Interpretive Communities, Cambridge, Mass., 1980.

10 H.G. Gadamer, *Truth and Method*, New York, 1984.

11 A. Schutz, *Collected Papers* (The Hague, 1962), pp.1, 7-9,74-5.

12 R. Rorty, J.B. Schneewind, and Q. Skinner (Eds.), *Philosopy in History,* Cambridge, 1984, pp 6-7.

13 J. Plamenatz, *Man and Society*, London, 1963, i.x.

14 See W.E. Connolly, *Political Theory and Modernity*, Oxford, 1988, p. vii; S. Wolin, *The Presence of the Past*, Baltimore, 1989, 1.

15 T. Ball, *Reappraising Political Theory.*

16 See e.g. C. B. Macpherson, *The Political Theory of Posessive Individualism*, Oxford,1962; N. Wood, *John Locke and Agrarian Capatilism*, Berkeley, Calif., 1984.

17 I Shapiro 'Realism in the Study of the History of Ideas', *HPT* 3,1982, 535-78.

18 See e.g. A. Bloom, 'Leo Strauss', *Political Theory,* 2, 1974, 372-92.

19 See, *inter alia*, J.G.A Pocock, 'The History of Political Thought: A Methodolgical Wnquiry', in P. Laslett and W.G. Runciman (Eds.) *Philosophy, Politics and Society*, 2nd ser. Oxford, 1964, 183-202; J.Dunn, 'The Identity of the History of Ideas', Philosophy, 43 1968, 85-116; Q. Skinner, 'Meaning and Understanding in the History of Ideas', *History and Theory*, 8, 1969, 3-53, repr. In J. Tully (Ed.), *Meaning and Context*, Quentin Skinner and his Critics, Princeton, NJ, 1988, 97-118.

20 See Ch. 11 below.

21 Cf. Shapiro, 'Realism'.

22 This is also K.R. Popper's conception of the social scientist's task; see the open Society, London 1969, ii, 95-6. This methodological similarity suggests one way of affecting a rapprochement between political theory and the social sciences. See J. Farr, 'Popper's Hermeneutics', *Philosophy of the Social Sciences*, 13, 1983, 157-76.

23 Dunn, 'Identity'.

24 See S.R. Suleiman and I. Crosman (Eds), *The Reader in the Text*, Princeton, NJ, 1980; H.R. Jauss, *Toward an Aesthetic of Reception,* Minneapolis, 1982; R.C. Holub, *Reception Theory*, London, 1984.

25 C.F. Gadamer, *Truth and Method*, 269-74.

26 A. Ryan, *Property and Political Theory*, Oxford, 1984, 3-4. To Ryan's list I would add, amongst many others, later Marxists (mis)reading of Marx; see below, chs. 9, 10.

27 A.C. Danto, 'Basic Action', *American Philosophical Quarterly*, 2, 1965, 141-8.

28 M. Butler, 'Early Liberal Roots of Feminism: John Locke and the Attacks on Patriarchy, *APSR* 72, 1978; and my critique, *APSR* 73, 1979, 549-50.

29 M. Leslie, 'In Defence of Anachronism', *Political Studies*, 18, 1970, 433-47.

30 T. Ball, 'Party', in Ball, J. Farr, and R.L. Hanson (eds.). *Political Innovation and Conceptual Change*, Cambridge, 1989.

31 Q. Skinner, 'Some Problem in the Analysis of Political thought and action', in Tully (Ed.), *Meaning and Context*, 112.

32 T. Ball and J.G.A Pecock (eds.), *Conceptual Change and the Constitution*, Lawrence, Kan., 1988, 2.

33 Q. Skinner, *Foundations of Modern Political Thought*, Cambridge, 1978, I, pp. xii-xiii.

34 Skinner, 'Some Problems', 112.

35 Ball, Farr, and Hanson (Eds), *Political Innovation*; Ball, *Transforming Political Discourse*, Oxford, 1988.

36 Locke, *Second Treatise*, Ch. VI, sect., 52.

37 J. Farr, 'Understanding Conceptual Change Politically', in Ball, Farr, and Harison (Eds.), *Political Innovation*, 34-6.

38 See my *Transforming Political Discourse*, ch.I.

39 A. MacIntyre, *A Short History of Ethics*, New York, 1966, 2-3.

40 G.J. Schochet, *Patriarchalism in Political Thought*, New York, 1975, 268-9.

41 The following is suggested by A.C. Danto's discussion of 'tensed sentences' in *Narration and Knowledge*, New York, 1985, 56-8.

42 I. Lakatos, 'Falsification and the Methodology of Scientific Research Programmes', in I Lakatos and A. Musgrave (Eds.), *Criticism and the Growth of Knowledge*, Combridge, 1970, 115.

43 See. Ch. To below

44 See Ch. 2.3 below

45 See, *inter alia*, J. Dunn, *The Political Thought of John Locke*, Cambridge, 1969; *A Discourse on Property*, Combridge, 1980 and *An Approach to Political Philosophy: Locke in Contexts,* Cambridge, 1983; R. Asheraft, *Revolutionary Political and Locke's 'Two Treatises of Government'* Princeton, NJ, 1986.

46 Q. Skinner, "The Ideological Context of Hobbes's Political Thought' *Historical Journal*, 9, 1966, 286-317; 'The Idea of Negative Liberty', in Rorty, Schneewind, and Skinner (Eds.), *Philosophy in History*, 193-221;

'More's Utopia and the Language of Renaissance Humanism', in A. Pagden (Ed.), *The Languages of Political Theory in Early-Modern Europe*, Cambridge, 1987, 123-57.

47 W.K Wimsatt and M. Beardsly, "The Interntional Fallacy', *Sewanee Review*, 54, 1946.

48 B. Parekh, 'The Rushdie Affair: Research Agenda for Plitical Philosophy', *Poltical Studies*, 38, 1990, 695-709.

49 H. Rechenbach, *Experience and Prediction*, Chicago, 1961, 6-7.

50 D. Baumgold, 'Political Commentary on the History of Political Theory', *APSR* 75, 1981, 928-40.

51 C. Condren, *The Status and Appreaisal of Classic Texts,* Priceton, Nj, 1985.

2

# Quentin Skinner On Reading a Text*

*–Anuradha Sharma*

This essay tries to discuss some of the problems created due to a certain way of reading the classical texts. The approach that is being discussed here is that of having a history of ideas. The author has attempted to bring out the flaws of this approach through various arguments and examples.

## What do the Historians of Ideas do?

The task of the historian of ideas is to study and interpret the classical texts. The attempt is towards bringing out the "dateless wisdom" or "universal ideas" present in moral, political and religious writings. The idea is to gain from these "timeless, elements" as they are believed to be of significance in all times, irrespective of the period in which they were written. The focus is kept on what was "said" about certain "fundamental concepts" related to morality, politics, religion and social life. These texts are re-read as though they were written by some contemporary thinker, for the present times. It is believed that while undertaking such studies one must not go into the details of when and in which social context were these written, as this would divert attention unnecessarily from the main concept and would lessen their importance/value.

## The Problem with this Approach

This point of view is being questioned in this essay. It has, for long, been believed that the classical theorists have a command over certain "fundamental concepts". This has caused much confusion over the years in the history of ideas. There are various

* Paraphrased version of the article by Quentin Skinner titled "Meaning and Understanding in the History of Ideas" in *Visions of Politics* Vol. I, Cambridge, 2002.

ways in which this thought is misleading. First of all, the problem is that a certain continuity of ideas in a given field of thought is unavoidable. The new concepts do have some links with the earlier concepts. Without these resemblances it would be difficult to relate activities to each other. History would become meaningless if we do not recognize these connections. Actually this leads to confusion.

Now, the problem can be clearly pinpointed. If we just concentrate on what the classical texts "say" about certain concepts then actually we will not be able to understand what those theorists meant by that concept. Our own preconceptions are bound to colour that concept (and in that case, it would certainly loose its original meaning).

Psychologists face this dilemma very often; as an observer sometimes his own mental set up sees the reality in that specific way.

Put in other words the problem is that in order to understand, classification has to be done but in order to classify, we must take the help of familiar categories. This poses the danger of seeing the new material through the old categories and which might not be the right categorization. May be we could have come up with some new forms of categorization otherwise. And we could be imposing our meaning on someone else's thought, someone else's concepts.

## The Problem with the Paradigm

A preset pattern/understanding is called a paradigm and this essay attempts to show that although such paradigms are important and have brought out significant results often, but sometimes such paradigms create an illusion where the concepts from the past are wrongly, forcibly conjoined with the study of the morality, politics, religion etc. in the present times. So much so that sometimes such accounts seem less of history and more of *mythology*.

This also involves assuming that a certain classical writer said such and such thing about an issue.

## History or Mythology?

One such way through which the historians come up with 'mythologies' is that of assuming that each classical writer must have had a doctrine of his own on all the concepts related to his area of study. Such attempts sometimes even 'create' these doctrines. *This happens in various ways.*

## Concepts Re-interpreted or Wrongly Interpreted

Any chance remarks by that theorist would be taken up and would be used as a point 'from his doctrine'. Such wrong, connection could be established by some biographer or by some historian of ideas who is working on building up some "unit idea"/ concept.

In the first situation, *a biographer could interpret a remark or comment made by a classical thinker in a way entirely unintended by the thinker himself.* There have been such instances of gross misinterpretation or superimposition of one's own notions on somebody else's words. For example Marsilius of Padua in his *Defensor Pacis* remarked that the executive role of rulers is in contract with the legislative role of the people. Now some modern commentator who is familiar with the doctrine (popular since the American Revolution) that one condition of political freedom is the separation of executive from legislative power, would propose that Marsilius should be taken to be the founder of this doctrine. Marsilius was not referring to the question of political freedom while making that, comment and yet, thanks to this form of imagined connection-making exercises that now it is a point of debate whether he was or was not referring to that doctrine although he was clearly not familiar with that line of the events.

Similarly a statement, given by Sir Edward Coke on Bohham case that the common law of England may sometimes override statute. The modern commentator (esp. American) would associate it with the doctrine of judicial review which came much later. Coke knew nothing of such a doctrine. He was making that statement in an entirely different context where a party politician of law is custom and not, as James believed, the will of the sovereign. What follows after such wrong interpretations is that a debate follows whether he meant to say so or not. People who disagree with this deep-connection between 'past' and present also ironically based their conclusion on Coke's text and do not question the attempt which in the first place assumed that Coke must have meant to say this.

Another danger such suppositions pose is that of 'finding'

doctrine in the classical texts where none existed.

For example, Richard Hooker commented in Book I of his *Of the Laws of Ecclesiastical Polity* upon natural sociability. Now he was merely distinguishing between godly origins of church from mundane origins of civil associations. But that comment was seen as the first step towards the "theory of social contract". Or when John Locke makes a remark somewhere in his *Two Treatises of Government* about trusteeship he is believed to be coming up with the 'doctrine' of 'the political trust'.

The point is that if the writer meant to propose such a such why did he himself not do so and why is it that the historian has to reconstruct their ideas through guesses and hints.

## The Danger of Half Truth-half Imagination

How half truth-half imagination brings out absurd notions can be seen from an illustration of what the pioneer of this approach, Arthur Lovejoy, has to say about the method of this approach. First of all one must create an ideal type of the doctrine to be 'traced back' in history—it could be that of equality, progress, reason of state, the social contract, the separation of power etc. Then one must trace its roots back in history and for that, each and every part of history where this was 'mentioned' in any form must be noted.

The danger with this approach is that the doctrine to be searched becomes an entity in itself, then the historian starts treating it as though it has always been present in the past too. It is argued that it has always been there but could not come up strongly, because may be it was 'not understood properly' then, or may be it 'faced obstacles' or may be it 'dropped from sight' several times etc.

Emergence of a doctrine is presented as though the story of development of an organism is being told. For example, we are told that the 'birth' of the idea of progress was quite an easy one, it 'overcame the difficulties' presented by the 16th Century and 'gained ground' through the next hundred years. But the idea of the separation of powers came into the world with greater difficulty. Although it almost 'emerged' during the English civil war, it look another Century for the three-fold division to emerge fully.

## The Absurdities Created due to this Mythicizatioin

Whenever this kind of approach is followed, two kinds of absurdities arise. The writers of the past are credited with having extraordinary almost magical capacity of foreseeing the doctrine of the future much before they actually emerged. For example, Marsilius of Padua is considered notable in this contributions because he 'foresaw' the emergence of Machiavelli's theory, Machiavelli is notable because he "laid the foundation" for Marx John Locke's theory of signs is notable 'as an anticipation' of Berkeley's metaphysics etc. They are even praised or criticized for 'being like us or 'not being like us. Machiavelli's political ideas are very much like our own so he is 'praiseworthy'. But other thinkers of his time were not like us so their views are 'completely unreal' etc.

Another absurd thing that happens as a result of such an approach is that extensive debates begin regarding whether that unit idea/concept was really present in the past in that form or not. An imagined course of movement is debated upon causing further absurdity. For example, when the history of ideas takes up the theory of separation of powers and "traces" its past– the debate begins whether the doctrine was present in the works of George Buchanan? No, he did not clearly express it, but he was the only one to 'come the closest' to it. So, it must have come up clearly by the royalists during the English Civil War, when they presented their constitutional proposals. No, it is not in its pure from ever there on. Or consider the theory of social contract, was it 'there' in the pamphlets produced during the French religious wars. No, because there it was incompletely developed. So, was it there in the works of the Catholics at that time? No not even there but definitely better expressed than the others.

So, the mythology of doctrines tends to convert stray, scattered remarks into 'hints' of doctrine by the classical writers – and interestingly these discovered doctrines are the ones that the historian had set to *discover* at the outset. They claim to have found what they started with.

## The Other Aspect of the Problem

The *opposite* of this also happens when this kind of approach is followed. A classical theorist who "fails" to provide any such 'clues' of doctrine in his work, is *criticized* for not having a vision for the future or for having serious drawbacks. Thomas Hobbes or sometimes Niccolo Machiavelli is made responsible for man's first disobedience. His works are termed "immoral and irreligious" by Leo Strauss (a chief proponent of this approach).

Basically however what these historians of ideas do is to supply the classical theorists with beliefs which were not their in the first place. Thomas Aduinas may not have called "civil disobedience" foolish but that "he would not have approved of it". Marsilius of Padua would have approved of democracy since 'the sovereignty he espoused pertained to the people'. *Such attempts are dangerous because through these the historian presents his own prejudices as the ideas of more popular thinkers in the name of 'understanding' their works*. Through this, history is made into a dirty game where the ideas of the writers *who are no more* are hugely misrepresented.

The most usual practice is to take up a doctrine, criticize some classical writer for having failed to mention it and show how imcompetent that theorist was. This approach is so dominant in the field of history of political ideas that ever the most anti-essentialist of theorists T.D. Weldon has not questioned it. In the first part of his book *State and Morals* — he has presented various definitions of state as "formulated" by several political theorists. He maintains that all the theories of the state fall into two main groups — 'some define it as an organism, others as a machine' and further adds that even the theorists considered to be the leading thinkers fail to present a clear, consistent theory of state. Their works are full of inconsistencies. Only Hegel comes closer to using one of the two 'main' models of describing state. Without these models, what sort of theory can one hope to come up with. So, in his opinion he has clearly cracked the code of what the theory of state should be like and he has 'discovered' that none of the earlier political theories have had the 'clarity of thought' to think on those terms. Everyone except Weldon himself has been 'confused'.

The literature on history of ideas is full of such imagined, constructed misguidances. For example, the question of importance of voting, role of public opinion etc. in the political theory. Now, these questions have gained importance in modern times with the introduction of representative democracies. This does not matter to commentators and they go on criticizing Plato's *Republic,* for 'leaving out' any discussion on 'influence of public opinion'. Or criticizing John Locke's *Two Treatises* for not 'being clear' on his understanding of the question of universal suffrage. In a historical context where popular rule was not an issue of discussion how can the historian find flaws with the writers of that time about not having paid any attention to points related to modern day issues like universal suffrage, voting, public opinion, people's rule etc.

Another aspect of such mythological constructions is that it is assumed that these classical writers wanted to put forth some great theories of modern concern. And then, when obviously their writings do not show that level of contribution, they are 'criticized', for presenting a 'flawed work', a 'weak theory', an 'unclear concept' etc. For example it is first assumed that one of Machiavelli's basic concerns in *IL Principle* was to explain 'the characteristics of men in politics' then obviously his work would seem 'one sided and unsystematic'. Again, if it is first assumed that Locke's *Two Treatises* talks of 'natural law and political society' then clearly his work would seem to be of poor quality since he fails to talk of 'a world state'. The question is whether, in the first place, these writers intended or even could have intended to do what then are criticized for not doing.

## A Second Type of Mythology

Another aspect of the mythical constructions by the historians of ideas is that they usually set out searching for theories in the works of the classical writers where there were none. In other words, it may not at all be necessary that those writers did not express themselves very coherently or did not elaborate much upon a certain point. Now, these historians of ideas often take on the responsibility of providing 'coherence' to these theories of the classical writers i.e. they fill up the 'gaps' in the theory. Thereby not only dangerously changing the meaning of what the original writer wanted to say but also coming up with an abstract 'message' which can be passed on because it is 'clear'.

In writing about the history of moral and political philosophy this 'coherence' is most essential. This they 'create' by all means, at all costs, by every effort. So, if Hobbes' political philosophy is not clear, his work *Leviathan* must be read, re-read till some coherence is 'visible'. Or, if Hume's work does not seem consistent, an effort should be made to go through all the works of his until consistency is displayed 'at all costs'. If Herder's political ideas are scattered throughout his work then it is the duty of the historian 'to present these ideas in some coherent form'. The attitude of the historian of ideas is that of effort and quest to find coherence where there may not be, need not be, could not be.

## "Who Needs the Details, just find some Coherence"

This attitude tends to restrict and close the ideas provided by these thinkers. *A forced coherence misrepresents their contributions, which could have been very expansive and wide ranging originally.* If, for example, it is assumed that a study of Rousseaou's philosophy must search for most 'fundamental thought', then it would belittle his contribution over several decades to several fields of enquiry. If Hobbes is assumed to have presented his views 'mainly' on a general 'Christian' system then it hides his major contributions to the relations between ethics and political life. If Edmund Burke is supposed to have worked on a 'coherent moral philosophy' then the variety of thoughts put forth by him would go absolutely unnoticed.

It could be so that a certain writer was interested in various issues and has reflected on a variety of topics but to force a coherent structure out of these would be incorrect.

In their attempt to come out with some 'clear' theory and not finding one the works of the classical writers, these historians of ideas criticize them for being incoherent, unsystematic, for example, great effort is made towards systematizing Marx's various remarks, ideas. But such an activity is difficult because Marx was concerned with a wide range of different issues at different times. After failing to 'systematize' his work he is accused of having presented his ideas in a 'fragmentary' manner.

*First these writers are categorized as having a certain 'model of thought' and then criticized for not really coming up to that model thought.* For example, first it is assumed that all conservative thinkers must hold some 'organic' conception of the state and then Lord Bolingbroke is criticized for not having that sort of an idea of state. First it is assumed that any philosopher who writes about the theory of justice, would write about one of the three 'basic' points on that subject and then, Plato or Hegel are shown to be rather incoherent about these points. It becomes completely unimportant that they were not writing in today's context or that they were expressing their views in an entirely different socio-political context. It does not remain a historical study anymore, it becomes something far from it. A mythological construction by the historian.

Even stating this problem clearly, with illustrations, has not had an impact. It still goes on and misguides in two ways. One, there is an attempt to dismiss what the writer himself wanted to say. His points are overlooked if they seem to 'disrupt' the line of thought 'discovered' by the historian. Sometimes complete works are ignored due to this. For example, Locke is treated as a 'liberal political theorist' but the information ignored here is that in his thirties he favoured conservative and authoritarian stances. It was only in his fifties that his views changed. He is not considered 'Locke' till his fifties.

Then there is Hobbes who has quite clearly presented his political theory on the issue of Civil Rights in *"The Sovereigns and the Duty and Liberty of Subjects"* and has undoubtedly related it to the 'mutual relation between Protection and Obedience' This work has been seen as indirectly referring to the "religious character" of the whole system and the historian wonders why Hobbes was not forthright about it.

*Another related tendency in this manner of thinking is that a contradiction less, clear theory must be extracted out of the varied works of the classical writers. It is believed that there has to be a single line of thought specific to that theorist.* No consideration is paid towards the path of development his ideas took. He might have changed his views under different intellectual influences, over the time but those complexities are forcibly ironed out. A simple generalized theory is created using the works of the thinker. For example, Machiavelli's two works – *IL Principle* (1513) and *Discorsi* (1519) are quite different in their notions and yet the usual attempt is to come up with a general theory of Machiavelli that integrates both the works in a manner where the two do *not* show any contradiction between them. Similarly, Karl Marx is not allowed to have changed his pattern of thinking from his days of *Economic-Philosophical Manuscripts to Das Kapital.* Instead of presenting the changes his ideas underwent over the time, the historian of ideas informs us that Marx was actually 'obsessed with a moral vision of reality' and is not a scientist of society but a moral-religious thinker.

## Complexity of Work Reduced to Contradictions in Work

Leo Strauss, a promoter of this approach maintains that often whenever such 'contradiction' in the works of a writer are observed, they are explained as an attempt by the writer to avoid persecution, social, intellectual criticism etc. He is only pretending to stand by those ideas in order to be away from any controversy. It is for the readers, the historians to see his true opinions and 'overlook' the seeming 'contradictions'.

Such a defence of historian's approach is problematic because it assumes two things at the outset. One, that the original works must have been against the popular ideas of that period. Two, uncovering the 'real' theory behind the 'presented' work of the writer is a very intelligent thing to do. Those who feel that two aspects of a writer work are plainly contradictory, they are simply being careless, unintelligent.

## Does the Author know Better or the Interpreter?

Till now we saw how having certain pre-conceived notions about the works of a certain writer can lead to misjudgements about his work. It is believed that such incorrect, misguiding references would only be possible at an abstract level. However, it has been observed that even while describing the finer details of some writer's work, preconceived notions exercise their influence.

When a historian of idea describes the work of a certain author, he leaves no space for what the author himself had to say. In discussing the importance of relevance of that work in present context he completely overlooks the context in which that work was put forth by the author at that time.

For example, it is often suggested that with Petrarch's ascent of Mount Ventoux, the age of Renaissance dawned. But did Petrarch himself intend to show this through his act does not concern the historian of ideas. Another crude version of such attempts is where Plato's political views in *The Republic* are said to be one of a 'totalitarian party politician'. Similarly, Rousseau is held responsible for the emergence of totalitarianism.

There is another less-noticeable fashion in which such misrepresentation of historical works takes place. For example Machiavelli is called the founder of 'modern political orientation' (this bit is historically significant) but where this phrase is used as a starting point of a discussion of the 'modern' elements in Machiavelli's thought then it becomes problematic. Not only certain ideas are 'discovered' through this but also the original meaning of that author's thoughts are lost. Similarly, Locke is seen as one of the founders of modern liberal school of political thought. But to then go on to say that he was himself a liberal political theorist would be going beyond the fact/truth.

While explaining the meaning of these writings, the interpreter might describe the meaning of it in an incorrect manner if he fails to connect the writings with the socio-political circumstances in which those were written. The usual mistake made is that of mixing up the classical works with the concepts the interpreter is familiar with. It is like trying to understanding some other culture *purely* on the basis of knowledge about one's own culture. It is unavoidable to use one's own knowledge but the problem begins when only that is used and the context in which the original work was created is totally ignored.

This sort of attitude leads to two kinds of problems. One, unnecessary links are assumed between two works where there is no link. The interpreter would find some similarity in a modern and a classical work and then would assume that the modern work must have been inspired by the classical one. It is true that works are inspired by other works but the connection must not just be assumed, it must be proved. The connections should not be mythological, imagined but real, for example, Edmund Burke's political views were supposed to be an answer to Bolingbroke's work, who himself is said to have written under the influenced by Hobbes, who in turn is said to have been influenced by Machiavelli.

Such connections are purely imagined. *If real connections are to be seen, then three conditions must exist, first, the 'inspired' author must have read the works of the earlier author, secondly, that inspiration could not have come from any other writer and finally the inspired writer could not have come up with those ideas for sure, on his own.*

None of the writers discussed above who are said to be linked by a chain of inspiration fulfil these conditions. They have not read the work they are supposed to be inspired by; the influence in none of the cases is specifically from the said authors (it could have come from many other writers of that time) and about the third test, one can never tell as to how far an idea can be called original (because somewhere or the other the direct/indirect influence does exist).

## Putting Meaning Where There is None

The other misguiding impact that a flimsy connection between theories of the past and concept of the present can have is that they give a certain meaning to the past activities or events which never was there.

For example, if a historian decide that a fundamental feature of the radical political thinking of the English Revolution during the mid-seventeenth century was to ensure the right to vote to all; then he will show that Leveler's demands were also in the same line when the demand of democracy was raised. The danger arises when the concept of a 'philosophy of liberal democracy' is used as a blanket term for understanding the Leveler movement. In such a case, some of the very important characteristic elements of Levelers ideology cannot be explained, they will seem out of line. For instance, then we cannot understand why did he raise his voice for monarchy, or why did he appeal to people's religious sentiments, because if he was for democracy then both these elements of his ideology go against democratic values, and they are the characteristics features of his ideology. Leveler is by some imagined connection associated with the fight for right to vote while he was not into any such efforts.

Similarly, there is the example of Locke's *"Two Treatises"*. In his work, he has talked about the right to resist tyrannical governments. A historian who thinks that this argument is about the importance of consent in any lawful political community would lead the readers towards a wrong argument. He has used a modern concept of 'government by consent' to explain the work of Locke's but what the concept really stands for and what Locke was talking about are actually two entirely different things. The words may seem similar somewhere but the context and meaning of the two thoughts are absolutely unconnected.

While the concept of 'government by consent' talks of the legal arrangement that must be there if a civil association is to be called legitimate; Locke's concept of consent arises in connection with a description of the *origins* of legitimate political societies.

## Can we Avoid Paradigms or Reference to the Past?

The problem discussed till now is that a historian of ideas cannot avoid being influenced by the present day paradigms in discussing the earlier works and that it is dangerous also. However, what can be done to surpass this danger is to understand that there are certain considerations that must be kept in mind before making statements or before understanding the statements made by other people. What follows is *a methodological solution to this unavoidable problem.*

If the author himself was so clear about the future significance of his ideas or if he was presenting a certain concept he is the best person to tell what exactly does he mean by his concept. If he himself has not connected it with some larger theory/idea then no one else has the authority to assume what he 'wanted' to say. If at all a need to interpret his concept arises then such an attempt must be very careful in doing so. It must be described within the range of descriptions that author himself would have used. The interpretation should remain clearly within the context given by the author himself. Otherwise the interpretation cannot represent that author's idea.

And if this consideration is kept in mind while interpreting some classical theorist's work then the criticism that he did not present his theory properly, clearly would also disappear because it is wrong to criticize a theorist for not being theoretically clear when he did not intend to discuss that aspect. *There is no sense in asking questions which the theorists did not seek to ponder upon, in the first place.* They were not writing in response to modern day queries, their works must be seen in their specific context if their real, actual meaning is to be understood.

The problem that arises due to imagined connections between the works of different theorists is that they mislead. They are more like stories, created, made up. They are far from the truth.

One last consideration that must be kept in mind while interpreting some thinker's work is that it must be realized that thinking is an effortful activity. In the course of thinking of problems, various sorts of activities and ideas come up; there are contradictory ideas that fight with each other, there emerge ideas that are beyond our pattern of thinking and they sometimes tend to create confusion in the mind of the thinker. He ponders over them, changes his earlier ideas, presents something totally new etc. So while he may come up with a coherent theory he may also given certain unclear concepts. This effort and this pattern is ignored when an attempt is made towards systematically presenting the 'scattered' thoughts of a classical writer. It must be kept in mind that this confusion, un-clarity all are equally important while discussing someone's work. These confusions actually explain how the ideas developed, what influenced them to come up etc. They form the context in which these works emerged originally.

## Is Having a History of Thoughts a Good Idea?

Till now the dangers of understanding the classical texts at a very surface level have been shown. (The danger of just picking up words from those texts and assuming their meanings). Now, it has also been argued that with some care, such danger can be overcome. *But actually the point remains that such an approach of interpreting the classical texts in the context of modern concepts, is basically wrong.*

From now on, the attempt would be on putting forth an argument even stronger than the one given till now. The approach being discussed here, in principle, cannot help us to arrive at an adequate understanding of the texts we study in the history long of ideas.

*The basic reason behind this is that if we wish to understand any such classical text, we must be able to not only give the meaning of what was said but also of what the writer himself may have meant by saying what he said.* A study that focuses just on what a writer *said* about some doctrine would be inadequate and misleading because meanings of terms we use to express our concepts sometimes change over time. So that, what a writer meant to say then may mean something else in today's context, if we just concentrate on *what he said.* For example, when Bishop Berkeley's doctrine of immaterialism was called by the critics as having a "egoism" in it, they did not mean to say that it had "Hobbism" in it, (which a historian of ideas would interpret). When they used the term 'egoism' they meant to say what we today mean by solipsism (a theory that the self is the only existing thing).

Another way in which what a writer said and the interpretation of his work fail to connect is when a certain irony is observed in their statements.

Using this argument that ironically what they said seems totally different from what they meant/would have meant also misguides.

*Taking the statements, remarks made by a classical theorist at their face value is misleading.* For example, Thomas Hobbes in discussing the laws of nature, somewhere claims that the laws of nature are the laws of God, and that we are obliged to obey the laws of nature. Now this is a statement that uses the term God to bring forth the importance of the laws of nature (just as people who believe in God follow his rules so everyone should follow the rules of nature). He was a known sceptic (critical of established traditions) and usually this statement is not taken too seriously by those who know his work. But the promoters of this approach (of having a history of ideas) insist that Hobbes must have meant what he said and that he was actually a believer. Similarly, Pierre Bayle whose *Dienonnam* contains theories appropriate to a Calvinist theology (a sect in Christianity opposed to the Catholic Sect) is not known as an anti-Catholic but some commentators argue that he was not a non-believer, he was a man of faith.

Now, the inadequacy of the approach used by the revisionist interpreters is being pointed out through these examples. The revisionists (the historian of ideas) claim that a study of the texts by these theorists in itself can show what they meant to say. Such an analysis wrongly assumes certain notions, not just about the writers, but also about the times they were living in. Their contemporaries, both the critics as well as the sympathises believed that Hobbes and Bayle were against the prevailing religious orthodoxies. Both these writers were well aware of the dangers of being against the religious orthodoxy in those times. Two assumptions follow, one, either they were in favour of religious orthodoxies (as the revisionists claim) or two, they were against the religious orthodoxy. The revisionists argument does not stand because the two writers lived in fear of being attacked for their writings at various points in their life and also, if they were so in favour of religious orthodoxy then why did they not change the major sections of their works which talk against religious orthodoxy.

## How to Read a Classical Text

So, just by reading the texts written by those writers again and again, we cannot hope to get to the meaning of their works. We would have to connect it with the information beyond the text, the information about the socio-political conditions in which they were writing.

Basically, the argument is that while trying to understand the meaning of any serious remark, just a study of what he said is not sufficient. To understand the meaning we need to know (1) What is said; (2) the intended force with which it is said i.e. (i) not just what these writers were *saying* but also (ii) what they were *doing in* saying it.

It is very important to know *what they meant by saying it,* and not just what is the meaning of their words.

## The Problems with the "Unit Idea" Quest

The approach that says that individual works from the past can be understood keeping in mind the development of a certain "Unit Idea" can be questioned by an argument of Wittgenstein. According to him, it is very important to ask the question – what were the writers doing when they made those statements, what was the problem that they were addressing while presenting those remarks and it is only then that the meaning of their work can be understood properly.

For exmaple, Descartes in his *Meditations* has argued in favour of the idea of unquestioned knowledge. The historians of philosophies have never asked the question why under what circumstances did Descartes presented this idea. Everyone takes for granted that since he was a philosopher, who deals with the question of certainty, so in that context he must have talked of this also. It was later found out by some of the scholars working on Descartes' theory (when he asked the question "under what circumstances did this remark/idea come up"). It was in fact in response to a very strong belief in scepticism (a belief that one should question each and every idea). This information throws a new light on the meaning of Descartes' works; it explains the special character of his work.

When Lovejoy (a promoter of the approach of history of ideas) attempts to "track the development of a unit idea through several individual texts" he is taking us in a wrong direction, because he is assuming that conditions in which an idea develops are not important and also that a ground, unit idea has existed, on its own and different works have just "approached" it differently. It assumes that an idea exists beyond the individual works where it has been found.

For example, an attempt to write the history of the idea of nobility in early Modern Europe. In one context, it has been used to refer to a marked noble quality; in another it stands for a class; in yet another context it means, one can have noble qualities even if not noble by birth; in another it means nobility is a quality attained by deeds but is often seen in people noble by birth; and in yet another context it is used in a disreputable sense.

It is not sufficient to understand a term in one context, if a history of that idea is to be written. It must be studied in all the contexts wherever it appeared, all the points that it was then trying to make in different contexts.

The mistake that historians of ideas like Lovejoy, make is that of looking for the "essential meaning of the idea" as something that "remains the same".

The second problem that such approach causes is that it ignores the theorist's contributions. They are merely shown to be contributors towards the development of that idea. This sort of approach ignores many important questions like (1) what role did this idea play in the thought of those thinkers; (2) what place did that idea hold in the intellectual climate of a given period. If these questions are asked then we get to know a lot.

We come to know how this idea was an answer to some problem of its time and what is its significance and what are the reasons that still make it relevant.

This exercise would actually show that there cannot be a history of a unit idea. There is no unit idea, the ideas that have emerged at different points in time have had their specific contexts and have not necessary emerged out of each other.

## But Connections with the Past are Important

To say so does not mean that we are saying that continuities in philosophies have not existed or there have never been certain key concepts in philosophies. What we are saying is that we need to move beyond the study of those continuities.

One reason is that they were not really answering similar questions when they gave their individual ideas.

The second reason for moving beyond such histories is that these tend to block out the individual contributions, the actual meaning of the ideas presented by a given thinker.

## Two conclusions

The appropriate method of studying the history of ideas involves an understanding of what these works wanted to say when they were put forward. The context in which that work appears is the best judge of what the writer intended/wanted to say.

The importance of studying the history of ideas lies in a possibility of mutual enrichment between historical evidence and philosophical analysis. How with time the meaning and concepts change form. The issues raised in the past, the solutions offered can guide the philosophers of today.

The main conclusion is that instead of looking for the answers the classical texts gave for the problems of that time and 'directly' using those for our present day problems we should do our own thinking for ourselves.

But this does not mean that the study of the history of idea is useless. What we can learn from them is how there exist various ways of thinking about issues. Different periods had different types of problems and answers were also different for each of those problems. This tells us that each case is unique, each social period has its own specificities and this must be kept in mind while looking for an answer to their problems. It is most important to learn that, there are no 'timeless' issues or 'evergreen' answers; and that issues and concepts are specific truths of specific societies at a certain point of time.

This is the best lesson we can learn, we should learn, from the history.

3

# Hind Swaraj: Contest and Content

*–Anil Dutta Mishra*

## Introduction

Hind Swaraj is Mahatma Gandhi's unique and fundamental work. It is an Indian contribution to Political Theory after Kautaliya's *Arthashastra*. Gandhi was a political activist responding creatively to the socio-political and economic circumstances in which he was located. Hind Swaraj is an alternative to modern socio-economic-political thought. It is a book, which cannot be ignored in any discussion and debate on human progress, socio-economic development and contemporary problems. It is a key to understanding not only Gandhi's life and thought but also the present dilemmas arising out of technology, industrialization and globalization. Hind Swaraj still continues to evoke critical interest the world over even now. It is not only a book on how to win political freedom for India. It is a Magna Carta for the freedom of mind and the evolution of human species from conscious and material beings to super-conscious and moral beings.[1] In fact Hind Swaraj is a manifesto for a new world order based on supremacy of ethics and morality over matter. It still represents voice of the voiceless, voice of the common man of India, and even of the common people of the whole world.

Hind Swaraj is one of the earliest of those few books which Gandhi wrote during his hectic public life. All other writing of Gandhi are in the form of articles, statements, letters and speeches. Hind Swaraj has a pivotal position in his writings, because in this small but 'severe' booklet is contained Gandhi's ideas, and which Mahadev Desai has aptly termed "seminal". The book, to quote Gandhi's own words has had a "chequered career".[2]

Margaret Chatterjee called Hind Swaraj "a very basic document for the study of Gandhi's thought'. B. R. Nanda called it Gandhi's "confession of faith". Erik Erikson called it 'a rather incendiary manifesto'. Dennis Dalton called it 'a proclamation of ideological independence.' And Judith Brown called it 'the nearest he came to producing a sustained work of political theory'. Similarly, Gerald Heard compared Hind Swaraj with Rousseau's *Social Contract*. George Catlin (1950) compared it with *The Spiritual Exercises* of St. Ignatitus Loyala.[3]

Hind Swaraj is a work, which Gandhi himself translated from Gujarati into English. Hind Swaraj is the seed from which the tree of Gandhian thought has grown to its full stature. For those interested in Gandhian thought in a general way, it is the right place to start; for it is here that he presents his basic ideas in their proper relationship to one another. And for those who wish to study his thought more methodically, it remains the norm by which to assess the theoretical significance of his other writings including the Autobiography.[4]

The unique beauty of the Hind Swaraj lies in its capacity to present a very scientific and philosophical discourse in the most ordinary language. In other words the book is written in perfectly Gandhian style-terse, simple and logical. The basic feature of Hind Swaraj is that every time you go through it, you will get a new interpretation and a new insight. It is in Hind Swaraj that we find Gandhi first announcing his own life-mission. This is nothing other than showing the way for the moral regeneration of Indians and the political emancipation of Mother India. Hind Swaraj teaches "*the gospel of love in place of that of hate. It replaces violence with self-sacrifice. It pits soul force against brute force*".[5]

## Context of Hind Swaraj

The immediate context of writing the booklet was Gandhi's encounter with the Indian anarchists in England and their cult of violence. It is not only the cult of violence that provoked Gandhi to write this tract. On the contrary, it goes much deeper and is more comprehensive in its sweep. The entire Western or material civilization forms the very backbone of his critique.[6]

One can discover three issues clearly emerging in Hind Swaraj. First is the then current politics in India, its leaders and political events and Gandhi's own position in relation to them. Second, and rather the most crucial issue is the entire question of material or 'modern' civilization. And, lastly, there is the question of passive resistance that is posited as an alternative to what Gandhi calls the brute force.[7]

In Hind Swaraj, three streams of thought merge and what emerges is a manifesto warning against what Gandhi called the mad race after civilization or (according to more recent usage) modernization. Hind Swaraj is a critique of modernization, which in Gandhi's words is identified with the Western, material, modern civilization. The critique does not stop there. One can discover the contours of what he called, "the whole theory of life," emerging from the discussion recorded therein. It is a theory of life, which is not static. No theory, which seeks to build up an alternative to the one in vogue, can be static. It is, indeed, a dynamic model theory, which acquires greater precision as Gandhi's experiences through his public life accumulate. Mahatma Gandhi considers 'Parliament' and 'machinery' to be the mainstay of modern civilization and therefore warns against their importation.[8]

On October 9, 1909, Gandhi [9] wrote to Lord Ampthill a letter, which contains ideas, which formed the bases of Hind Swaraj;

1. Impatience with the British rule was widespread in India and so was the hatred of the British;
2. The above being the case, repression would be counter-productive;
3. British people were obsessed with commercial selfishness and hence the British Government would not concede the rights of the Indians;
4. The fault lies not with the British people but with modern civilization which is a negation of the sprit of Christianity;
5. All that shines as modern—the railways, machines, the style of life etc. are a true badge of slavery of the Indian people, as they are of Europeans;
6. Rise of large cities like Calcutta and Bombay was a matter

of sorrow, not of congratulation;

7. India has lost because her villages are destroyed;
8. Violent methods are built in the modern civilization and so is immorality;
9. I share the national sprit but I do not agree with those who want to use violence directly or indirectly to win freedom for the country because it is immoral and against the sprit of Indian civilization; and
10. Rulers must rule according to the wishes of the people; the moment they fail in their primary duty, people must refuse to recognize them and cooperate with them.

Hind Swaraj raises fundamental questions. India's encounter with Britain was not political and economic but civilizational. Even today, the situation is no different from the one when Gandhi wrote Hind Swaraj. For proper understanding of Hind Swaraj, it is necessary to refer to the historical context of Hind Swaraj, which, in the main, consisted of six situations or developments:

(a) The general developments in India since 1857;

(b) The emergence of new professional classes;

(c) The circumstances prevailing in India with special reference to the partition of Bengal;

(d) The Russia-Japanese War, and the revolutionary fervour in Czarist Russia;

(e) The situation in South Africa and Gandhi's experiences and experiments there; and

(f) The immediate provocation for Gandhi to write Hind Swaraj.[10]

The book is addressed to a mixed audience: the expatriate Indians greatly attracted to terrorism and political violence, the Extremists and Moderates of the Indian National Congress, the Indian nation (means ordinary Indians), and the English (means both the British ruling class living in India and Britons living in Great Britain).

As to why Gandhi wrote the book, there was first of all the question of an inner illumination and the consequent urge to communicate. Gandhi's intentions in writing Hind Swaraj have been grouped by Anthony J. Parel[11] under six rubrics. These are:

1. Gandhi harboured the ideas contained in Hind Swaraj for quite some time. Gandhi was inpatient to communicate them to people around him and world over specially the Indians who were his immediate concern;
2. He wanted to clarify the meaning of Swaraj, which was far wider and deeper than political independence;
3. Gandhi wanted to re-open a peaceful path of conflict resolution perfected by Indian civilisation and convince the people of India, especially the youth, to abjure terrorism and return to the Indian way;
4. Gandhi wanted to tell his countrymen that it was not the British colonialism, which was their real enemy. The real enemy was Western civilisation. So long as they remain mesmerized by Western civilisation, they would remain slaves even if they get political independence;
5. Gandhi was keen to see that Indians and British part political company as friends, not as enemies. He did not consider the British to be the enemies of Indians; the enemy was the modern (industrial) civilisation, which afflicted them both; and
6. He wanted to use Hind Swaraj as a vehicle to give to India an updated version of *dharma*, which even a common man could understand and which would fit its people for life in the modern world. "I have used the language of politics, but I have really tried to offer a glimpse of *dharma*". Thus, Gandhi wanted to make British occupation of India as an opportunity to realise fully the potential of Indian civilisation.

Parel [12] then looks into the historical contexts in which Gandhi wrote the Hind Swaraj. These contexts include:

1. The hold of modern industrial civilisation on the minds of the people all over the world, especially in the West. Hind Swaraj challenged this civilisation and branded it as satanic. According to Parel, "Its critique of that civilisation is one of its main contributions to modern political thought". While criticizing modern civilisation, Gandhi was not negative and

vindictive. He commended some of its contributions which Indian civilisation lacked or did not pay the attention they deserved–civil liberty, equality, human rights, prospects of improving the economic conditions of the poor, emancipation of women from tradition and religious toleration. He was critical because its tendencies were lop sides, because its concept and practice of freedom did not amount to Swaraj, in fact it negated it. It promoted rights at the cost of duties, economic progress at the cost of moral and spiritual progress, and divided the world into We and They using religion, political dispensation, economic status, military might, education, etc. as dividers. It negated human brotherhood and the concept of vasudhaiva kutumbakam.

2. The political situation in South Africa where he evolved as a Mahatma was another historical context in which Hind Swaraj was written. It was in South Africa that he first acquired the vision of Indian nationalism. In fact South Africa was the foundation on which he realised himself as a leader. Parel rightly says that South Africa enabled him to transcend colonialism as the cause of the plight of Indians there. The culprit was the modern civilisation, which had caught as whole humanity by its neck.

   South Africa freed Gandhi from man of the constraints he would have got, had he been in India. He could not work without any social and religious pressures but also experiment with his ideas in places like Phoenix settlement. But for his being in South Africa, he would not have got the opportunity to go to London on lobbying missions in 1906 and 1909 and thus acquire his diplomatic skills.

3. The third historical context Parel identifies is the politics of expatriate Indians, especially of those based in London, which centred on preparation for violent struggle against the British. This brought Gandhi closer to many of the revolutionaries and prompted him to write Hind Swaraj.

4. The Indian nationalist movement was yet another context in which the book was written by Gandhi.

5. Gandhi's acquaintance with Western people, philosophers and

thoughts was a major factor that shaped and sharpened Gandhi's views contained in Hind Swaraj.

The above mentioned ideas were developed in Hind Swaraj or Indian Home Rule, a small book of about 30,000 words (96 pages), written in Gujarati on board the ship S.S. Kildonan Castle during Gandhi's return trip from England to South Africa after an abortive mission to London. It was written in ten days between 13 to 22 November 1909. The whole manuscript was written on the ship's stationery, and the writing went on at such a furious pace that when the right hand got tired Gandhi continued with the left. He worked day and night on the manuscript. Forty of the 275 manuscript pages were written with left hand. And he wrote as if under inspiration. In the entire autograph, only sixteen lines have been scratched out and only a few words changed here and there.[13] As stated by Gandhiji himself: "*I wrote the entire Hind Swaraj for my dear friend Dr. Pranjivan Mehta. All the argument in the book is reproduced almost as it took place with him.*"[14]

The book first appeared serially in the Indian Opinion and later it was published in book form, to be proscribed in March 1910, by the Bombay Government, because it contained '*matter declared to be seditious*'.[15] On that, Gandhi published the English translation from Natal to show the innocuous nature of its contents. The ban was finally lifted on 21 December 1938. When Gokhale saw the translation, he thought it so crude and hastily conceived that he prophesied that Gandhi himself would destroy the book after spending a year in India. In 1921, Gandhi said: "*with deference to the memory of the great teacher, I may say that his prediction has failed to come true.*" Gandhi writing of the book said: "*I withdraw nothing except one word of it, and that in deference to a lady friend*".[16]

The Hind Swaraj or Indian Home Rule is a severe condemnation of modern civilization. It is divided into twenty chapters and two appendices. It deals in detail with swaraj, civilization, lawyers, doctors, machinery, education, passive resistance and other matters. It deals with practical questions in a most scientific and original way. It is written in dialogue form, reaching great heights in some places. It is a faithful record of conversations he had with workers, one of whom was an avowed terrorist.

Divided into four themes elaborated or enunciated in various parts of the book, viz., (a) core concepts: non-violence, education, and technology; (b) criticism of Parliament, of machinery and of the Congress view of Swaraj; (c) Hind Swaraj as an assessment and a critique of the Western civilization with reference to non-Western civilization with non-Western criteria; and (d) prescription. [17] Hind Swaraj is the quintessence of all that Mahatma Gandhi had read, thought and experienced by the age of forty. While a student in England, he came in contact with radical and liberal groups and individuals. It was there that he read extensively, thought deeply and gained first-hand experience of the working of Western civilization. The most distinctive influence on the formation of his ideas was through the works of Tolstoy, Ruskin, Thoreau and Edward Carpenter, all vehement critics of industrial life and advocates of simplicity.

The substance of Gandhi's attacks in Hind Swaraj is 'machinery', that is, technology. It "*is the chief symbol of modern civilization; it represents a great sin*".[18] In Hind Swaraj Gandhi declared "Parliament" as a "prostitute and a sterile woman". Indicates that Hind Swaraj posits an ideal state of things in which there will be no machine, no railways, no doctors, lawyers and such other things as are the symbols of modern civilization. It is not Rousseau's state of nature, but the ideal society of Marx in which the state will wither away, minus the modern type of technology (machinery) to which the former (Marx) was wedded unconditionally.[19]

Gandhi's thinking about the whole question of industrialization seems to be running along two parallel levels. At one level, Gandhi seems to be concerned with the problem of poverty and unemployment. Gandhi was very clear about this in mind. He knew that the Western pattern of industrialization involved per capita investment of a magnitude, which India could hardly afford to generate unless it took to authoritarian or totalitarian methods. Gandhi's aim was to revive cottage and village industries. In other words what he was seeking was the resuscitation of the village through the revival of its handicrafts. Must not be supposed that Gandhi believed in the static, archaic mode of production in the village prevalent in the past. He welcomed every improvement in the village craft (small unit) if it led to increase in productivity. The only condition attached was that the improvement must not render people unemployed. He was even willing to accept the use of energy (electricity, etc.) if it could be useful for village industries, in case the village owned the power plant. At another level Gandhi had a more fundamental objection to Western pattern of industrialization. It is in this respect that his approach differs both from the liberal and the Marxian approach. Liberal and the Marxian approaches put their faith in an ever-growing material standard of life. And for this purpose, they depend upon an intensive exploitation of natural resources, minerals and fossil fuels. This leads them to multiply machinery which Gandhi called the 'craze for machinery'. Agriculture, therefore, becomes the backbone for pushing ahead with such a pattern of industrial development. Exploitation of agriculture leads to the growing desolation and ruination of the village and the pauperization of the village population, which eventually finds its sanctuary in the cities, in the slums and in overcrowded, cramped spaces. This leads to an unrestrained urbanization with all its attendant evils of crime, prostitution and has been aptly termed as 'street corner societies'.[20]

A very critical element in Gandhi's critique of modern machine technology is that it leads to conflict among nations and ultimately to war. "Blueprint for Survival," statements by thirty- three of Britain's most distinguished scientists have reaffirmed the faith in Gandhi. Recent critics who question the very basis of its dependence on the present-day technology reinforce Gandhi's objection to modern civilization. Since technology is predicated upon increasing consumption of natural resources, which, the critics point out, are limited, the entire superstructure of the so-called civilization is threatened with destruction. Gandhi cried a halt to this mad pursuit after indiscriminate multiplication of machinery.[21]

Gandhi questioned all these assumptions. He was not against science as such. Modern science is grounded on two fundamentals. The first is the kind of science which penetrates the nature of reality, tries to go deep into problems of the universe, raises issues of a philosophical nature and tries to establish or reject them by its experiments, and makes an effort through its findings at unification of man with the deeper reality in which he has his being and becoming. But there is yet another dimension of science, that is, the dimension of its application to solving the physical needs of the humankind.[22]

Gandhi warned and suggested restraint. It is in this context that he prescribed the application of science only when its usefulness had been assessed in all its multi-dimensional relationship with man, society and nature. We are witnessing today a civilization crisis. It is a crisis because the entire system of machine technology is in crisis, rather threatened with a crash as sensitive minds, scientists and others, are warning us today. Gandhi was perhaps the first in the present century who realized the deeper and long-range implications of this technological progress. His whole response to it is one of caution, restraint and limitation. It originated in Hind Swaraj as a response of a particular civilization, namely, of the Indian civilization to the Western. Gandhi's thinking evolved within the orbit of the world developments (including the two World Wars), his response acquired a universal character embracing the whole mankind verging on a precipice where the large-scale high technology has brought it.[23]

Gandhi could easily reconcile it with his basic philosophical position. What emerged from this was a way out of the present civilizational crisis. We may now chart out the basic ingredients of the Gandhian scheme. In Gandhi, man emerges at the centre of all social, economic and political development. This man is the spiritual man, aligned and wholly integrated with his community and his surroundings.[24]

Hind Swaraj is a warning against indiscriminate large-scale mechanization of life and a pointer to the future. The rudimentary model presented therein is, as we have indicated, not static. It is, on the contrary, dynamic in so far as it assumes a more sharply defined shape as Gandhi's thinking becomes global in character through time. Hind Swaraj, therefore must be placed within the framework of Gandhi's thought as it developed through his active life.[25]

In Hind Swaraj, Gandhi re-opens the debate, which had raged in India in the second half of nineteenth century, and he raised his voice against modern, Western civilization. He also offered a concept of normal society having its roots in India's past and its values. Gandhi revalidated the essence of Indian civilization; he made the plea that it be accepted as the starting point of the next phase of India's growth in order to transform it in the long run. Two other factors determined the format and the content of Hind Swaraj. The patriotic Indians in London had come to the conclusion that India should "*adopt modern methods of violence and modern civilization to drive out the British.*"[26]

Gandhi had evolved a different approach to life on the basis of his experiments in South Africa; he disagreed with the patriotic Indians about their diagnosis and prescription.[27] As a point of clarification, we should like to point out that Gandhi's denunciation of railways, lawyers, and doctors and parliaments and machinery and brute force should not be taken literally. These have only an emblematic or metaphorical significance. Gandhi means more than what he says.[28] Gandhi enunciates a 19-point programme of action entitled *Chhutkara*, which means "the emancipation".[29]

Hind Swaraj provides a scathing critique of Western civilization. The three recurrent themes are : (i) colonial imperialism; (ii) industrial capitalism; and (iii) rationalist materialism.[30] According to Gandhi, colonialism triumphed in India not because of its strength but because of Indians' inherent weaknesses, which allowed 'this intimate enemy' to take root. Gandhi was the first person to have attributed the British rule in India to a 'moral decline' affecting the entire nation.[31] Attributing colonialism in India to 'our weakness', Gandhi thus argued that '*The English have not taken India; we have given it to them. They are not in India because of their strength, but because we keep them....*'.[32] According to Gandhi, the British conquest of India was solely due to the Indians' moral failure.[33] In Hind Swaraj Gandhi produced the most effective trans-cultural protest against the hyper-masculine worldview of colonialism. In other words, Hind Swaraj is the most creative response to the perversion of industrial capitalism.[34] For Gandhi, industrialization remained the driving force behind Western civilization. 'Machinery is the chief symbol of modern civilization;

it represents a great sin...If the machine craze grows in our country, it will become an unhappy land.' [35] '*It is necessary to realize that machinery is bad. We shall then be able gradually to do away with it ... If, instead of welcoming machinery as a boon, we should look it as an evil, it would ultimately go.*'[36] According to Gandhi, '*a snake-bite is a lesser poison than the mill industry because, while the former merely harmed the body, the latter destroys body, mind and soul.*'[37] According to Gandhi, there remained a tension between true civilization and a civilization based on machine. While the former is based on brute rationalist materialism, the latter draws its sustenance from dharma. In modern civilization, *artha* (money) and *kama* (desire) are totally divorced from *dharma* on the basis of the alleged superiority of rational materialism.[38]

On the one hand, Hind Swaraj was Gandhi's creative response to the theoretical basis of Western civilization. Drawing on the civilizational resources of Hindu religion and its tradition, he put forward a new theoretical framework to conceptualize both colonialism and industrial capitalism. On the other hand he developed the fundamental precepts of what later became Gandhism. The three important themes that recur not only in his writings but also in his deeds are *swaraj*, *swadeshi* and *satya*. Swaraj was rule of self by the self. It was therefore more than a political idea for to the Mahatma it meant India's spiritual liberation through a fundamental change in each individual's perception. *Swadeshi*, which meant self-respect, self-realization and self-reliance was not merely glorification of traditional and indigenous methods of production but a creative application of the available means meaningful to the people in consideration. His debate is not on '*whether India needs technology*'; his debate is on '*the kind of technology that India needs*'. *Satya* is truth-force and only *ahimsa*. Together with *ahimsa, satya* constituted *satyagraha*. It was a method of securing rights by personal suffering. *Satyagraha* was an indigenous combination of reason, morality and politics; it appealed to the opponent's head, heart and interests.[39]

## Contents of Hind Swaraj

The opening chapters 1-3 deal with the Indian National

congress and the Indian awakening. Chapter 4 explains the true meaning of Swaraj. A critique of modern industrial civilization is presented in chapters 5-6. The pitiable condition of India is elaborated in chapter 7-12. Why Gandhi considered the Indian civilization to be a truly modern civilization is given in chapter 13. The potency of *satyagraha* or passive resistance is explained in chapters 14-17. Chapters 18-19 discuss the problem associated with modern education and technology. The last chapter 20 gives conclusions. Appendix I lists twenty references for further reading, including six by Tolstoy, two by Thoreau, two by Ruskin, one by Plato (Defence and Death of Socrates), and one by Mazzini (Duties of Man), and one each by Dadabhai Naoroji, and R.C. Dutt on the economic condition of colonial India.

In a letter to a friend in India, Gandhi [40] summarized the contents of Hind Swaraj in the following words:

1. There is no impassable barrier between East and West.
2. There is no such thing as western or European civilization, but there is a modern civilization which is purely material.
3. The people of Europe, before they were touched by modern civilization, had much in common with the people of the East; anyhow the people of India, and even today Europeans who are not touched by modern civilization, are far better able to mix with Indians than the offspring of that civilization.
4. It is not the British people who are ruling India, but it is modern civilization, through its railways, telegraph, telephone, and almost every invention, which has been claimed to be a triumph of civilization.
5. Bombay, Calcutta, and other chief cities of India are the real plague-spots.
6. If British rule were replaced tomorrow by Indian rule based on modern methods, India would be no better, except that she would be able to retain some of the money that is drained away to England; but then India would only become a second or fifth nation of Europe or America.
7. East and West can really meet when the West has thrown

overboard-modern civilization, almost in its entirety. They can also seemingly meet when East has also adopted modern civilization, but that meeting would be an armed truce, even as it is between, say, Germany and England, both of which nations are living in the Hall of Death in order to avoid being devoured, the one by the other.

8. It is simply impertinence for any man or any body of men to being or to contemplate reform of the whole world. To attempt to do so by means of highly artificial and speedy locomotion is to attempt the impossible.
9. Increase of material comforts, it may be generally laid down, does not in any way whatsoever conduce to moral growth.
10. Medical science is the concentrated essence of black magic. Quackery is infinitely preferable to what passes for high medical skill as such.
11. Hospitals are the instruments that the Devil has been using for his own purpose, in order to keep his hold on his kingdom. They perpetuate vice, misery and degradation and real slavery. I was entirely off the track when I considered that I should receive a medical training. It would be sinful for me in any way whatsoever to take part in the abominations that go in the hospitals. If there were no hospitals for venereal diseases, or even for consumptives, we should have less consumption, and less sexual vice against us.
12. India's salvation consists in unlearning what she has learnt during the past fifty years or so. The railways, telegraphs, hospitals, lawyers, doctors, and such like have all to go, and the so-called upper classes have to learn to live consciously and religiously and deliberately the simple life of a peasant knowing it to be a life giving true happiness.
13. India should wear no machine-made clothing whether it comes out of European mills or Indian mills.
14. England can help India to do this and then she will have justified her hold on India. *There seems to be many England today who think likewise.*

15. There was true wisdom in the ages of old having so regulated society as to limit the material conditions of the people: the rude plough of perhaps five thousand years ago is the plough of the husbandman today. Therein lies salvation. People live long under such conditions, in comparative peace much greater than Europe has enjoyed after having taken up modern activity, and I feel that every enlightened man, certainly every Englishman, may, if he chooses, learn this truth and act according to it.

Similarly R.P. Misra [41] beautifully in a nutshell, summarizes the contents of Hind Swaraj:

1. The so called modern civilization is not western civilization because there was no difference between East and West before the modern industrial civilization engulfed the West.
2. The exploitation of the East by the West is not because of the civilization they have been bitten by.
3. India has not been invaded by the British; Indian were so lured by the industrial civilization that they invited the British to rule over them.
4. Exploitative urbanization symbolizes modern civilization.
5. The problem is not the removal of the British and their replacement by Indians but how to change the system to bring in a truly modern civilization.
6. Improvement in the material welfare does not, in any way, uplift man morally. Improvement in the moral standards of life, ennobles even materials progress.
7. Medicine, as it is practiced, is the major cause of diseases.
8. Legal system generates discord among the people; it rarely brings people together.
9. Craze for machinery is a dangerous proposition; labour saving machinery is good if everyone has work for livelihood and creativity.
10. Violence breeds violence; *Satyagraha* is the weapon of strong, not of the weak.

11. Ends and means are inseparable; we cannot achieve noble ends by wrong means. Right means will always lead to right ends.
12. 'Simple living and high thinking' alone can bring peace and harmony.
13. Primary education means moral education.
14. There was true wisdom in the saying of the sages having so regulated society as to limit the material conditions of the people.
15. India will be free the moment Indians cast away the lure of modern civilization.

## Gandhi on Hind Swaraj

Writing the introduction to the Gujarati edition, translated and published in the *Indian Opinion* of 22 November 1909, Gandhi said: "*The views I venture to place before the reader are, needless to say, held by many Indians not touched by what is known as civilization but I ask the reader to believe me when I tell him that they are also held by thousands of Europeans.*"[42] However, when the English translation was published, Gandhi wrote a comparatively longer introduction on 20 March 1910: "*the British government in India constitutes a struggle between the Modern civilization, which is the Kingdom of Satan, and ancient civilization, which is the Kingdom of God.*" In the same year he wrote to Gokhale that the ideas contained in the book "*have been matured in the course of the struggle ...*" Again writing to Manganlal Gandhi , he said : "*My present state of mind is such that even if the whole world is against what I have written, I would not be depressed.*"[43]

Gandhi published Mr. Wybergh's criticism written in the form of a letter dated 3 May 1910 in the *Indian Opinion* of 21 May 1910.[44] In reply Gandhi, in his letter dated 10 May 1910 concentrated mainly on an exposition of passive resistance, because most of the remarks in Mr. Wybergh's letter centred round it. However, in answer to Wybergh's criticism of his views on modern civilization, Gandhi categorically stated: "*I have ventured utterly to condemn modern civilization because I hold that the spirit of it is evil .It is possible to show that some of its incidents are good but I have examined its tendency in the scale of ethics.*"[45] In 1914, when the second Gujarati edition was brought out, Gandhi wrote: " *I find that the convictions I started in the book have grown stronger.*"[46] Further, "*The key to an understanding of Hind Swaraj lies in the worldly pursuits should give way to ethical living.*"[47] Writing to Maganlal Gandhi in 1919, Gandhi said: "*Besides, the more experience I gain, the more I realize that machinery will keep us in personal slavery and I find what I said it in Hind Swaraj is literally true*".[48] In 1920, answering the critics, he said: "*I do not ask India to follow today the methods prescribed in my booklet. If they could that, they would have Swaraj not in a year but in day. What I am doing today is that I am giving the country a pardonable programme for the attainment of parliamentary Swaraj*".[49]

In 1921, he carried the explanation still further. In his foreward to the book, he sounded a note of caution to the reader.

"But I must warn the reader against thinking that I am today aiming at the Swaraj described therein. I know that India is not ripe for it. It may seem an impertinence to say so. But such is the conviction. I am individually working for the self-rule pictured therein. But today my corporate activity is undoubtedly devoted to the attainment of parliamentary Swaraj in accordance with the wishes of the people of India. I am not aiming at destroying railways or hospitals, though I would certainly welcome their natural destruction. Neither railways nor hospital are a test of a high and pure civilization. At best they are a necessary evil. Neither adds one inch to the moral stature of a nation. Nor am I aiming at a permanent destruction of law courts, much as I regard it as a '*consummation devoutly to be mills. It requires a higher simplicity and renunciation than the people are today prepared for.*"[50]

In 1924 answering some objections, Gandhi wrote: "I have nothing to withdraw from what I have written in the Indian Home Rule... It must be remembered that it is not the Indian Home Rule depicted in that book that I am placing before India. I am placing before the nation parliamentary, i.e., democratic Swaraj. I do not suggest today a destruction of all machines, but I am making the spinning-wheel the master machine. The Indian Home Rule depicts an ideal state....The fact that I cannot come up to the ideal condition of things laid down therein is to be attributed to my weakness.. What I have said about hospitals is also true. And yet I suppose I shall resort to the few medicines I hold lawful so long as I retain the least attachment for my body".[51]

In 1929, he wrote to Satis Chandra Dasgupta that "*there is not one word in Hind Swaraj that cannot be substantiated if I have to rewrite it today, I may change the language but never the thought.*"[52] In 1938, the Aryan Path bought out its special number devoted to Hind Swaraj. Giving a message to the Aryan Path on the eve of the publication of its special number, Gandhi categorically stated:

"*I may change the language here and there, if I had to rewrite the booklet. But after the stormy thirty years through which I have passed, I have seen nothing to alter the views expounded therein.*"[53]

In 1939, a friend, according to Gandhi, pointed out the contradiction between what he wrote in Hind Swaraj and what he practiced. Gandhi commented with his usual forthrightness.

"*The Key to understand that incredibly simple ( so simple as to be regarded foolish) booklet is to realize that it is not an attempt to go back to the so-called ignorant dark ages. But it is an attempt to see beauty in voluntary simplicity, poverty and slowness. I have pictured that as my ideal. I shall never reach it myself and hence cannot expect the nation to do so. But the modern age is for variety, for flying through the air, for multiplicity of wants, etc. which have no fascination for me. They deaden the inner being in us. The giddy heights which man's ingenuity is attempting, take us away from our Maker who is nearer to us than the nails are to the flesh which they cover.*"[54]

In October 1939, Gandhi had a discussion with the members of the Executive of Gandhi Seva Sangh. He told the members present on that occasion: "*I would ask you to read Hind Swaraj with my eyes and see therein the chapter on how to make India non-violent. You cannot build non-violence on factory civilization, but it can be built on self-contained villages.*"[55]

Two of his last pronouncements on Hind Swaraj need to be extensively quoted. Both of them are in the form of letters. In a letter to one Mr. Krishnachandra on 14 June 1945, he wrote:

"I still abide by whatever I wrote about railways, etc., in Hind Swaraj. But that applies to be an ideal state. It is possible that we may never reach that state. Let us not worry about it. It is for this reason that I have said that if we do not feel unhappy. At the same time, we should also not make a duty of giving up these things. We should have a free and essay attitude in such matters. We must use these facilities as little as possible. There will be all types of people in the society. There certainly are today. We have to live with them. Non-attachment is the only proper *dharma* under these circumstances. The only thing we must be careful about is that we do not deceive ourselves. Your statement that trains, etc., should shunned, even as theft, adultery and falsehood, is not correct. The important reason for this is that even society considers theft, etc., to be immoral. Trains, etc., have not been, nor need they be so considered. All that we may say is that we should not consider trains, etc., as means of enjoyment."[56]

The last letter he wrote was to Jawaharlal Nehru in which he explicitly referred to Hind Swaraj. "*I have said*", he wrote, that "*I fully stand by the kind of governance I have described in Hind Swaraj...My experience has confirmed the truth of what I wrote in 1909.*"[57] Then he went on:

"*It is better that I re-draw the picture today in my own language... What is worth knowing is only what I have to say today. I believe that if India, and through India the world, is to achieve freedom, than sooner or latter we shall have to go and live in village, in huts, not in places. Millions of people can never live in cities and places in comfort and peace... We can have the vision of that truth and non-violence only in the simplicity of the villages. That simplicity resides in the spinning wheel and what is implied by the spinning wheel... The sum and substance of what I want to say is that the individual person should have control over the things that are necessary for the sustenance of life.*"[58]

One can analyse from the above statements that Gandhi's own evaluation of Hind Swaraj has undergone a change.

## Methodology

In studying Hind Swaraj, the first problem that confronts a student is that of methodology. Is Hind Swaraj to be taken as a final blueprint, which the Mahatma was trying to realize in reconstructing the Indian society? Or is it outburst of an Indian disgusted with the ills of modern civilization and its institutions, e.g., parliament, etc.? Or is it a message that calls for rethinking of the entire approach of linear progress, which was the hallmark of the nineteenth and early twentieth centuries?[59]

All these questions are immediately arise as soon as one goes through the Hind Swaraj. To understand Hind Swaraj both with reference to India and the world at large, we will have to put the tract in a historical perspective. But before we do so, a word about the methodology of studying it is called for.[60]

From the point of view of methodology, Hind Swaraj cannot be taken to be the final blue print along which Gandhi wanted to refashion Indian society as well as the world order. Hind Swaraj "has reference to an ideal state." "Gandhiraj was an ideal condition," and he warned the reader "*against thinking that I am today aiming at the Swaraj described therein*."[61]

One can see that Gandhi had a flexible mind. Yet from the series of citations, which we have mentioned above, it is clearly visible that the Mahatma was not willing to yield ground on the ideas propounded in the booklet. In the letter written to Nehru, which perhaps suggests his latest thinking, he said he fully stood by the kind of governance he described in Hind Swaraj and went on to say, "*what is worth knowing is only what I have to say today*." And then he proceeded to redraw the picture that he had in mind.[62]

It will appear, therefore that the Mahatma expresses apparently contradictory opinions, which, it is assumed in some quarters, persisted till the end. Yet in Gandhi's own words:

"*I am not at all concerned with appearing to be consistent. In my search after truth, I have discarded many ideas and learnt many new things. Old as I am in age, I have no feeling that I have ceased to grow inwardly or that my growth will stop at the dissolution of my flesh. What I am concerned with is my readiness to obey the call of Truth, my God, from moment to moment, and, therefore when anybody finds any inconsistency between any two writings of mine...he would do well to choose the later of the two on the same subject.*"[63]

And Mahadev Desai very aptly expressed this when he said that while "*the views expressed in the first edition of Hind Swaraj have remained in substance unchanged, they have gone through a necessary evolution.*"[64]

This only means that there are some very basic and fundamental propositions on which Gandhi tried to build up what he called the whole theory of life. These basics remained unchanged and unmodified. In response to challenges posed to him by the limitations with which both the individual 'man' and the 'social situation' were constrained, he was willing to compromise on details.[65] Explore the fundamental propositions of Gandhi right from Hind Swaraj until his death in 1948. What we are aiming at is to show that while the basic model he conceived remained the same in working it out it was open to adaptation.

## Studies on Hind Swaraj

Not until 1919, Hind Swaraj became widely known in intellectual circles in India. All of them, however, did not like it. S.A. Dange, a noted communist leader, in his book *Gandhi versus Lenin* (1921) and M.N. Roy in his book *India in Transition* (1922) dismissed it as mere humanitarianism based on ignorance of the laws of class struggle. It is quite another thing that at least Dange changed his views so enormously in the later stages of his life that he almost became a Gandhian. Sir Shankar Nair, a leading lawyer of India (he was also the president of Indian National Congress) in his book *Gandhi and Anarchy* (1922), castigated Gandhi for advocating anarchism through *Satyagraha*.

Gandhi's Hind Swaraj, which contains his seminal ideas and basic approach to the problems of contemporary civilization, has not received the attention it merits. It is notable that during the period 1920-47, when Gandhi dominated the national movement, the book Hind Swaraj was widely ignored. Even the intellectual community in the universities and in other centres of learning, research and public education did not evince much interest in Hind Swaraj. We know of only five major studies. Firstly, in 1938, Sophia Wadia devoted an entire issue of *Aryan Path (London) to Hind Swaraj*. Secondly ,T.K. Mahadevan in 1973 brought out a special number of *Gandhi Marg (New Delhi) on Hind Swaraj*. Thirdly, Nageshwar Prasad brought a book entitled *Hind Swaraj: A Fresh Look* in 1985. Fourthly, Anthony J. Parel brought a book entitled *Gandhi: Hind Swaraj and Other Writings* in 1997. And recently Prof. R.P. Misra made a deep study of *Hind Swaraj* in 2006.

## Conclusion

Hind Swaraj is one of the most significant treatises that Gandhi wrote to clarify his views. Hind Swaraj is perhaps the most systematic exposition of Gandhi's ideas of state, society and nation. Although Hind Swaraj is an original tract, while writing it Gandhi was heavily influenced by some of the leading Western thinkers[66] as well as Indian philosophy. It contains a statement of some of the fundamental tenets in Gandhi's politics. In other words, Gandhi stated his position quite clearly in Hind Swaraj and held on to it all his life. In fact, Hind Swaraj laid the most crucial theoretical foundation of his entire strategy for winning swaraj for India.[67] It is also the most authentic text of Gandhian social and political ideas dealing with *swaraj* and *satyagraha.* In Hind Swaraj , Gandhi depicted the dichotomies between the spiritual, moral fabric of Indian society, and the violent, politically corrupt nature of European states more dramatically than any of his predecessors.

The aim of Hind Swaraj was 'to confront the anarchist and violence-prone Indian nationalists with an alternative to violence, derived from Gandhi's earliest experiments with *satyagraha*'. Hind Swaraj served two purposes: on the one hand, it was a detailed commentary on Western civilization that thrived on naked force; it also laid down, on the other, the fundamental pillars later to become basic precepts of Gandhi's social and political ideas.[68]

Hind Swaraj is a foundational text for understanding Gandhi and his ideology. An outcome of a cross-fertilization of ideas, Indian and Western, Hind Swaraj was perhaps the most powerful exposition of Gandhian social and political ideas.[69] It is a significant text with refreshing ideas (a) critiquing the Western civilization; and also (b) seeking to build 'a vernacular model of action' that the people of India understood.[70]

Gandhi's Hind Swaraj is not a rejection of the liberative contribution of modernity: civil liberties, religious tolerance, equality, poverty alleviation. Rather his effort can be interpreted as an attempt to integrate these positive elements with a liberating re-interpretation of tradition. With his critique from within the tradition, Gandhi becomes the great synthesizer of contraries within and across traditions.[71]

Hind Swaraj is a Gandhi's response to the immediate, contemporary problems arising out of inner and outer conflicts at individual, state and society level. Hind Swaraj also provides a vision, strategies, blueprint to future and an alternative to solve the contemporary problems. Future hope lies in Hind Swaraj.

Hind Swaraj is echoed in recent well-known studies like– *The Ages of Gaia* by James Lovelock; *The Turning Point* by Fritj of Capra; *Entropy: New Worldview* of Jeremy Refkin; *Human Destiny* by Lecompte du Nouy; *Clash of Civilization* by S.P. Huntington; *The Third Wave* by Elwin Toffler; *Deschooling Society* by Evan Ellich and *Mega Trends* by John Naisbistt. It is high time for both our policy makers and the people, to turn the torch within so that they may be inspired to adopt the way shown in Hind Swaraj, if not for any other consideration, but for its pragmatic strength to solve our present day maladies of India as well as of the whole world.

## Notes

1. R.P. Misra, *Hind Swaraj*, New Delhi, Concept Publishing Company, 2006 ( Under Publication).
2. Nageshwar Prasad (Ed.), *Hind Swaraj: A Fresh Look*, New Delhi, Gandhi Peace Foundation, 1985, p. 1.
3. Anthony J. Parel, *Hind Swaraj and Other Writings*, Cambridge, Cambridge University Press, 1997, p.XII.
4. *Ibid.*, p. XIII.
5. Mahatma Gandhi, *Hind Swaraj or Indian Home Rule*, Ahmedabad, Navajivan Publishing House,1938, p.13.

6. Nageshwar Prasad, p.16.
7. *Ibid.*
8. *Ibid.*, pp.16-17.
9. D.G.Tendulkar, *Mahatma*, Vol.1,Bombay, Vithalbhai K. Jhaveri, 1951, pp.127-28.
10. Devdutt, Hind Swaraj: Context and Text, in Nageshwar Prasad (Ed.), *Hind Swaraj: A Fresh Look*, New Delhi, Gandhi Peace Foundation, 1985, p.30.
11. R.P. Misra, *op. cit.*
12. *Ibid.*
13. Anthony J. Parel, *op.cit.*, p. XIV.
14. *CWMG*,Vol. 71, p.238.
15. *CWMG*, Vol. 10, p.245.
16. *CWMG-CD*, Vol. 22, p.260.
17. Devdutt, *op.cit.*, p.33.
18. M.K.Gandhi, *op. cit.*, p. 94.
19. Nageshwar Prasad, *op.cit.*, p.17.
20. *Ibid.*, pp. 18-19.
21. *Ibid.*, pp. 20-23.
22. *Ibid.*, p. 23.
23. *Ibid*, pp. 23-24.
24. *Ibid.*, p. 24.
25. *Ibid.*, p. 28.
26. Devdutt, *op.cit.*, p.32.
27. *Ibid.*
28. *Ibid.*, p. 35.
29. *Ibid.*, p. 38.
30. Bidyut Chakrabarty, *Social and Political Thought of Mahatma Gandhi*, London,Routledge, 2006, p. 24.
31. *Ibid.*
32. M.K.Gandhi, *op.cit.*, p.24.
33. Bidyut Chakrabarty, *op.cit.* p.25
34. *Ibid.*
35. M.K.Gandhi. *op.cit.*, p. 81.
36. *Ibid.*, pp. 83-84.
37. *Ibid.*, p. 82.
38. Bidyut Chakrabarty, *op.cit.*, p. 26.
39. *Ibid.*, pp. 26-27.
40. D.G. Tendulkar, *op.cit.*, pp. 129-31.
41. R.P.Misra., *op.cit.*
42. *CWMG*, Vol.10, p. 7.
43. *CWMG*, Vol.10, p. 139.
44. *CWMG*, Vol 10, pp. 507-11.
45. *CWMG*, Vol.10, p. 247.
46. *CWMG*, Vol.12, p. 411.
47. *CWMG*, Vol.12, p. 412.
48. *CWMG*, Vol.15, p. 340.
49. D.G.Tendulkar, *op.cit.*, p. 17.

50. *CWMG*, Vol. 19, pp. 277-78.
51. *CWMG*, Vol. 24, p. 548.
52. *CWMG*, Vol. 42, p. 125.
53. *CWMG*,Vol. 67, pp. 169-70.
54. *CWMG*, Vol, 70, p. 242.
55. *Ibid.*, p. 296.
56. *CWMG*, Vol.80, p.325.
57. *CWMG*, Vol.81, p.319.
58. *CWMG*, Vol. 81, pp.319-20.
59. Nageshwar Prasad, *op.cit.*, p.12.
60. *Ibid.*
61. *Ibid.*
62. *Ibid.*, pp. 12-13.
63. *CWMG*, Vol. 55, p.61.
64. M.K.Gandhi, *op.cit*, p.5.
65. Nageshwar Prasad, p. 13.
66. Bidyut Chakarabarty, p. 23.
67. *Ibid.*
68. *Ibid.*, p. 24.
69. *Ibid.*
70. *Ibid.*
71. Rudolef C. Heredia, Interpreting Gandhi's Hind Swaraj, *Economic and Political Weekly*, Vol. XXXIV, No.24, June 12-18, 1999, p.1501.

# 4

# Satyagraha with Special Reference to Bhiku Parekh

*– Sweta Mishra*

*Satyagraha* was not originally coined by Gandhiji. Even before him, the idea of *Satyagraha* was found in religious books, like the *Upanishads*, the *Ramayana*, the *Mahabharata*, the *Gita*, the *Quran* and many others. It was also practised by Indians as well as Westerners like Prahlad, Raja Harishchandra, Socrates, Plato, Jesus, King Ashoka and many others. Prahlad, the first individual *Satyagrahi*, offered *Satyagraha* against the tyranny of his cruel father. It was not known then that it was what *Satyagraha* meant.[1] According to Gandhiji, "the principle called *Satyagraha* came into being before that name was invented. Indeed when it was born, I myself could not say what it was".[2] Some of the westerners believe that Gandhiji derived the idea of *Satyagraha* from Christ's *New Testament*, specially the Sermon on the Mount. Some others believe that he got this idea from the writings of Tolstoy, though Tolstoy himself deduced it from the *New Testament*. In fact Gandhi derived his idea of *Satyagraha* neither from Christ nor from Tolstoy, but from his own Vaishnavite faith.[3]

## Satyagraha - Meaning and Genesis

The word *Satyagraha* is Sanskrit in origin. It is a compound word formed of *Satya*, meaning truth and *Agraha*, meaning clinging, holding fast, adherence, insistence. In other words, *Satyagraha* means clinging to truth, holding fast to truth, insistence on truth, or firm adherence to truth come what may. Defining the term Satyagraha, Gandhi once wrote:[4]

Truth (*Satya*) implies love and firmness (*agraha*) engenders and therefore serves as a synonym for force. I thus began to call the Indian movement *Satyagraha,* i.e. the force which is born of truth and love or non-violence and gave up the phrase passive-resistance in connection with it".

Gandhiji described *Satyagraha* as "firmness in a good cause"[5] in Indian Opinion. In *Young India,* he pointed out that *Satyagraha* was just a new name for "the law of self-suffering".[6] And in Hind Swaraj, he proclaimed that "sacrifice of self is infinitely superior to sacrifice of others", and that a self-sufferer does not make others suffer for his mistakes.[7]

*Satyagraha,* which was Gandhi's supreme invention, discovery or creation, stands for a ceaseless and relentless pursuit of truth without resorting to hatred, rancour, ill-will or animosity. His concept does not imply passivity, weakness, helplessness or expediency. It is essentially an attitude of mind and a way of life based on the firm desire for vindicating just causes, correcting wrongs and converting among-doers by voluntary self-suffering and by patient and active use of the means which are non-violent and intrinsically just. In J.B. Kripalani's words, "*Satyagraha* is strike plus something more. This something makes for better morals amongst those who carry on the fight. It also means greater loss of morals for the opponent. A *Satyagrahi* is better non-cooperator than a striker".[8] Infact *Satyagraha* is action-oriented search for and adherence to truth and a non-violent fight against untruth.

*Satyagraha* also implies an assertion of the power of the human soul against political and economic domination, because domination amounts to a denial of truth since it takes recourse to falsehood and manipulation for maintaining itself. Thus, *Satyagraha* is the vindication of the glory of the human conscience. The latter (conscience) reinforces the non-violent battle for the victory of truth.[9]

*Satyagraha* is utter self-effacement, greatest humiliation, greatest patience and brightest faith. It is its own reward.[10] *Satyagraha* is a relentless search for truth and a determination to reach truth.[11] It is a force that works silently and apparently slowly. In reality, there is no force in the world that is so direct or so swift in working.[12] It implies the exercise of the purest soul-force against all injustice, oppression and exploitation. Literally, it means "truth pressure" and denotes the operation of the soul or spirit suffering, confidence, self-purification and trust are attributes of soul-force.

The theory of *Satyagraha* is not a new innovation. It is as old as Patanjali. Gandhiji emphatically asserted that its origin had deep linkage with the idea of purity. Calling *Satyagraha* as Kamadhenu, he believed that it was useful both for a *Satyagrahi* and his adversary.[13] *Satyagraha* has also 'been linked with Yajna of Indo-Aryan days. 'Between the original form of human and animal sacrifice and its contemporary manifestation in *Satyagraha*, it has "undergone the intellectual refinement of the *Upanishads* and humanistic transfusions from Jainism and Buddhism'.[14]

Gandhi discovered this term during his endless non-violent resistance movement against racial discrimination in South Africa. In 1906 Gandhi organised the Indians in South Africa and led a new kind of resistance movement against the unjust laws under which they were then suffering. In the beginning, Gandhi used the term passive "Resistance", but as the time passed and his struggle for justice advanced, this phrase gave rise to confusion and was considered as the weapon of the weak. As a result, it appeared shameful to use an English word which could not be easily understood. He felt that the movement he had started was essentially different from what was ordinarily known as passive resistance. Gandhi, thus, felt the need for an appropriate word for the new kind of resistance and announced a small prize in his weekly, Indian opinion for the best suggestion in this regard. One of the competitors, Shri Maganlal Gandhi, suggested the word 'Sadagrha' meaning firmness in a good cause. Gandhi liked the word but he felt it did not represent the whole idea he wished it to connote, namely truth-force or the power of truth, force born of truth and love or non-violence. He, therefore, corrected it to "*Satyagraha*", which literally means insistence or truth or the pursuit of truth.

Discussing the origins of *Satyagraha* with Joseph J. Doke, Gandhi is represented to have stated:

'I remember', he said, 'how one verse of a Gujarati poem, which, as a child, I learned at school, clung to me'. In substance it was this:

'If a man gives you a drink of water and you give him a drink in return, that is nothing. Real beauty consists in doing good against evil.

As a child, this verse had a powerful influence over me, and I tried to carry it into practice'. Then came the sermon on the mount'.

"But, said I, 'surely the *Bhagavad Gita* came first? 'No', he replied' of course I knew the *Bhagavad Gita* in Sanskrit tolerably well, but

I had not made its teaching in that particular a study. It was the New Testament which really awakened me to the rightness and value of passive resistance. When I read in the 'sermon on the mount' such passages as 'Resist not him that is evil but whosoever smiteth thee on thy right cheek turn to him the other also', and 'love your enemies and pray for them that persecute you, that they may be sons of your Father which is in heaven', I was simply overjoyed, and found my own opinion confirmed where I least expected it. The *Bhagavad Gita* deepened the impression, and Tolstoy's *The Kingdom of God is Within You* gave it permanent form.[15]

## *Satyagraha* and Passive Resistance

Until the invention of this term *Satyagraha*, the South African movement was called 'Passive Resistance'. But so long as the phrase passive resistance was used, the *Satyagraha*, were mistaken to be a danger to person and property which the suffragists in England were, and the movement was regarded as a weapon of the weak. Gandhi apprehended the possible psychological effect of characterising the South African movement as a weapon of the weak and the helpless and sharply contrasted *Satyagraha* to passive resistance:

"The power of suggestion is such, that a man at last becomes what he believes himself to be. If we continue to believe ourselves and let others believe, that we are weak and helpless and therefore offer passive resistance, our resistance would never make us strong, and at the earliest opportunity we would give up passive resistance as a weapon of the weak ... Again, while there is no scope for love in passive resistance, on the other hand, not only has hatred no place in *Satyagraha* but is a positive breach of its ruling principle. While in passive resistance there is a scope for the use of arms when a suitable occasion arrives, in *Satyagraha* physical force is forbidden even in the most favourable circumstances".[16]

Thus if a passive resister does not use violence, it is due to his incapacity or under the force of circumstances, whereas a *Satyagrahi* refrains from using violence even if he were in a position to use violence effectively. A *Satyagrahi* never seeks to take advantage of the opponents weakness. Passive resistance may, therefore, sometimes be looked upon as a preparation for the use of force while *Satyagraha* can never be utilised as such. It may also be offered side by side with the use of arms. *Satyagraha* and brute force, being each a negation of the other, can never go together.

Passive resistance is a new technique of fighting wrongs or a policy resorted to by the unarmed against superior force, while *Satyagraha*, as seen by Gandhi, is a matter of faith or creed. Hence, the latter is grounded in an integrated philosophy of the universe life and fundamental ethical principles.

In passive resistance, the aim is to embarrass and harass the adversary and eventually to defeat him; but in *Satyagraha* the effort is towards not causing the slightest harassment or injury to the other party. In passive resistance, the resister's aim is to gain a victory over the adversary, while terms like 'victory' or 'defeat' have no place in the *Satyagrahi's* vocabulary. The latter's aim is the moral and mental conversion of the other party.

Passive resistance may be undertaken against persons while *Satyagraha* is never directed against a person as such. It is directed only against institutions, systems, political and other vested interests, and wrongdoings (and not strictly against the wrong doer).

Passive resistance may arise from hatred, anger or frustration and may thus be motivated by a feeling of retribution or retaliation, but not so with *Satyagraha* which is accompanied with love for the other party and possibly with a prayer that he may see reason without coming to personal harm.[17]

*Satyagraha* may be offered to one's nearest and dearest; passive-resistance can never be offered to them unless, of course, they have ceased to be dear and become an object of hatred to us.

*Satyagraha* goes beyond passive resistance in the stress on a spiritual and moral teleology because the final source of hope and consolation for the *Satyagrahi* is God. Hence Gandhi wrote:

"*Satyagraha* differs from Passive Resistance as the North Pole from South. The latter has been conceived as a weapon of the weak and does not exclude the use of physical force or violence for the purpose of gaining one's end whereas the former has been conceived as a weapon of the strongest and excludes the use of violence in any shape or form".[18]

Thus passive resistance is, according to Gandhi, a 'negative' concept and has little in common with the active' principle of love on which *Satyagraha* is based.[19]

## Basic Postulates of *Satyagraha*

There are some essentials or basic postulates of *Satyagraha* like Truth, Non-Violence, Faith in God, Brotherhood of Man, Supremacy of Moral Law and Purity of Means.[20] These are discussed below:

## Truth

Truth is the core of Gandhian philosophy of *Satyagraha*. *Satyagrahi* minus truth or *satya* is zero. In fact, *Satyagraha* is based on truth or soul force. Inner voice is the voice of truth and justice. Howsoever man might be selfish or crooked, the voice of truth, besides in his innermost depth and *Satyagrahi* tries to appeal to that voice of reason and truth.

Truth is derived from the Sanskrit word *Sat* which means being existing living. Thus truth means "that which exists". Since the existence of nothing is more obvious than that of the various laws governing the universe, truth, according to Gandhi, is nothing but a law operating in the universe. "The world", he says, "rests upon the bedrock of *Satya* or Truth".[21]

For Gandhi, it was not mere perception of truth which mattered what was more important for him was speaking the truth, acting the truth and realising the truth in every breadth of life and action. Self-realisation was another name for realisation and establishment of the truth of life and being.

Gandhi identified God with truth. Hence his famous proposition "God is truth". The reason for his identification, according to Gandhi, was that God alone is that law which governs all life. But in 1929, he reversed the earlier proposition and asserted that "truth is God". This inversion of the proposition does not change its basic meaning yet there was a reason behind this change of formulation Gandhi said "I found that the nearest approach to truth was through love. But love has many meanings in the English language. But I never found a double meaning in connection with truth and even the atheists had not demurred to the necessity or power of truth. And it was because of this reason that I saw that rather than say that 'God is Truth', I should say that 'Truth is God'. Accordingly, in our fight for social change, we must hold fast to truth and truth alone".[22]

## Non-Violence

To Gandhi, the path of truth is narrow as it is straight.[23] As a result, truth and non-violence are inseparable and it is impossible to realise perfect truth so long as we are imprisoned in the moral frame without non-violence, it is not possible to seek and find truth. Hence, non-violence and truth are so intertwined that it is practically impossible to disentangle and separate them. So, *Satyagraha* is impossible without non-violence.[24]

Non-violence literally means non-killing or non-injury. According to Gandhi, every act of injury to a living creature and endorsement of such act by refraining from non-violent effort, whenever possible.

Historically, or chronologically speaking, to prevent it, is a breach of *ahimsa*.[25] Gandhi's active non-violence emerged as a result of his experiences in South Africa especially his painful experience at Maritzburg. But, it also followed logically from his conception and quest for truth. Gandhi said, "without non-violence it is not possible to seek and find truth... They are like the two sides of a coin. Truth is the end".[26] The principle of non-violence is hurt by every evil thought, undue haste, lying, hatred and wishing ill-will to anybody. It is such a state of physical and mental discipline that can move the chord of human heart and bring a change of heart in the so-called enemies.

## Supremacy of Moral Law

*Satyagraha* does not depend upon physical or brute force. It is based on moral force—the force of truth and justice, the force of self-purification and self-suffering, love and service, courage and discipline. Gandhi says, "Purity of means is based upon the recognition of the supremacy of moral law". Therefore, the entire gamut of the philosophy of *Satyagraha* is based on the fact that truth and morality alone can be victorious, and we cannot adopt immoral principles to create a moral society. Hence Gandhi made *Satyagraha* "the moral equivalent of war". It is a way of life based on the laws of love and holiness.[27] However, insistence on moral means does not imply that evil, injustice, tyranny and exploitation are to be tolerated. On the other hand, he believed that evil must be resisted and eliminated but resisted through means that are in consonance with morality, not with hate, war, violence and ill-will.

## Faith in God

Gandhi emphasises that a *Satyagrahi* must be a believer in God. A *Satyagrahi* has no other stay but God, arid one who has any other stay or depends on any other help, cannot offer *Satyagraha*, because he may be a passive resister, a non-cooperator and so on, but cannot be a true *Satyagrahi*.

## Brotherhood of Man and Faith in the Goodness of Man

Gandhi believed in the principle of one universal soul. To Gandhi, brotherhood of man means that we are one of another. It means that you cannot injure your neighbour without injuring yourself or *vice versa*. Hence the entire edifice of *Satyagraha* rests on the faith in the goodness of man. *Satyagraha* aims at change of heart through non-violent, noble and friendly action.

Gandhi mentions the following as the basic assumptions for successful *Satyagraha*.[28]

(a) There must be common honesty among *Satyagrahis*.

(b) They must render heart discipline to their commander. There should be no mental reservation.

(c) They must be prepared to lose all, not merely their personal liberty, not merely their possessions, land, cash etc., but also the liberty and possessions of their families, and they must be ready cheerfully to face bullets, bayonets, or even show death by torture.

(d) They must not be violent in thought, word or deed towards the 'enemy' or among themselves.

## Vows of *Satyagraha*

For the success of *Satyagraha* and in order to make the *Satyagrahi* intellectually, morally and spiritually strong enough to withstand enough all temptations, provocations and inflictions, Gandhi prescribed certain cardinal disciplines (eleven vows) a code of conduct, to be observed by them–more by the *Satyagrahi* leaders than by the *Satyagrahi* masses–in their daily life. The vows fall into two categories–principal and subsidiary.[29]

## Principal Vows

### Truth

Of all disciplines, the observance of the vow of truth comes first. The observance of the vow of truth is generally understood as merely confined to speaking the truth. But, according to Gandhi it really means that we must be truthful in thought, word and deed. Thus the observance of truth rules out the practice of secrecy, cunningness and deception. Truth is to be realized by devoted constant practice and indifference to all other interests in life. It means ceaseless striving and complete detachment. The realization or darshan of truth, said Gandhi, "can only be attained by the man of pure detachment. Anger, greed, pride not fear, all these things draw it evil across the seeker's eyes".

### *Ahimsa* (non-injury)

*Ahimsa* or non-violence literally means non-killing or non-injury. It is not enough not to take the life of any living being. The follower of this vow may not hurt physically or mentally even those whom he believes to be unjust, he may not be angry with them, he must love them; thus he would oppose the tyranny and injustice, whether of parents, governments or others, but will never hurt the tyrant. The follower of truth and *ahimsa* will conquer the tyrant by love; he will not carry the tyrant's will but he will suffer punishment even unto death for disobeying his will until the tyrant himself is conquered.

## Celibacy or *Brahmacharya*

It is well-nigh impossible to observe the foregoing two vows unless ceilbacy is also observed; for this vow, it is not enough that one does not look upon any woman with a lustful eye; he has to control his animal passions so that they will not move him even in thought; if he is married, he will not have a carnal mind regarding his wife but will consider her as his life-long friend and will establish with her the relationship of perfect purity.

## Control of the Palate

Until one has overcome the temptations of the palate, it is difficult to observe the foregoing vows, more especially that of celibacy. Control of the palate is the first essential in the observance of the vow of *brahmacharya*. Sex is indeed so tightly bound up with the palate that one who has not mastered taste cannot control animal passion either. An aspirant and striver for *brahmacharya* should, therefore, cultivate a feeling that he is eating not to satisfy the palate but just to keep body, mind and soul in perfect health.

## Non-Stealing

To take another person's property without his knowledge or permission or in the belief that it is an unclaimed property is, no doubt, an act of stealing. But stealing according to Gandhi, also includes taking of something from another without really needing and working for it, or taking it in larger quantity than is required for the immediate use, or to use it for a purpose different from one intended by the leader or to use it for a period longer than fixed with him, needless multiplication of wants, needless accumulation and hoarding for future use while others are in need of it at the moment, etc. In his opinion all amassing of wealth, above and beyond one's legitimate requirements; is theft.

## Non-possession or *Aparigraha*

It is not enough not to possess and keep much, but it is necessary not to keep anything which may not be absolutely necessary for our bodily wants; thus if one can do without chairs, one should do so. The follower of this vow will, therefore by constant reflection simplify his life.

## Subsidiary Vows

## Social and Religious Equimindedness

A *Satyagrahi*, according to Gandhi, should be firm believer in social and religious equality and in the equality of sexes. He should cultivate perfect equimindedness towards all people irrespective of their caste, colour, occupation, sex, religion, birth-place and habitation and should cultivate equal reverance for all the principal religions of the world. He should try to eradicate all kinds of unreasonable distinctions and discriminations, including untouchability, from the society; should try to establish communal harmony and to elevate the position of the fallen sections of the society, including those of the untouchables, the aboriginals and the women.

## Bread-Labour

The vow of bread-labour means that everybody, especially a *Satyagrahi*, must earn his bread and other primary needs of life by labouring with his hands, since production of every essential article involves bodily labour. "Bread-labour is a veritable blessing to one who would observe non-violence, worship truth, and make the observance of *brahmacharya* a natural act." It develops habits of obedience, self-respect and reliance, tenacity of will, sense of unity with others, endurance of hardships, sense of order and cooperation, energy, courage, equanimity, and practice in handling moral equivalents of weapons. Gandhi recommended hand-spinning as only universal form of bread-labour. But he never ceased to regard agriculture to be the ideal. In addition to spinning, everybody must, according to Gandhi, be his own scavenger. He felt that "there must be something radically wrong where scavenging has been made the concern of a separate class in society." Everyone should therefore, commence bread labour as a scavenger. Scavenging thus intelligently taken up, will help one to a true appreciation of the equality of man.

## *Swadeshi*

It is inconsistent with truth to use articles about which or about whose makers there is a possibility of deception. Therefore, for instance, a votary of truth will not use articles manufactured in the wills of Manchester, Germany or even in his own country, for he does not know that there is no deception about them. The vow of *Swadeshi* requires the use of simple and simple made clothing to the exclusion of even fancy buttons, foreign cuts, etc., and so will *Swadeshi* be applied to every department of life.

## Fearlessness

Truth and non-violence or love are the principal keystones of *Satyagraha* and these require sufficient fearlessness. One who fears cannot seek and follow truth. *Satyagrahi's* will, therefore, endeavour to be free from the fear of kings, people, caste, families, thieves, robbers, ferocious animals such as tigers and even death. Cultivation of courage and preparedness for sacrifice and sufferings which are necessary for a non-violent fighter also demand fearlessness. "He who has not overcome all fear cannot practice *ahimsa* to perfection".[30] A truly fearless man will defend himself against others by truth force or soul force.

## Humility

Arrogance, egotism, self-importance, anger, and the pride of achievement—all these draw an evil across a truth seeker's eyes. Detachment, openness and tranquility of mind, absence of prejudice and of the idea of doership in action, mildness, sublimity, forgiveness, fortitude—these are the real attributes of dispassionate seeker after truth and follower of non-violence. All these qualities taken together are called humility. Hence Gandhi writes in his Autobiography: "The instruments for the quest of truth are as simple as they are difficult. They may appear quite impossible to an arrogant person, and quite possible to an innocent child, the seeker after truth should be humbler than the dust".[31]

## Code of *Satyagraha*

After discussing vows of *Satyagraha*, in detail, in the preceding pages, we now take up the code of *Satyagraha*.

A *Satyagrahi* bids good-bye to fear. He is, therefore, never afraid of trusting the opponent. Even if the opponent plays him false twenty times, the *Satyagrahi* is ready to trust him the twenty-first time, for an implicit trust in human nature is the very essence of his creed.[32]

A *Satyagrahi* is nothing if not instinctively law-abiding, and it is his law-abiding nature which exacts from his implicit obedience to the highest law, that is the voice of conscience which overrides all other laws.[33]

. Since *Satyagraha* is one of the most powerful methods of direct action, a *Satyagrahi* exhausts all other means before he resorts to *Satyagraha*. He will, therefore, constantly and continually, approach the constituted authority, he will appeal to public opinion, educate public opinion, state his case calmly and coolly before everybody who wants to listen to him, and only after he has exhausted all these avenues will he resort to *Satyagraha*. But when he has found the impelling call of the inner voice within him and launches out upon *Satyagraha*, he has burnt his boats and there is no receding.[34]

The *Satyagrahi,* whilst he is ever ready for fight, must be equally eager for peace. He must welcome any honourable opportunity for peace.[35]

My advice is *Satyagraha* first and *Satyagraha* last. There is no other or better road to freedom.[36]

In the code of the *Satyagrahi* there is no such thing as surrender to brute force. Or the surrender then is the surrender of suffering and not to the Wielder of the bayonet.[37]

As a Satyagrahi I must always allow my cards to be examined and re-examined at all times and make reparation of an error is discovered.[38]

## Qualifications of a *Satyagrahi*

The following are the qualifications. I held as essential for every *Satyagrahi* in India:

1. He must have a living faith in God for he is his only rock.
2. He must believe in truth and non-violence as his creed and therefore 'have faith in the inherent goodness of human nature which he expects to evoke by his truth and love expressed through his suffering.
3. He must be leading a chaste life and be ready and willing for the sake of his cause to give up his life and his possessions.
4. He must be a habitual khadi-weaver and spinner. This is essential for India.
5. He must be a teetotaller and be free from the use of other intoxicants in order that his reason may be always unclouded and his mind steady.
6. He must carry out with a willing heart all the rules of discipline as may be laid down from time–to–time.
7. He should carry out the jail rules unless they are specially devised to hurt his self-respect.

The qualifications are not to be regarded as exhaustive. They are illustrative only.[39]

## Forms and Techniques of *Satyagraha*

The technique of *Satyagraha* admits of various methods to be used in successive stages, and many of them simultaneously, the most important being Basic Education and other items of the Constructive Programme, persuasion through reason, persuasion through change of heart by self-suffering and persuasion through non-violent direct action or non-violent non-cooperation which may take the forms of strike, picketing, boycott, and hijrat, ultimately culminating in civil disobedience.

## Basic Education

Gandhi wanted every individual to be a full-blooded, fully developed member of society and aimed at the allround development of man's personality, that is, his physical, mental, moral and spiritual faculties. He knew that "man is neither mere intellect, nor the grass animal body, nor the heart or soul alone. A proper and harmonious combination of all the three is required for the making of the whole man".[40] Thus, he devised a scheme of basic education which aimed at" an allround drawing out of the best in child and man-body, mind and spirit. He aimed at a perfect, well-balanced, allround education in which the body, the intellect and the heart have all simultaneous and full development into a natural harmonious whole. He described the system of basic education as "the spearhead of a silent social revolution fought with the most far-reaching consequences"[41] which will lay the foundation of a juster social order in which there is no unnatural division between the haves and the havenots.

## Constructive Programme

Constructive Programme was an integral and positive aspect of Gandhi's post-1920 *Satyagraha* movements. It was adopted for the achievement of economic self-sufficiency and inculcation of the *swadeshi* spirit amongst the masses. It was employed for the promotion of communal harmony and removal of social evils like untouchability, unemployment and illiteracy.

Constructive Programme according to Gandhi is designed to build up the nation from the very bottom... it must mean complete independence in every sense of the expression. Indeed his claim that Civil Disobedience is not absolutely necessary to win freedom through pure non-violent effort if the cooperation of the whole nation is secured in the Constructive Programme. For Gandhi constructive work was the heart of the matter. He described it as the permanent part of the non-violent effort. Handling of *Satyagraha* without the constructive programme will be, in his words, "like a paralysed hand attempting to lift a spoon."[42]

Gandhi adopted constructive programme as a method of *Satyagraha* for the first time during his Non-violent Non-cooperation Movement of 1920. In the course of this movement, national schools and institutions were started, arbitration courts and panchayats were established, and spinning on *Charkha* began with the sole object of replacing government schools and colleges, law courts, and foreign goods which were to be completely boycotted.

Spinning and social welfare activities were continued

throughout the Bardoli *Satyagraha* of 1928 with an emphasis upon the entire Khadi programme. Even during his *Salt Satyagraha* of 1930, the wearing of hand-spun cloth was imperative for all *Satyagrahis*, and welfare and self-sufficiency work was undertaken as a way of achieving *swaraj*. However, the constructive programme as a definite method of achieving complete Independence found its clear and full exposition only in the post-individual *Satyagraha* period of December 1941.

Constructive programme was not conceived by Gandhi for a single day. It took several years to give shape and form to the programme. It was during the post-individual *satyagraha* period that Gandhi expounded his whole philosophy of constructive programme and published a 25-page booklet entitled *Constructive Programme.* In 1941, Gandhi had listed the following thirteen items:

1. Communal Unity,
2. Removal of Untouchability,
3. Prohibition,
4. Khadi,
5. Other Village Industries,
6. Village Sanitation,
7. New or Basic Education,
8. Adult Education,
9. Uplift of Women,
10. Education in Health and Hygiene,
11. Provincial Languages,
12. Propagation of Rashtra Bhasa, and
13. Promotion of Economic Equality.

On 15th February 1945, Gandhi addressed Kasturba Nidhi workers. The booklet on Constructive Programme was revised with some more items added to the already existing thirteen. The items added were:

14. Kisans,
15. Labour,

16. Adivasis,
17. Lepers,
18. Students.[43]

After Gandhi's death, the following items were added by his followers to strengthen the movement:

19. Cow Protection,
20. Nature Cure,
21. Bhoodan,
22. Gramdan, and
23. Shanti Sena.[44]

## Conversion through Persuasive Argumentation

Simultaneous with mass education and other constructive activities, it is necessary in order to bring about any lasting revolution or radical change, first to change the attachment of individuals and groups to certain ideas, sentiments and assumptions. This is possibly only by conversion through rational and gentle persuasion, not by coercion and compulsion.

In *Satyagraha*, persuasion takes two forms, to be applied in successive stages. The first stage is largely characterised by rational argumentation. The opponent is sought to be convinced by reason. Gandhi said: "I have no desire to carry a single soul with me if I can not appeal to his or her reason. My conventionality I carry to the point of rejecting the divinity of the oldest Shashtras if they cannot convince my reason."[45] In his opinion, one of the greatest qualities of a *Satyagrahi,* particularly a *Satyagrahi* leader, is to possess the capacity for independent thinking and convincing others by reason. Thus a *Satyagrahi* has first of all to try to convince his opponent by reason and mobilize public opinion against the evil which he is out to eradicate. When public opinion is sufficiently roused against an evil the strongest will not dare to practice or openly to lend support to it. An awakened and intelligent public opinion is the most potent weapon of a *Satyagrahi.*[46]

## Conversion through Self-Suffering

According to Gandhi, the next step that the Satyagrahi has

to take in the direction of meaning the evil-doer from the evil is, to appeal to his heart by patient self-suffering, sympathy, sincerity, chivalry and humility. "You cannot inject new ideas into a man's head by chopping it off; neither will you infuse a new spirit into his heart by piercing it with a dagger."[47] Voluntary self-suffering opens the eyes of the evil-doer which are otherwise what to the voice of reason. Thus a *Satyagrahi* has to appeal continuously to the evil doer's head and heart combined.[48] Having failed to convince the evil doer merely by reason or in case he refuses even to listen to his arguments, the *Satyagrahi* seeks, by means of self-suffering, to get through to his unprejudiced judgement so that he may willingly come again onto a level where he may be persuaded through reason "...the hardest metal yields to sufficient heat. Even so must the hardest heart melt before sufficiency of the heat of non-violence. And there is no limit to the capacity of non-violence to generate heat."[49]

## Fasting

The most delicate form of *Satyagraha* is fasting. Unlike some other forms of *Satyagraha*, Gandhi was himself the author of fasting. Fasting is chiefly, a way of personal cleansing and penance.[50] It is a potent and "infallible weapon in the armoury of *Satyagraha*". It is a fiery-weapon.

Gandhi enunciated certain general principles and conditions under which a *Satyagrahi* could resort to fasting: "A *Satyagrahi* should fast only as a last resort when all other avenues of redress have been explored and have failed. Suffering even unto death and, therefore, even through a perpetual fast is the last weapon of a *Satyagrahi*. That is the last duty which is open to him to perform.[51] He was of the considered view that fasting should be undertaken only by an "expert" and by him, too, only according to his capacity to fast. Fasting should be undertaken either for self-purification or self-restraint, or for appealing to the better nature of the opposite party, in order to make him reconsider his stand and realise his wrong. It may be undertaken to check acts of violence, to remove bitterness or even purify political atmosphere. It should, however, be employed only as "a species of tyaga", and never as a method of exercising under pressure on the opposite party.

As an expert in *Satyagraha*, Gandhi himself undertook fasts on as many as seventeen different occasions during his life, but he warned his friends and followers against imitating him blindly or out of false or hysterical sympathy. Of these fasts, his three fasts were against official injustice, four against the institution and practice of untouchability, three against Hindu-Muslim riots, and four against other acts of violence. Further, three of his fasts were for self-purification and penance,[52] and one to encourage the Ahmedabad Mill workers in the strike which they were continuing on his advice in order to secure increase in their wages.[53]

## Non-Violent Non-Cooperation

Gandhi admittedly learnt the technique of non-violent non-cooperation from Leo Tolstoy. Non-violent non-cooperation is a sacred duty and an alternative to anarchy. It is the most expeditious method known to the world of winning over opponents. Non-cooperation with the evil-doer is a mild form but can be an immensely potent technic when undertaken on a mass scale. It is the activisation of love for the redress of wrongs. There can be non-cooperation between a father and his sons as well between an imperial oppressor and the citizens. Non-cooperation indeed means renunciation of the benefits of a system with which we non-cooperate. A non-cooperator has therefore, to renounce the benefits of schools, corporations, courts, titles, legislatures and other institutions set up under an evil system.

Gandhi's scheme of non-cooperation presupposed ability on the part of *Satyagrahi* masses to control all the forces of evil. His scheme also presupposed suffering and losses to the non-cooperator. According to Gandhi, non-cooperation is a "measure of discipline and self-sacrifice, without which no nation can make real progress."[54]

Gandhi started his first Non-cooperation Movement in India in 1920. It aimed to redress the wrongs of the Khilafat and the Punjab massacres and for the attainment of *swaraj*. The items of the programme were as follows:[55]

(a) Surrender of titles and honorary offices and resignation of nominated posts in local bodies.

(b) Refusal to attend government levies, durbars and other official and semi-official functions held by government officials, or in their honour.

(c) Gradual withdrawal of children from school and colleges in the various provinces.

(d) Gradual boycott of British Courts by lawyers and litigants and establishment of private arbitration courts by them for settlement of private disputes.

(e) Refusal on the part of the military, clerical and labouring classes to offer themselves as recruits for service in mesopotamia.

(f) Withdrawal by the candidates from election to the reformed councils and refusal on the part of the voters to vote for any candidate who may despite the congress advice, offer himself for election.

(g) Boycott of foreign goods. Laying down of arms and the suspension of taxes were the two last stages of Non-cooperation.

Non-violent non-cooperation may take the form of strike, picketing, boycott, *hartal* and hijrat, ultimately culminating, in Civil Disobediences.

## Strikes

According to K.L. Shridharani, the strikes as such "is labour's instrument for the acquisition of a desired standard of treatment and living from the employer."[56] Strikes may be employed directly and openly to achieve political ends. For example, during his South-African *Satyagraha* Movement, he advised and himself conducted a strike of Indian Coalmine workers and railway-men in the months of October-November, 1913, for the singular object of persuading the Government to repeal £-3 tax.[57]

However, whether the strike method is employed to achieve economic ends, or to secure political betterment, it must fulfil certain preliminary requisite in order to find a definite place in the *Satyagraha* scheme. Firstly, a peaceful strike must be limited to the actual sufferers and must, at the same time, be justifiable on its own merits. Secondly, it should be spontaneous and not manipulated. During his Ahmedabad *Satyagraha*, Gandhi laid down the other conditions of a successful strike. These were:[58]

1. Never to resort to violence,
2. Never to molest black-legs,[59]
3. Never to depend upon alms, and
4. To remain firm, no matter how long the strike continued, and to earn bread, during the strike by any other honest labour.

Gandhi, however, warned against the use of strikes in the public utility services thought that the strike or abstention from work in essential services was against the spirit of Satyagraha for it puts the community or at least a substantial section of it, to loss, harassment or inconvenience. He thought that "dislocation of these would dislocate public life".[60]

## *Hartal*

*Hartal* or peaceful stoppage of work is another form of *Satyagraha. Hartal* means voluntary suspension of business in protest against some evil authority. It is a way of signifying protest, and its purpose is to strike the imagination of all the people as well as the government. According to Gandhi, it is an "act of self-purification".[61] It is the best method of making our strong disapproval of the action of the government. It is a means, more powerful than monster meetings expressing national opinion.[62] *Hartals*, however, should be absolutely voluntary; otherwise they would cease to be non-violent. *Hartal* forcibly brought about cannot be considered *Satyagrahi hartal.* They should be brought about by persuasion, gentle argument and propaganda.

In any case, there should be no element of compulsion or force in it. Besides, *hartals* should not be organised too frequently, for then they would be hardly effective.

## Boycott

Another *Satyagraha* method advocated by Gandhi was .the boycott of economic, social, political, educational, legal and other institutions with the object of lodging protest against, and putting pressure on, the opposite party in order ultimately to seek redress of grievances. It is a sort of punishment and is conceived in a vindictive spirit.

Economic boycott is implied in the vow of *Swadeshi.* It implies the boycott of commodities of universal use, for they must always be locally produced. According to Gandhi, foreign cloth is such a commodity. Hence in 1920-22, he went so far as to urge the destruction of foreign cloth in India. Gandhi himself inaugurated the bonfires of foreign cloth in Bombay in July 1921.

In the social sphere, boycott takes the form of non-violent social ostracism. But Gandhi tells us that in the complex conditions of the modern world, social ostracism is of a very limited application. It may be employed only in extreme cases "when a defiant minority refused to bend to the majority, not out of any regard for principle, but from sheer defiance or worse".[63] Social boycott should be applied only in such a way that it is not felt as a punishment by the object of boycott. "It must cause pain to the party using it, if it causes inconvenience to its object."[64]

In the political sphere, boycott takes the form of civil disobedience. It includes resignation of offices and titles and refraining from making use of the services of those who do not represent popular will and flout public opinion. Voters "mustratify their verdict by complete abstention from any encouragement of the so-called representatives. The public will be bound, if they are non-cooperationists, to refrain from giving these representatives any prestige by attending their political functions or parties".[65]

The boycott of educational, legal and other institutions means setting up of such parallel institutions on the non-violent model in the light of the ideal.

## Picketing

Peaceful picketing is also a valid and useful form of *Satyagraha*. Picketing, like *hartal*, should also be persuasive and coercive. Both during the Non-cooperation Movement and the Civil Disobedience Movement of 1930-34, Gandhi urged picketing, preferably by women, of foreign as well as country liquor shops and foreign cloth shops. However, Gandhi does not favour *dharna* as a method of picketing. He considered *dharna* as a form of barbarity, a crude and cowardly way of using coercion. Picketing as a species of *Satyagraha* has to be entirely non-violent.

## Hijrat

Hijrat or *deshatyaga* is an age-old technique - individual as well as corporate—of meeting wrongs. It means voluntary emigration by people from the land they have hitherto believed to be theirs,[66] when they are grievously oppressed and terrorised and when they have no other recourse. But in Gandhi's opinion, in the purest form of *Satyagraha*, there is no need for doing *hijrat.* But in case of incapacity of offering non-violent or even violent resistance to the oppressor, Gandhiji's alternative to cowardly submission to oppression and demoralization was hijrat. "It is wisdom to vacate houses or places that are plague infected. Tyranny is a kind of plague and when it is likely to wake us angry or weak it is wisdom to leave the scene of such temptation."[67]

Gandhi advised hijrat to the Hindus of Sindh province during communal riots in 1939-40.[68] He also advised hijrat to the city women of India during Second World War to escape criminal assaults and violation by foreign soldiers stationed in India.[69] Earlier he had commended hijrat to the *Satyagrahis* of Bardoli in 1928, and those of Junagadh and Vitthalgad in 1939.[70]

*Hijrat,* however, should be resorted to in extreme cases. It should be a planned, and not a cowardly fight. But "planned hijrat requires courage and forethought".[71]

All these various species of non-cooperation culminate in civil disobedience which is the next logical weapon.

## Civil Disobedience

It is an active, strong and extreme form of *Satyagraha.* According to Gandhiji, civil disobedience is a necessary part of non-cooperation.[72] Gandhi conceived it as "a substitute for violence or armed rebellion. It is a non-coercive method which any law-abiding citizen can adopt, provided he is saturated with the spirit of non-violence and is ready for the utmost sacrifices.[73]

According to Gandhi, complete civil disobedience implying a refusal to render obedience to every single state-made law can be a very powerful movement.[74] In Gandhiji's opinion, civil disobedience should be "so complete that if an order was issued on us by the government saying go to the right', we must not hesitate to move leftward". It is a complete, effective and bloodless substitute of armed revolt.

Civil disobedience can be undertaken for the deliberate breach certain unmoral statutory enactments, or as the symbolic non-violent revolt against the state. In either case, it does not reflect want of respect for the constituted authority. Its ultimate aim is to substitute voluntary cooperation for involuntary cooperation and willing obedience for forced obedience. This underlying objective alone can make the *Satyagrahis* adhere to their inner voice.[75] Civil disobedience can be practiced "only as a last resort and by a selected few in the first instance at any rate".[76]

Civil disobedience is primarily of two types - offensive or assertive and defensive. Either of the two types may be offered by single individuals as completely independent units or by masses collectively. But whereas individual civil disobedience is self-led, mass civil disobedience needs a leadership. Gandhi considered civil disobedience as essentially an individual affair and he regarded individual civil disobedience as more effective, almost irresistible. According to him, "offensive compromise is based on give and take, but in *Satyagraha* 'there can be no give and take in fundamentals. Any compromise on fundamentals is a surrender because it is all give and no take."[77]

However, this list like any other list, cannot be said to be complete and exhaustive. There can be as many forms and techniques of *Satyagraha* as there are forms of injustices, their different grades of intensity, different nature of the agents and their relations with others. It is through the advocacy and use of these techniques that Gandhi delivered his supreme message of substituting willing obedience to forced obedience and voluntary cooperation for involuntary cooperation. In the words of Diwakar, "It is not Gandhiji who made *Satyagraha* but *Satyagraha* which has made Gandhiji... If it is a matter of obligation between two, it is *Satyagraha* which has obliged Gandhiji rather than it reverse.[78]

## Bhikhu Parik on *Satyagraha*[79]

For Gandhi, rational discussion and persuasion were the best way to resolve conflict. This was peaceful, non-coercive, and respected the moral integrity and autonomy of each party. Gandhi acknowledged that, taken to its logical extreme, his theory of 'relative truth' undermined the very basis of action, for no man could ever act if he constantly entertained the nagging doubt that he might be wholly mistaken. However, he thought that one should at least acknowledge one's fallibility and leave room for reflection and reconsideration, and that, being irreversible and emotionally charged, violence did not allow this.

Gandhi also rejected violence on moral grounds. Morality consisted in doing what was right because one believed it to be right, and required unity of belief and conduct. Since the use of violence did not change the opponent's perception of truth, it compelled him to behave in a manner contrary to his swabhava and sincerely held beliefs, and violated his moral integrity.

Gandhi further argued that violence rarely achieved lasting results. An act of violence was deemed to be successful when it achieved its immediate objectives. However, if it were to be judged by its long-term consequences, our conclusion would have to be very different.

Finally, for Gandhi the means-end dichotomy lying at the heart of most theories of violence was false. In human life the so-called means consisted not of implements and inanimate tools but of human actions, and by definition these could not fall outside the jurisdiction of morality. Besides, the method of fighting for an objective was not external to but an integral part of it. The so-called means were really the ends in an embryonic form, like seeds, of which the so-called ends were a natural flowering. As such, the fight for a just society could not be conducted by unjust means.

Gandhi argued that we needed a new method to fight against injustice, as the two methods—rational discussion and persuasion, were inadequate or deeply flawed. The new method, according to Gandhi, should activate the soul, mobilize its enormous latent energy, and generate a new kind of spiritual power that had hitherto not been given its due place in political life. The new method should aim to open up the opponent's mind and heart so that rational discussion could take place in a climate of goodwill and critical self-reflection. He thought that his method of *satyagraha* met this requirement.

Gandhi first discovered *satyagraha* and tried it out during his campaigns against social discrimination in South Africa. In the course of his struggles against British rule in India and the unjust practices of his own society, he kept on perfecting it. According to Gandhi, *satyagraha* meant civil insistence on or tenacity in the pursuit of truth. It aimed to penetrate the barriers of prejudice, ill-will, dogmatism, self-righteousness, and selfishness, and to reach out to and activate the soul of the opponent. Every human being had a soul, however, degenerate or dogmatic he might be. Thus, he had the capacity to feel for other human beings and to acknowledge their common humanity.

*Satyagraha* was a 'surgery of the soul', a way of activating Soul-force'. For Gandhi 'suffering love' was the best way to do this, and formed the inspiring principle of his new method. The *satyagrahi*, whenever confronted with an injustice, sought a dialogue with his opponent. He did not confront the latter with a dogmatic insistence on the justice of his demands, rather he invited his opponent to join him in cooperatively searching for the truth of the matter in dispute, as he knew he could be partial and biased. Since his sole concern was to evoke a moral response in his opponent, he did everything possible to put him at ease and nothing to harass, embarrass, anger, or frighten him, hoping thereby to trigger in him a slow, intensely personal, and highly complex process of self-examination. He suspended the struggle, the moment his opponent showed willingness to talk in a spirit of genuine goodwill, and gave reason a chance to work in a more hospitable climate.

Gandhi, like Kant and John Rawls, argued that every community required a widespread sense of justice to hold it together. But unlike them he argued that the sense of justice was highly cerebral and needed a deeper and emotionally charged sense of shared humanity to give it depth and energy. The sense of humanity consisted in recognition of the fundamental ontological fact that human well-being was indivisible, that in degrading and brutalizing others people degraded and brutalized themselves, and that they could not sustain a communal life without a spirit of mutual concern and love.

Gandhi observed certain basic principles in all his *satyagrahas*. They were preceded by a careful study of the situation, patient gathering of facts, a reasoned defence of the objectives, a popular agitation to convince the opponent of the intensity of the *satyagraphi's* feeling, and an ultimatum to give him a last chance for negotiation. Throughout the *satyagraha*, the channels of communication with the opponent were kept open, the attitudes on either side were not allowed to harden, and intermediaries were encouraged. A pledge, not to use violence or to resist arrest or confiscation of his property, was to be taken by the *satyagrahi*. The *satyagrahi* prisoner, too, was to follow these rules. He was expected to be courteous, to ask for no special privileges, to do as he was ordered, and never to agitate for conveniences 'whose deprivation does not involve any injury to his self-respect'.

The effectiveness of *satyagraha* was explained by Gandhi in terms of the spiritual impact of suffering love. The *satyagrahi's* love and moral nobility disarmed his opponent, weakened his feelings of anger and hatred, and mobilized his higher nature. And his uncomplaining suffering denied his opponent the pleasure of victory, mobilized neutral public opinion, and created in him a mood conducive to calm introspection. The two together triggered the complex process of critical self-examination on which a *satyagrahi* relied for its ultimate success. Neither love by itself nor suffering by itself was enough. Love spiritualized suffering, which in itself had only a psychological value; suffering gave love its psychological energy and moral power. According to Gandhi, it was not easy to explain rationally how non-violence worked, as we knew so little about the operations of the human soul. 'There is nothing invisible in violence. On the other hand, non-violence is three-fourth invisible', and it acted in a 'silent and undemonstrative' manner.

Although Gandhi continued to maintain that suffering love was omnipotent and, when pure, capable of 'melting even the stoniest hearts', he knew that reality was quite different. Not surprisingly, Gandhi introduced such other forms of pressure as economic boycott, non-payment of taxes, non-cooperation, and *hartal* (cessation of work), none of which relied on the spiritual power of suffering love alone. Even his vocabulary increasingly underwent a radical change, at times becoming merely an obverse of the language of violence. He started talking about 'non-violent warfare', 'peaceful rebellion', a 'civilised form of warfare', a 'war bereft of every trace of violence', and 'weapons' in the 'armory' of the *satyagrahi*, all intended to 'compel' and 'force' the opponent to negotiate. Gandhi's political realism triumphed over his moral idealism, and, despite his claims to the contrary, the *satyagraha* was not always a purely spiritual method of action.

Apart from these methods, Gandhi introduced the method of fasting, which was highly controversial. He argued that his fast was a form of suffering love which had a fourfold purpose. First, it was his way of expressing his deep sense of sorrow and hurt at the way in which those he loved had degraded themselves and disappointed him. Second, as their leader he felt responsible for them, and his fast was his way of atoning for their misdeeds. Third, it was his last desperate attempt, an 'intense spiritual effort', to stir their sluggish conscience', to 'sting them into action', and to mobilize their moral energies. Finally, the fast was intended to bring the quarrelling parties together and to get them to resolve their differences themselves, thereby both deepening their sense of community and developing their powers of self-determination and conflict resolution.

Gandhi agreed that his fast exerted considerable pressure on his intended target, but thought it on balance fully justified. The fast did exert moral pressure, but there was nothing improper in it. And it was not coercion or blackmail because it did not threaten others with personal harm.

Gandhi imposed strict limits on fast as it could be misused for selfish purposes and even degenerate into blackmail. These limits were: (i) it could not be undertaken against those with whom one was bound by the ties of love; (ii) it must have a concrete and clearly specified purpose and not vague and abstract goal; (iii) the purpose must be morally defensible in the eyes of its intended target; (iv) it should not in any way be designed to serve one's own interests; (v) it should not ask people to do what they are incapable of doing, or involve great sacrifices; and (vi) it should only be undertaken by one who is an acknowledged moral leader of his people, has a long record of working for their welfare, and an unblemished moral character.

## The limits of *Satyagraha*

Gandhi's *satyagraha* had moral and political significance, but it also suffered from several limitations. Although he was right to stress the unity of reason and morality, or the head and the heart as he called it, he was wrong to think that all or even most social conflicts could be resolved by touching the opponent's heart. They sometimes occur because men of goodwill take very different views of what human well-being consists in. It is difficult to see how Gandhi's method can resolve these differences and the consequent conflicts.

Gandhi rightly argued that human beings are generally affected by the suffering of others and regret that suffering even if they are unable or unwilling to do anything about it. However, he overlooked the fact that, if they thought the suffering deserved, their reaction would be different. Not the suffering *per se* but one's judgement of it determines one's response to it, and hence it has different effects on different individuals, depending on their beliefs and values.

Gandhi was wrong to argue that *satyagraha* never failed and that it was effective under all conditions. If he had said that it was as a self-chosen way of being in the world and that one would die rather than kill, he view would have made moral but not political sense. To his credit he insisted that it was meant to succeed and achieve results. And that subjected his claim to a different kind of scrutiny. It was an article of faith for him that all human beings had souls which could be 'touched' and 'activated'. As a result he did not and could not acknowledge that some souls might be profoundly distorted and pathological. Contrary to what he said, *satyagraha* pre-supposes a sense of decency on the part of the opponent, an open society in which his brutality can be exposed, and a neutral body of opinion that can be mobilized against him.

Gandhi's *satyagraha* has much to be said for it, but it cannot be a catholicon. Although Gandhi insisted otherwise, violence need not be accompanied by hatred and ill-will or be uncontrolled. Like non-violence it too can be restrained, measured, born out of love for both the victims and the perpetrators of injustice, and used to arrest human degradation.

Although Gandhi's *satyagraha* had its limitations and he was wrong to claim 'sovereign efficacy' for it, it is a powerful, novel, and predominantly moral method of social change. Not surprisingly, it has been borrowed and tried out in different countries with suitable adjustments to local circumstances. The United States is an excellent example of this.

## Conclusion

*Satyagraha* is, in fact, a growing science. Gandhi has demonstrated the efficiency and efficacy of *Satyagraha* not only in getting political freedom but against exploitation, oppression, social injustice and social evils in his life time. *Satyagraha,* moreover, is not the weapon of the weak or coward, rather it is a weapon of the strong or brave which demands for a new real civilization and culture for the humanity as a whole.

In fact, *Satyagraha* is the most powerful and permanent weapon to solve political, social and economic as well as religious problems. It holds good even today in our democratic setup against any perpetrated evil. Gandhi claimed that the Sarvodaya social order would be free from moral degradation, economic exploitation, and political subjugation.

## Notes

1. Gouri Kant Thakur, *Mahatma Gandhi's Philosophy of Satyagraha,* Kishore Vidya Niketan, Varanasi, 1988, p.3.
2. M. K. Gandhi, *An Autobiography or the Story of My Experiments with Truth,* Navjivan, Ahmedabad, 1956, p.239.
3. Gouri Kant Thakur, *op. cit.,* p.3.
4. M.K. Gandhi, *Satyagraha in South Africa,* I Edition, S. Ganesan, Madras, 1928, p.173.
5. *The Collected Works of Mahatma Gandhi,* Vol. VIII, The Publications Division, Ministry of Information and Broadcasting, Government of India, Delhi, 1962, pp. 22-23.
6. *Ibid.,* Vol. XVIII, 1965, p.133.
7. M.K. Gandhi, *Hind Swaraj* or *Indian Home Rule,* 'I Edition, III Reprint, Navjivan, Ahmedabad, 1958, p.79.

8. J.B. Kripalani, *Gandhian Terminology* (Unpublished MSS) AICC Papers, File No. 15,1936, p.27.
9. V.P. Varma, *The Political Philosophy of Mahatma Gandhi and Sarvodaya,* Lakshmi Narain Agarwal, IV Edition, 1980-81, p.162.
10. *Young India,* 26-2-1925, p.73.
11. *Young India,* 19-3-1925, p.95.
12. *Young India,* 4-6-1925, p.189.
13. *Tire Collected Works of Mahatma Gandhi,* Vol. XIII, p.522.
14. K.L. Shridharani, *War Without Violence,* Bombay, 1962, p.162.
15. V.P. Varma, *op.cit.,* pp.163-164.
16. M.K. Gandhi, *Satyagraha in South Africa, op. cit.*, p. 114.
17. S.C. Gangal, *Gandhian Thought and Techniques in tire Modern World,* Criterion Publications, New Delhi, 1988, pp. 154-155.
18. V. P. Varma, *op.cit.*, p. 168.
19. *Harijan,* 14.5.1938, p. 111.
20. Ramjee Singh, *Gandhi and the Modern World,* Classical Publishing Company, New Delhi, 1988, p. 79.
21. M.K. Gandhi, *Satyagraha in South Africa, op.cit.*, p.433.
22. Anil Dutta Mishra, *Fundamentals of Gandhism,* Mittal Publications, New Delhi, 1955, p.22.
23. M.K. Gandhi, *Satyagraha,* Navajivan, Ahmedabad, 1954, p.40.
24. M.L. Sharma, "Mahatma Gandhi's View of *Satyagraha*", *Gandhi Bhavan News Letter,* University of Delhi, VoL.II, No.1, January 1989, p.52.
25. *Young India,* 11-8-1920.
26. S.C. Gangal, *op.cit,* p.152.
27. Ramjee Singh, *op.cit,* pp.82-83.
28. *Harijan,*22-10-1938.
29. R. R. Diwakar, *Saga of Satyagraha,* Gandhi Peace Foundation, New Delhi, 1969, p.225.
30. *Harijan,*1-9-1940.
31. M. K. Gandhi, *Autobiography, op.cit.*, p.15.
32. M. K. Gandhi, *Satyagraha in South Africa,* 1950 Edition, *op.cit.*, p.159.
33. *Speeches and Writings of Mahatma Gandhi,* G. A. Natesan and Company, Madras, 1933, 4th Edition, p.465.
34. *Young India,* 20-10-1927, p. 353.
35. *Young India,* 19-3-1931, PAO.
36. *Harijan,* 15-9-1946, p. 312.
37. *Young India, 30-4-1931,* p. 93.
38. *Harijan,* 11-3-1939, p. 44.
39. *Harijan,* 25-3-1939, p. 64.
40. *Harijan,* 8-5-1937.
41. *Harijan,* 9-10-1937.
42. M.K. Gandhi, *Constructive Programme,* 1941, p.29.
43. *Ibid.,* p.3.
44. Anil Dutta Mishra, *op.cit.,* p.77.
45. *Young India,* 14-7-1920.

46. *Young India,* 8-8-1929.
47. Louis Fischer, *The Life of Mahatma Gandhi* (Bhavan's Library), Vol.I, p.93.
48. Quoted in D. G. Tendulkar, *Mahatma,* Vol. II, p.265.
49. *Harijan,* 7-1-1939.
50. M. K. Gandhi, *Autobiography, op.cit.,* p. 419.
51. *Harijan,* 18-2-1933.
52. For details see Ram Rattan, *Gandhi's Thought and Action,* Kalinga Publications, Delhi, 1991, pp. 289-292.
53. *The Collected Works of Mahatma Gandhi,* Vol. XIV, *op.cit.,* 1965, pp. 254 and 268.
54. D. G. Tendulkar, *op.cit.,* p.13.
55. *Ibid.,* p.12.
56. K. L. Shridharani, *War Without Violence: A Study of Gandhi's Method and Its Accomplishments,* I Edition, Victor Gollancz Ltd., London, 1939, p.36.
57. The *Collected Works of Mahatma Gandhi, op.cit,* Vol. XII, 1964, pp. 658-68.
58. M. K. Gandhi, *Autobiography, op.cit.,* p. 27.
59. Black-leg is a person who offers to work when the regular workers are on strike.
60. *Harijan,* 10-8-1947, p.274.
61. M. K. Gandhi, *Autobiography, op.cit.,* p.562.
62. D.G. Tendulkar, *op.cit.,* Vol.1, p.312.
63. D. G. Tendulkar, *op.cit.,* Vol.1, p.312.
64. *Young India,* 16-2-1921.
65. *Young India,* 8-12-1920, p.298.
66. *Young India,* 31-5-1928.
67. M. K. Gandhi, "Bardoli on Trial", *Young India,* 31-5-1928.
68. *Non-Violence Peace and War,* Vol.I, Navjivan Publishing House, Ahmedabad, 1948, pp.253-54.
69. *Ibid.,* Vol.II, p.377.
70. *Harijan,* 20-5-1939.
71. *Non-Violence in Peace and War, op.cit.,* p.253.
72. *Young India,* 27-3-1920.
73. *Harijan,* 24-6-1939, pp. 159-60.
74. *Young India,* 4-8-1921.
75. *Harijan,* 15-10-1938, p. 290.
76. *Young India* , 23-3-1921.
77. *Harijan,* 30-4-1940.
78. R.R. Diwaker, *Satyagraha: Its Technique and History,* Hind Kitabs, Bombay, 1946, p.91.
79. Excerpted from Bhikhu Parikh, *Gandhi,* Oxford University Press, London, 1997.

# 5

# The Critique of Modernity with Special Reference to Bhiku Parekh

*– Jai Narain Sharma*

Indeed it is like a paradox that a man who was once regarded as an avowed critic of modern civilization is being acclaimed today as the saviour of the Modern World. Only a few years ago more than 60 Noble Prize Winners, in a joint statement, while expressing their concern and anxiety over the deepening of world crisis have looked towards Gandhi as the hope of humanity. The modern world is facing an unprecedented crisis. Violence has replaced the law of love, machine has replaced man and individual has become a mere cog in the wheel of the state. The old world is worn out and dead but the new world is yet to be born. The values of materialism, industrialism and consumerism are being challenged but the mainfesto of the alternative civilization remains hazy. In such a scenario the message of Gandhi must be spread by one and all.

The Mahatma's life work and position in world history were memorably summed up by Albert Einstein, the greatest scientist of the last century: "The veneration in which Gandhi has been held throughout the world rests on the recognition, for the most part unconscious, that in our age of moral decay he was the only statesman who represented that higher conception of human relations in the political sphere to which we must aspire with all our powers. We must learn the difficult lesson that the future of mankind will only be tolerable when our course in world affairs, as in all other matters, is based upon the justice and law rather than the threat of naked power. Generation to come will scarce believe that such a one as this ever in flesh and blood walked upon this earth."[1]

Gandhi gave a decisive new direction to history. What was it about this man which held the human race in thrash who was this individual? And how did he come to yield such influence our the rest of mankind? He himself said that he was a very average individual. He confessed that he was not intellectually brilliant, but he added that while there are limitations to the development of mind there are no limitations to the development of heart.

But Gandhi has also been dubbed by a large number of persons as a reactionary. The more generous of his critics have described him as a revivalist. Some call him irrelevant specially in the present scenario. Even a mature mind like V.S. Naipal in his classic work 'India: A wounded civilization', opined "No Government can survive on Gandhian fantasy ; and the spirituality the solace of a conquered people which Gandhi turned into a form of national assertion, has soured more obviously into the nihilism that it always was."[2]

Gandhi is one of the most resolute critics of modernity in the twentieth century. He sees modernity, unless unchecked, sweeping away everything that stands in its way as it tries to take "charge of the world." Taking charge of the world implies that we can know how to organize the world (through science and rational, neutral theorizing) and how to implement our plans (through research, technology, and instrumental reasoning). At the heart of modernity is a questioning of dissatisfaction with the present and a faith that reason and the changes it fosters will lead to a progressively better future. In mounting his challenge, Gandhi confronts the foundational principles of the modern world and, in their place, he offers an idealized conception of traditional life in rural India, which he sees providing an alternative to the complexity, materialism, and poverty he detects in modern society.

The usual reading of Gandhi presents him as relentlessly anti-modernist: Ramashray Roy, for example, argues that "Gandhi's critique of modern civilization is total."[3] However, this is not the last word about his critique of modernity. Not only does he write about the ways it can be part of the good society, but his theory is also closely tied to such modern concepts as autonomy and equality.[4]

However much Gandhi builds on important modern conceptions such as secular equality and universal rights, his encounters with modernity do not prompt him to merge it with tradition. Unlike some of the leading Indian thinkers of the time, he does not want to synthesize modernity and Hinduism or to self consciously borrow aspects of modernity. His reconceptualization of autonomy and equality, allied as they are with community, duty, and cohesion, are oppositional to modern ones, and he seeks to buttress these goods by mounting a critique of modernity and modernization that is simultaneously conservative and radical. He wants a reformed tradition to stand, erectly and resolutely, to confront modernity. Only in this way, he reasons, can the dangerous elements of modernity be exposed and the modern project be made to explain itself. In advancing his position, Gandhi seeks to complicate modernity and rob it of its certainty.[5]

If we are to understand Gandhi's thought in its proper perspective, we must assign to the word 'modern' its proper content.

Modernity is a complex phenomenon, with a layered history of meanings. Its exact origins in time and space remain a matter of controversy, but is generally acknowledged as evident in seventeenth century Europe. At the time it was confined, innocuously enough, to a small group of philosopers-*cum*-scientists, who remained, on the whole, circumspect in their presentations and public statements in view of the paranoia of the Church with regard to innovative thought. Three names associated with certain momentous revolutions in scientific and philosophical attitudes, Descartes, Bacon and Newton, have become symbolic of the new approach to scientific learning which changed the face of the world. It is characterized by the need to put all true propositions to a philosophic test (methodological skeptism); the need to submit all truths about the world to a practical test (experimental proof); the postulation of two fundamental and dirremptive spheres of mind and matter, with the mathematical approproation one over the other; the assumption of a mechanical uniformity and lawlessness in nature, and the goal of an anthropocentric assertion of power over nature. Philosophical speculation had to be grounded in epistemology, which however remained as prone to multiple interpretations as the earlier metaphysics. If reason was subordinate to faith in the European Middle Ages, by the seventeenth century it began to assume primacy in the field of secular learning; it invaded eithics and politics in the eighteenth century, overtook befief in the nineteenth, and twentieth century stands, without any further obstacle to overcome, confronted with its own contradictions and limitations.[6]

Modernization as a conscious and deliberate pursuit has acquired currency in the post-world war. If development is the governing idea for the majority of Asian and African nations, modernization is their goal and objective. Though comparable to westernization, the two are not the same. Indeed, modernization could theoretically be conceived of as an endless, neverending process. Western societies have been modernizing at a rapid pace and catching up with them may involve some repetition of the process by covering the same ground and to that extent the two may appear identical. But the process need not go through the same stages or take the same time and it is here that modernization of under developed society may be differentiated from westernization.

Modernization indicates swift widespread change and transformation of societies and the broad lines of the process are industrialization, urbanization, and mass communication. Broad trends indicative of modernity could be spelt out as follows : (1) peoples' commitments and associations change from the local to the universal; (2) individual as a unit of society begins to play a more important role as against group; (3) association depending upon accident of birth is replaced by association of choice; (4) in place of fatalistic beliefs, there comes a sense of mastery over environment; (5) individual and group identities are not ascribed but chosen and achieved; (6) individual's work is less influenced by his family, residence and community; (7) rational and scientific attitudes replace emotions and non-rational approaches; (8) there is a change in social life in that authority is not necessarily associated with seniority or sex; youth and women acquire a new place and identity; (9) government, far from being a manifestation of power, come to be regarded as instrument of society with more popular participation, element of consent and accountability. A modern society, is differentiated, pluralistic, and is broadly participatory and democratic.[7]

Students of modernization have constructed models of societal behaviour under broad heads of tradition and modernity, the one being opposed to the other. A traditional society depends more on ascription than achievement, particularistic and diffuse in its orientation, more affective than rational and less differentiated and mobile in its structure and movement. It is predominantly agricultural and rural; a vast number of its people are illiterate and less susceptible to change.

But the dichotomy between tradition and modernity has limited validity applicability. Tradition and modernity are to be viewed as a continuum rather than two extreme and exclusive poles. A traditional society may have aspects of modernity and even the most modern society may have traits of tradionality.

Models of tradition and modernity are certainly helpful in our attempt to identify the predominant character of society. They greatly facilitate perception analysis and comparison. But no traditional society remains un-changed and even the most modern societies continue to live with many traditional elements. There is, in fact, an intricate mosaic of co existence of tradition and modernity and societies display a variety of combinations. At any rate, while societies can be identified as predominantly modern or traditional, elements of modernity and tradition co mingle in almost all societies.

The process of modernization may take various paths. Some traditions persist, some undergo change and some of them, indeed, may help in the very process of modernization. Modernization as a social process is a continuum that carries forward the past traditions and brings about a new pattern, a fresh combination. Since there never is a complete divorce between tradition and modernity, transition to modernity has often been effectcd through the use of traditional idiom, symbol and behaviour. Tradition may thus become an instrument through which an appeal for modernization may be made. Tradition may, therefore, serve the purpose of acting as a hand maid for a new birth. Which tradition, to what extent and when, would permit of change, is perhaps the most intricate and baffling question of human history. Possibilities of change and transformation of societies remain hidden as latent potentialities till they are evoked and tapped by some one in short the movement of modernization is often the modernization of tradition.[8]

While continuity and survival of reformulated tradition into modernity may be conceded, the process of modernization need not be taken as merely a cyclical and repetitive development of old time tradition. Modernization involves structural change and an element of innovation almost always accompanies it. Innovation, and an inclination and effort to sustain it may be the very foundation of modernization. While continuity may not be broken, there occurs a shift when modernization takes place. As innovation proceeds, flexible response of society help sustain its growth and produce congenial atmosphere for further leaps in the direction.

Under the spell of Gandhi's leadership, India's traditions were re-furnished, mobilised and galvanized to serve new goals and objectives. Gandhi's capacity for innovation was stupendous. He was, in fact, a great builder. He built institutions womens' institutions, labour unions, institutions like *Satyagraha* Ashram, political movement like Indian National Congress, Harijan Sangh, Hindi Bhasha Pracharini Sabha, Khadi Gramodyoga Sangh, and all this along with his ubiquitous contacts with India's millions. Gandhi was keen to apply the most appropriate technique in his agricultral and artisanal activities. Ashramities were for example sent from Phoenix to learn from Trappist to learn how to make sandals, the resulting product providing a valuable source of income for the institution. He advocated a careful study of horticulture and the establishment of model farms that would provide an example for surrounding farmers. He encouraged his followers to undertake socio-economic surveys of villages, so as to be able to obtain the facts on which appropriate campaigns for rural improvement could be based. "Gandhi did not therefore reject rational and scientific approaches to problems", admitted David Hardiman, "so long as they accorded with his moral principles."[9]

It was the singular genius of Gandhi that he perceived India's traditions with an instinct of a leader who knew what to do with them and how to do it. He was a strange mixture of the old and the new. Some of the richest and higest traditions of Indian civilization were embodied in him. For the vast multitudes of India, he was another *avatar* and his *darshan* was sought with avid interest. His prayer meetings, his revival of songs of worship, were indicative of his deep roots in India's traditions of *bhakti,* asceticism and self-sacrifice. In his personal life, he was a saint who abjured worldly pleasures and lived a life of self denial and devotion. The symbols he popularised, the technique he adopted, contained rich elements of past traditions. The future Indian polity was to be a *Ram Rajya,* the down trodden untouchables became Harijans and the fight against the British was *satyagraha.* His non-violent, non-cooperation, though defiant of laws, was full of humility and he called it savinay bhang. Gandhi's weapon of non-cooperation had its roots in Indian traditions. Inflicting pain upon oneself for self-realization was a hoary tradition in India. It was also well adopted for usage by an unarmed nation. Likewise, it was a potent instrument for reviving courage, fearlessness and honour, serving as a tonic for the Indian people by making them aware of the tremendous energies that lay untapped within themselves. It also served the purpose of integration through participation. The old symbolism was serving the new goal of political liberation.

He wanted to provide work for the half starved and half naked millions unemployed and underemployed, living in lakhs of villages in India, this he thought could be done through the revival of the spinning wheel and other cottages and village industries. Viewed uncritically in an age of highly, sophisticated technology, this looks like 'reaction', 'revivalism'. The putting back of the clock of progress or whatever else the so called modernist may choose to call it.

Before the invention of steam and its application to industry, the production of cotton and woolen yarn was a necessity both in the East and the West. The re-introduction of Khadi and other crafts in this age was necessity but not in the sense, it was a necessity in the past. It was not a physical necessity but a moral social economic and political necessity, if unmitigated poverty resulting from unemployment and semi-employment was to be relieved. Here also Gandhi took the help of science. He offered a prize of one lakh of rupees to a scientist or technologist who invented a *charkha*, which could yield more yarn and which could be produced and repaired in the villages. What Gandhi objected was a mad craze for industrialisation which replaces our human beings.[10]

Gandhi is also dubbed as conservative on account of his approach to religion. No doubt, he believed in God whose existance he admitted, he could not logically prove. For him truth was God. The moral law was God. He held that whoever believed in truth and non-violence was spiritual and godly. This, he held, could not be practised in a cave or on a mountain top. It must manifest itself in every activity of man in society.

But does belief in God militate against rationality and science? All great scientist are not non-believers. They hold that science has little to do with the primordial cause or the causeles cause. As a matter of fact, the scientists today have discarded the very idea of cause. They only investigate and find out the process by which change is brought about. Great and famous scientist like Newton, Einstein, J.C. Bose and many others are for belief in God. Only they did not take God inside their laboratories. And their search was for 'truth' which according to Gandhi is God.

It was not a personal God that the Mahatma believed in. He had the very, very deep and profound Hindu concept of *Brahma*. The all pervading Reality, which is God in its various manifestations. To quote his own words "To me God is Truth and love: God is ethics and morality: God is fearlessness: God is the source of life; Light and Life, and yet he is above and beyond all this. He is even the atheism of the atheist: he transcends speech and reason".[11]

Gandhi entitled his autobiography as *Experiments with Truth*. The idea of experimentation was in itself modern. All through his life Gandhi experimented with himself. He experimented with food, apparel, medicine, personal hygiene, social customs, language, public sanitation, not to mention his married life. His ceaseless endeavour to strike new paths, make fresh efforts evoked in the minds of people a symbolism of successful change and transformation. Gandhi's private life became a public topic for discussion as well as a model for imitation. Gandhi had conquered his self and he was a liberated soul. He had transcended earthly attachments, including the laws imposed by the alien empire. Perhaps the greatest value of his autobiography lay in its exemplifiation of the process of self development and integration of his personality. The way Gandhi struggled within himself for the attainment of perfection was a story that helped in the revival of national self-respect. Given will and motivation, one could reach heights of greatness this was the message of Gandhi's personal life. Conquering one's own self was the first step before one could challenge the foreign yoke; and the way Gandhi lived and developed, the conscious and deliberate attempt to live and utilise every moment of his life, served to show the drama of self realization that was open to all without let or hindrance. The most subtle and pervasive influence of the British Raj lay in spreading the psychology of self defeatism among the Indian people. The root of Indian slavery, according to Gandhi, was in the psychology of fear; and his personal life served to eradicate it and revive the ego and self-esteem of the Indian people.

Nothing would escape Gandhi's all embracing perspective. Nothing was too small or too big to serve the great cause of nation building and integration. Gandhi propounded healthy, progressive and modern ideas about several aspects of Indian life. His.views on Hindu Muslim question, India's national language, cow slaughter, child marriage, widow re-marriage, education, to name only a few, showed not only his tremendous capacity but also a rare gift for instilling new ideas and outlook on various facets of Indian life.

Before Gandhi's entry into Indian politics, the freedom struggle had proceeded into two broad channels : (1) the terrorist methods; and (2) the constitutional approach through appeal to the good sense of the British. Both the approaches had dismally failed and the country was in need of new leadership and fresh approach. Here was a call for innovation, for channeling the hopes, aspirations and energies of the people into new but acceptable ways. India had reached a blind alley and was groping in the dark. Gandhi's new technique of non-violent non-cooperation suddenly illumined the minds of the people. Here was a technique that grew out of India's traditions. It was perfectly applicable to a disarmed nation and it was based upon Gandhi's understanding of, and insight into, the British political culture.

Like J. S. Mill, Gandhi clearly understood that a liberal Government, in his case free India, cannot be sustained without a liberal society. Gandhi never used the term modernization. But his programmes, movements and approach gave eloquent proof of his perception of the need for modernity in India. Modernization was needed from three points of view. Firstly, it was the emergent need in as much as India had considerably lagged behind during the years of dependence and the lag had to be bridged. Secondly, the idea of nationalism, in itself new and modern, needed modernism as its pre-condition. India had to he a modern society before it could successfully fight against the foreign rule. This needed mobilisation and activisation of a vast number of people. India had to reform itself socially and religiously before it could think of demanding freedom. Lastly, as Gandhi realised, a modernized society alone could stand the stress and strain of independent nationhood, the goal of the Indian national movement. Modernization was necessary for self sustaining, integrative growth of India's nationalism.[12]

Into the status conscious, hierarchically organized, society of India, Gandhi's reformist zeal brought new ideas of eaualization. He was opposed to the practice of untouchability and was deeply aware of the evils that grew out of the traditional caste system. "Caste", said Gandhi, "has injured Hinduism because of its implications of superior and inferior status and of pollution by which are contrary to the law of love".[13]

Perhaps Gandhi's Western education and stay abroad had given him an opportunity to view Indian society in an objective way. He could easily distinguish the substance from the shadow, the form as against the essentials, the vital as against the ephemeral, the relevant against the irrelevant. Like many before him, he went to the root of the Hindu religion and scriptures. Having had the opportunity of living with Western people, he was impatient about the cant and hypocrisy that prevailed in Indian society. The reforms of Indian society that he advocated were needed for the very survival of Indian society, apart from it being instrumental in winning the struggle for independence. Though pragmatic to the core, he seemed to be in a hurry to put Indian society on a modern base. Gandhi brought the Western touch but he had the insight and understanding to make them relevant in the Indian context and conditions. Caste was to be modified, untouchability was to be removed, dignity of labour was to be instilled, not because Western countries were doing so but because they were the emergent needs of India.

Gandhi appears to be a strange mixture of tradition and change. Perhaps it is one of the reasons of his wide appeal, national stature and general acceptability, Gandhi symbolised India in transition, the India that found herself and the India that welcomed modernism. Some of the deepest and most significant founts of tradition were tapped to support and legitimise the newest needs of national awakening and exertion. Here was a man who never allowed even a shadow of an astrologer near him, a perfect specimen of *Bhagavad Gita karmayogi,* a Kautilya in action. Traditional in his exterior, Gandhi breathed modernism in every sector of national life. There was, for instance, the time factor. India was to be modernised within a time span that Gandhi laid down as it were. Every minute counted, every gesture mattered, every move significant, in the overall plan that had to be fulfilled. Gandhi perceived his role in the context of the total situation that prevailed in India. Otherwise tradititional in appearance, Gandhi dangled on his waist a watch, the symbol and emblem of modernity. Time was the essence and the given tasks were to be performed in a given time. Punctual to the minute, Gandhi had a fetish for cleanliness and order. People close to him have remarked that he was never seen unshaven; his nails were always cut; he did not use soap but his standards of cleanliness were very high.

Through personal example of self-discipline and self-development, embodying in his self the pre-dispositions and cultural configurations of India's traditions, Gandhi successfully carried out a thrust of modernity into the otherwise dull and stagnant society. With his arrival, India's politics gained primacy, involving a large number of people. With Gandhi, politics became participative, National and largely secular. He imbued India' millions with a purpose that was at once national and total. Narrow, sectarian outlook was challenged and new commitments came to the fore. People's hearts vibrated to the new symbolism of national identity. India's traditions coalesced in Gandhi, got transformed and released to serve the modern goals of nation building and national liberation. Old clusters of values and commitments stood exposed to the wind of change that now swept all over India. There was a new air of emancipation, a feeling of liberaion and a clearer, definite perception of the goal to be achieved. Country's resources were mobilised, and harnessed for national development and integration. A new leadership emerged, a mass-based, programme-oriented party built and efforts channelised into constructive activities of durable and national significance.

Gandhi acquired wide and convincing legitimacy for himself, reinforced national identity, achieved a rare degree of political penetration among the vast masses of India and brought forth an unusual deree of popular participation through empathy and mobility. All this was richly indicative of a fast pace of modernization.

The extent to which Gandhi went beyond his predecessors, espcially the so-called conservatives, was evident in the way he defined the nature of the cultural encounter between Britain and India. While they had argued that the conflict was between the Indian and European or between the Eastern and Western civilisations, Gandhi insisted that it was really between the ancient and modern. As he put it, there is 'no such thing as Western or European civilisation, but there is a modern civilisation'. His apprently trivial redefinition according to Bikhu Parekh, was in fact intended to alter the terms of the debate in his favour and achieve several ideological and political advantages. First, he was able to reject the currently fashionable view among many British and Indian writers that the East and the West were radically different and shared nothing in common. For Gandhi such a doctrine had no basis in facts, denied the fundamental unity of mankind and bred cultural parochialism. Second, he was able to attack modern civilisation without attacking the West. He greatly admired Socrates and Christianity, such modern writers as Tolstoy, Ruskin and Thoreau and several Western values and practices, and wished to exclude them from his criticism. Third, the distinction enabled Gandhi to argue that modern civilisation was of relatively recent origin in the West and that its pre modern counterpart was very different and more like Indian. He hoped thereby to remind the West of its earlier tradions and values, evoke its temporarily suppressed historical memories and elicit its support for his fight against modern civilisation. He was able to argue that since Indian civilisation stood for values to which the West had itself for centuries subscribed and was only trying to preserve their common heritage, by attacking and undermining it the West not only betrayed its own great past but also damaged its chances of future redemption. Fourth, by arguig that industrial civilisation was modern and 'still very young', Gandhi intended to suggest that it lacked the wisdom and matuity conferred by age, an important argument in a country that revered age. Finally, Gandhi hoped to convince his countrymen that in fighting modern civilisation they were not being reactionary. They were only combating the arrogance and impetuosity of an historical upstart and helping to preserve the permanent values of the whole of mankind, including the West. The idea of saving the soul pof their misguided masters tickled Indian pride and made Gandhi's harsh message ore acceptable.[14]

For Gandhi, then, India was a great battlefield, the modern kurukshetra on which the modern and ancient civilisations, the past and the present, were locked in a momentous battle for the future. The British were the best representatives of modern civilization and the Indians of the ancient. The former had fancied themselves as the missionaries of modern civilisations; Gandhi turned the Indians into missonaries of universal civilisation based on the great ancient values enriched by some of the valid insights of the modern. The hold of the colonial ideology was such that even its shrewdest critic did not transcend but largely reinterpreted its terms of debate.

Gandhi's critique of modern civilisation was far more complex than is generally imagined and quite different from that of such other writers as Rousseau, Carlyle, Ruskin, Tolstoy and Thoreau, by the last three of whom he was deeply influenced. In his view modern civilisation was grounded in a fatally flawed theory of man. Unlike ancient civilisation which was soul or spirit centred, the modern was body centred and in that sense 'materialistic'. For Gandhi the body had two basic characteristics. First, it was distinct, self-enclosed and separated from and only capable of preserving its integrity by maintaining its separateness from other bodies. As such it was the ontological basis of the human sense of particularity, and the source of the illusion that each individual was an independent and self centred ego only externally and contingently related to others and constantly concerned to preserve his identity by keeping the invasive others at a safe distance. Second, the body was the seat of the senses, and thus of wants and desires. By their very nature desires recurred with rhythmic regularity and were never satiated. They were also interrelated and one desire always gave rise to others. Qua sensual and desiring being, man was necessarily propelled by his inherently limitless desires and was always restless and dissatisfied.

A body centred or materialist view of man thus attributed two basic properties to him and regarded them as natural and legitimate, namely 'selfishness' and an 'infinite multiplicity of wants'. A civilisation based on such a flawed view necessarily suffered from several basic and interrelated limitations. First, it lacked moral and spiritual depth. Second, since it had no guiding principles to decide what desires deserved to be satisfied and within what limits, it led to a way of life devoid of meaning and purpose. Third, it de-humanised man and had a profound anti-human bias. Fourth, it perverted the human psyche and was suffused with the spirit of violence. Finally, it reduced wisdom to knowledge and the latter to a form of power only useful as an instrument of control over nature and other men. It thereby not only perverted the pursuit of truth but also lacked a system of knowledge capable of 'critically evaluating its basic assumptions and objectives'.[15]

Before concluding the chapter we might make a few general comments on Gandhi's critique of modern civilisation. Although a strong resemblance to the criticisms of such writers as Rousseau, Ruskin, Crlyle, Tolstoy, Nietzsche and Marx. Gandhi's critique contained original and important insights derived from the two great advantages he enjoyed over them. First, as a colonial native belonging to a despised race and an oppressed country, he experienced the darker side of modern civilisation not directly acessible to them. Second, as an heir to the rich and differently structured Indian civilisation, he brought to his critique an intellectual perspective and moral sensitivity not available to its Western critics.

Coming specially to the question, Was Gandhi Modern? Achariya J.B. Kripalani has very rightly said that if adherence to truth and supremacy of the moral law is modern, Gandhi was modern. If keeping one word and fulfilling one's engagement; eating for the sake of not satisfying a sophisticated palate but keep one's body fit for work recognition of the dignity of physical labour; tolerance and good understanding; feeling at home with those who differ from one or who are opponents; identification with the lowly and lost; untiring work for the poor, needy and down trodden, the unfortunate Daridranaryana last but not least dying for noble cause is modern, Gandhi was definitely modern. If, however the adoption of western forms in dress, food etc., drinking and smoking, dinning in fashionable and costly hotels and restaurants; using pleasure houses and night clubs; using time in scandal, mongolism and gossip is modern, surely Gandhi was not modern.[16]

The fact is that every son of a father is more modern than his parent. Like wise, every scientist or technologist working in recent times is more modern than the old masters. The word modern without its contents is merely a time judgement. It is not quality or value judgement. Modernity is like a fashion which is something fleeting and transitory. The latest fashion is for the hour. Modernity like fashion may pass even while we are writing or talking about it. Individuals and nations must order their lives by ideas and ideals which are more stable and permanent.

## Bhiku Parekh on the Critique of Modernity[17]

Modern industrial civilization emerged in the early years of the nineteenth century. Its characteristic features are rationalism, secularization, industrialization, the scientific culture, individualism, technological mastery of nature, globalization and liberal democracy. Whether it happened for good or bad is a point of debate since then. The answers to it varied, depending on the viewpoint of the commentator. Writers like J.S. Mill, Tocqueville, Thoreau, Tolstoy, Marx, Max Weber and Emile Durkheim viewed it in their own ways but theirs was a European standpoint.

Gandhi was familiar with both, the European as well as the

non-European viewpoints but found the non-European perspective more significant. Gandhi clearly separated the term modern from western, because although modernity came in the west, the west had seen an other form of civilization also before the modernity came. Modernity is a period that came in the west at a certain point in time; west has not been modern all along.

## No Self-Restraint

He found modern civilization to be basically, fundamentally flawed as it gave no respect to the basic nature, the qualities, and the 'swabhawa' of the individuals. It gave more importance to the body and neglected the soul. It was imperialist, violent, exploitative, unhappy and had no sense of purpose.

Since the modern civilization gave more importance to the body, it gave importance to the idea of individualism and to greed. It encouraged unending desires, an unsatisfied want for more and more material goods and gave no importance to morality. The centre of this material civilization was the capitalist economy which produced for the market, where people were tempted to keep buying with no sense of self-discipline or regulation of desires.

Capitalism encouraged the use of machines. Mechanization could have been a good source of betterment of human lives but due to a lack of moral principles, and with the only aim of gaining profit, it caused suffering for many. It threw many out of work, when introduced in places where there was an abundance of human labour. Mechanization and modern economic life created a new kind of slavery of material goods.

Modern civilization believes in always being on the move. The sense of identity that comes with social roots, established communities is being replaced by emptiness, mutual indifference and even hostility.

Moral life is been seen as a burden to be endured, just a means of keeping people from harming each other. Morality is much more deeper than just this. It shows the way to human dignity but in modern times it is seen just as a set of rules to be followed. Morality should be driven by sentiments of goodwill and mutual concern, instead, it is now being driven by a non-moral element, fear. Morality is seen, in modern times, as a means to self-interest. Modernity has robbed the morality of its most key quality – the quality of the soul. The only aim of the modern man is to somehow get on in the world, even at the cost of the purity of soul. Qualities like sensitivity, generosity, tender heartedness etc. have been rendered unimportant, instead, aggression, ambition, toughness, self-centredness are considered important.

Modern civilization exploited the poor and the weak European imperialism was a key expression of the aggressive and exploitative modernity. It rested on violence, both personal and collective. It even got extended against nature. Gandhi feared that after a certain time, the modern man may become so used to this violence that he will not even notice its damaging existence. Although modernity claims to be based on values like freedom, equality etc. it was actually violent and exploitative.

## The Limits of Rationality

Although Gandhi understood and appreciated the importance of reason, he was critical of the way it was treated in modern times. The modernity considered reason to be the ultimate test of all knowledge, while its own flaws and limits were overlooked grossly. Reason has its own place since it questions but not all aspects of human life are governed by reason. There is faith which goes beyond reason. Morality, wisdom, tradition, intuition, conscience are some faculties which are as valuable as reason. In fact, they are sometimes a step ahead than reason.

This attitude of modernity tends to consider, all those systems of knowledge which are different from reason, as inferior, backward and useless. It has no respect for diversity of thought patterns. It believes that rationalism is the best form of thinking, everything else is lesser, lower.

## State Culture

Since modernity promotes aggressive perusal of self-interest at all costs, such a system has to be managed by an equally ruthless, violent state. Such a system is governed by impersonal rules through a powerful bureaucracy.

The centralized economy created problems of a higher magnitude, requiring a centralized political power. The State becomes all powerful, it does not let individuals or groups solve their own problems. It creates big problems and shows that only a big power has the capacity to solve these. It also monopolizes all morality. Since people are no more bound by values, morality etc. they are controlled by State. State became the highest body of moral order—whoever followed its rules was good the others were bad. Gandhi argued that although State claimed to be the supreme power that worked in the interest of the larger good, it was just a battleground where powerful groups fought amongst themselves for power. It was in the hands of morally shallow people, hungry for power. The modern democracy was hardly democratic. In the name of people, some grabbed the power, misused it and no one was concerned about the interests of the common man.

## The Three Achievements of Modernity in Gandhi's View

Despite being critical of modernity, Gandhi appreciated it for its three good qualities. One, its scientific spirit; two, greater human control over the material world; three, a new culture of respect for rules.

What Gandhi found problematic about modernity was that it brought these three things but it failed to see the limitations of these aspects. It is very important to know where and how do these qualities can prove to be weak. For example it is right to emphasize on the importance of rules but it is wrong to not see that they are useless if the basic morality, basic value system is weak.

Gandhi could see the problems with the modern civilization better because he belonged to that part of the world which had suffered due to it. He clearly saw that the Europeans were very biased in the implementation of their great humane values like freedom, dignity, and equality. They believed that only their people were entitled to these values.

Gandhi's viewpoint was special for another reason also – the fact that he belonged to a different culture, a different civilization.

## Conclusion

Gandhi's perspective was unique because of his position; his being a non-European but that was, in a way, a disadvantage also. He oversimplified it. Although modern civilization is materialistic but it promotes the search for personal independence also; it promotes social justice, it discourages social inequality in its own ways. It does promote greed but it also encourages creativity, equality, liberty, an all round human development. Modernity has its own morality.

Gandhi failed to see that the good qualities of modernity were a result of the total structure of modernity and these were not just accidental by-products. In order to understand the true spirit of modernity both its virtues and vices need to be seen in a complete context. They are not exclusive of each other. Modern civilization should not just be criticized, its other positive potentials need to be appreciated

## Notes

1. B.R. Nanda, *In Search of Gandhi, Eassays and Reflection,* New Delhi, Oxford, 2002, p. 26.
2. V. S. Naipal, *India : A Wounded Civilization,* New Delhi Vikas, 1997, p. 172.
3. Ramashray Roy, *Self and Society*, New Delhi, Sage, 1985, p. 38.
4. Anthony Parel, (ed.), *Hind Swaraj*, Cambridge, Cambridge University Press, 1997, p. XVI, Introduction
5. Ronald Terchek, J., *Gandhi Struggle for Autonomy*, New Delhi, Vistar Publications, 2000, p. 78.
6. Madhuri Santanam Sondhi, *Modernity, Morality and the Mahatma,* New Delhi, Har Anand, 1998, p. 21.
7. Lloyd I. Rudolph, and Susanne, Hoeber, Rudolph, *The Modernity of Tradition*, Chicago, University of Chicago Press, 1967, p. 3.
8. D. N. Pathak, "Gandhiji : Trad ition and Change" in S. C. Biswas (ed.), *Gandhi Theory and Practice, Social Impact and Contemporary Change,* Shimla, Indian Institute of Advanced Study, 1969, p. 152.
9. David Hardinman, *Gandhi in His Time and Ours*, New Delhi, Permanent Black, 203 p. 77.
10. Jai Narain Sharma, *Alternative Economics*, New Delhi, Deep and Deep, 2003, p. 47.
11. *Young India*, 05-03-1931, p. 81.
12. D. N. Pathak, "Gandhiji : Tradition and Change", *op. cit.*, p. 154.
13. M. K. Gandhi, *Ashram Observences in Actions*, Ahmedabad, Navajivan

Publishing House, 1975, p. 115.

14. Bikhu Parekh, *Gandhi's Political Philosophy: A Critical Examination*, New Delhi, Ajanta, 1995, p. 20.

15. *Ibid.*, p. 21.

16. J. B. Kripalani, *Gandhi: His Life and Thought*, New Delhi, Publications Division, Ministry of Information and Broadcasting, Government of India, 1991, p. 423.

17. Paraphrased version of the chapter. *The crilique of Modernity* written by Bhiku Parekh in his book.

# 6
# Sarvodaya Philosophy

*– Anil Dutta Mishra*

## Introduction

Sarvodaya, today, does not represent a mere vision or utopian notion but makes an attempt of reorienting human mind to reconstruct human society. It has assumed the dimensions of a movement and a socio-economic force of great potentialities. It is a dynamic philosophy, which can make possible the advent of a radically transformed humanity. Sarvodaya seeks to build a new society on the foundations of old spiritual and moral values of India and attempts to meet the challenge of the contemporary problems.[1] The world has witnessed the propagation, experimentation and implementation of various socio-economic ideologies–capitalist, socialist and communist, time-to-time. But, in overall consideration, sarvodaya is undoubtedly far more superior to other attributive models. It envisages a well-balanced and integrated development of the nation with no distinction among have and have nots, privileged and under-privileged, ruler and ruled. The essence of sarvodaya thought lies in socialising matter through the strength of the spirit. Dogmas have no place in sarvodaya. "The philosophy of sarvodaya is not a set of dogmas, in its essence, it is compatible with an attempt of the spirit to prevail over matter and to socialise itself."[2] Sarvodaya is a redeemer's philosophy of social and political orientation, where suffering is, sarvodaya goes to mitigate it. It is the culmination of human emotional integration and the highest intellectual aspiration. It is a symbol of platonic detachment and Gita's Anasakti.[3] It is the highest manifestation of love and attempts at a mental transformation of the people. Gandhi denounced the utilitarian principle of the greatest good of the greatest number, and advocated the sarvodaya philosophy.

Gandhi did not originally coin the word "Sarvodaya". Even before him, the idea of sarvodaya was found in religious books: *Vedas*, *Upanishads*, *The Ramayan*, *The Gita*, *Quran* and many others. It was also preached by Indian and Western saints as well as philosophers. But Gandhi gave to these age-old principles and ideals an extended meaning and application. In fact, after the death of Gandhi, the word "Sarvodaya" came into greater prominence, when his fellow-workers assembled at Sevagram (Wardha), in March 1948, and decided to form an organization named 'Sarvodaya Samaj'. This name was chosen in preference to that of '*Satyagraha* Mandal' (*Satyagraha* Circle) because the word '*Satyagraha*' had come to acquire a restricted meaning which did not include constructive work. Since then the school of thought which accepts Gandhi's philosophy in all its aspects and of which the central figure is Vinoba Bhave, has come to be known as the 'Sarvodaya School' and its philosophy as the 'Sarvodaya Philosophy.'[4] The prominent thinkers of this school were Acharya Vinoba Bhave, Kishorlal Ghanshyam Mashruwala, J.C. Kumarappa, Kaka Kalelkar, Shanker Rao Deo, Dhirendra Mazumdar, Loknayak Jayaprakash Narayan and Acharya J.B. Kripalani. Except Jayaprakash Narayan, all of them had been associated with Gandhi in his constructive work.

## Sarvodaya: Meaning and Genesis

'Sarvodaya' is Sanskrit in origin which is comprised of 'Sarva' meaning all and 'Udaya' meaning rising. The etymological meaning of sarvodaya is the rising of all. This all includes all living beings.[5] In other words, sarvodaya as the word means welfare of all. The word first appeared in the form of the title for the Gujarati translation of John Ruskin's book entitled '*Unto The Last*'.[6] Sarvodaya was the title of series of nine articles, which Gandhi wrote and got published in Gujarati in the *Indian Opinion* weekly in South Africa in 1908.[7]

Sarvodaya is essentially a spiritual activity, which has two meanings, viz., negative and positive. As a negative concept, Sarvodaya is not limited to one person or to one group of persons. Nobody is excluded from enjoying anything from other.[8] It is not something which one man or set of men can gain or enjoy to the exclusion of others.[9] As a positive concept, Sarvodaya implies the participation of all kinds of people irrespective of class, caste, creed and religion. It also stands for the total blossoming of all the faculties – physical, mental and spiritual of the human being. It is an activity in which all may partake and if it is to amount to a full realization of the human faculties of the human soul.[10]

According to Acharya Vinoba Bhave, the term Sarvodaya commands a two-fold meaning. Firstly, Sarvodaya means making all happy by removing suffering and poverty with the help of scientific knowledge. Secondly, establishing a world state full with divinity, kindness and equality is called Sarvodaya.[11] Sarvodaya aims not at the rise of the few or the many, or for that matter the rise of the greatest number. It is not utilitarianism, which stands for the greatest good of the greatest number. It contains the germ of minority and majority. Contrary to utilitarianism stands for the good of one and all, of the high and the low, of the strong and the weak, the intelligent as well as the dull. As against the Laissez-faire theory, that is the survival of the fittest, Sarvodaya believes in the survival and development of all. To Vinoba, "The idea of Sarvodaya, as preached by the *Gita* is to merge oneself in the good of all."[12]

Apart from connoting the welfare of all, Sarvodaya commands two more meanings, firstly, the universal welfare and secondly, the integrated development of all. The Laissez-faire philosophy stands for the exploitation of many by a few. The utilitarian school supports the majority, totally neglecting the minority. Sarvodaya rejects these theories, which stand for the joy of few, advocates the welfare of all, irrespective of class, costs, creed, colour, race, region or religion. The philosophy of Sarvodaya makes the attempt or reorienting human mind, of reconstructing human society. It means welfare and prosperity of all. All must progress together without collision of interest.[13] Interpreting the purport of Sarvodaya, Dada Dharmadhikari said: "Sarvodaya is a term with a wider connotation since it conceives of assimilation of all and not only of many or most.[14] Sarvodaya is a philosophy, which provides checks against the imperfections of human mind and soul.

As regards the meaning of the word "Sarvodaya", there are broadly two views: the first, in its micro-form, means simply the rise of one and all; secondly, the macro-form connotes the rise of all, the universal welfare and the all round development of all.[15] But it connotes several other meanings. In its negative sense, it never omits even a singly person from enjoying anything from the rest of the mankind. As a positive concept, it promotes the development of all the faculties of man. According to Vinoba Bhave, it stands for not only making all happy by eliminating suffering from all but also for bringing a world state based on equality. For Gandhi, Sarvodaya as a broader concept stands for the merger of one in all with self-sacrifice and a selfless service. It aims at not only fulfilling the minimum material needs but also developing the ethico-spiritual aspects of all people.

## Sources of Sarvodaya

The following sources helped Gandhi to develop his concept of Sarvodaya. These were-Ruskin's book *Unto The Last*, Tolostoy's *The Kingdom of God is Within You*, Thoreau's *Civil Disobedience*, *The Bhagvad Gita*, *Isavasyopanisad*, Buddhism, Jainism, and Islam.

## Ruskin's 'Unto The Last'

The Gandhian philosophy of Sarvodaya can be traced to the central teachings of India's spiritual and religious heritage although Gandhi admits the fact that he had immediate inspiration from Ruskin's *Unto The Last* of which the term Sarvodaya is his rendering.[16] The welfare of all became the basic idea of Gandhi's philosophy right from the days when he wrote in Gujarati his most world famous thirty thousand words book '*Hind Swaraj or Indian Home Rule*' in 1909.

Gandhi called one of the chapters of his Autobiography '*The Magic Spell of Book*' wherein he describes the effects of Ruskin's *Unto The Last* (meaning uplift of the last). He translated it later into Gujrati claiming it Sarvodaya. It is a book from which Gandhi drew great inspiration and he at once determined to change his view of life in line with the ideals embodied in Ruskin's book *Unto The Last*.[17]

The central teaching of *Unto The Last*, according to Gandhi are:

(i) That the good of the individual is contained in the good of all.

(ii) That a lawyer's work has the same values as the Barber's in as much as all have the same right of earning their livelihood from their work.

(iii) That a life of labour, i.e. the life of the tiller of the soil and the handicraftsman is the life worth living.

There is a controversy with regard to the meanings of the terms "*Unto The Last*" and "Sarvodaya". Gandhi himself acknowledged that he translated it later into Gujrati, entitling it Sarvodaya. On the one hand, Benudhar Pradhan opines that the idea of welfare of all formed a part of his mental make-up even before he read this book.[18] This view is further strengthened from what Gandhi has expressed in his own words — "The first of these I knew".[19] On the other hand, Geoffery Ashe doubted whether the idea of Sarvodaya is contained at all in Ruskin's *Unto The Last*. Persons like Benudhar affirms that "it will be a travesty of truth to say that the objective of 'welfare of all' does not remain couched in the pages of *Unto The Last* of Ruskin."[20]

Ruskin and Gandhi both, were earnestly concerned with social welfare. While Ruskin aimed at the social welfare of 'the greatest number', Gandhi aimed at the welfare of all. Therefore, Vinobha Bhave feels that Gandhi is the real author of the term Sarvodaya, since the term, *'Unto The Last'* would mean only the uplift of the last *(Antyodaya)*. In fact, one has to accept that Ruskin's *Unto The Last* had directly or indirectly had a profound influence on Gandhi in fulfilling the ideal of *Sarvodaya*, which he had already cherished as his life's mission.

## Leo Tolstoy's The Kingdom of God is Within You

Gandhi was greatly influenced by Leo Tolstoy, through his book '*The Kingdom of God is Within You*' and his essay on 'Christianity and Patriotism'. Tolstoy's simplicity of life and purity of purpose influenced Gandhi deeply. His views on Christianity, its church, its teachings roused Gandhi's feelings. Tolstoy accepted love to be the law of life. The principles of non-violence, is based on love for the entire mankind. Tolstoy and Gandhi, both adopted the instrument of love to solve all problems in their lives. In his celebrated book *The Kingdom of God is Within You*, we find a political force creating an indelible mark on Gandhi. Gandhi confessed that its reading cured him of the skepticism and made him a firm believer of *Ahinsa*. Both Tolstoy and Gandhi firmly believed that non-violence could cure all social maladies, remove political ills, and establish peace on the earth and goodwill among mankind. In fact, both Tolstoy and Gandhi believed in the efficacy of love for the cure of evil and suffering in this world. Tolstoy perceived the truth, love and non-violence and Gandhi grasped the essence of these virtues and led his life directed towards these paths.[21]

Tolstoy also impressed upon Gandhi's mind the importance of bread labour. For Tolstoy, the man who abstains from manual labour is a thief of the society. Gandhi acknowledged his debt to Tolstoy. He says, 'the law that to live man must work, first come home to me upon reading Tolstoy's writing, 'On Bread Labour'- only those man deserve to eat bread who actually till the ground, spin cloth and produce things'. Tolstoy says, 'let us get off the shoulder of our neighbours' and Gandhi adds that if everyone performed that simple operation, he would have rendered all service God requires of him. Since every man has an obligation to himself as well as to the society, bread labour becomes an imperative duty which must be performed by each and every man.[22]

Gandhian philosophy of Sarvodaya comes very close to Tolstoyan philosophy of anarchism. The pure ideal of Gandhi's conception of *Sarvodaya* is an ideal of philosophical anarchism, a stateless society marked by voluntary co-operation. Profound faith in God, commiseration from the exploited, inherent aversion to violence, deep-rooted belief in the dignity of man led the two philosophers to the same goal and objective. But Gandhi is not a through going Tolstoyan. The difference between the two philosophers arises out of the fact that Gandhi is far more practical than Tolstoy. Tolstoy recoils from all expressions of violence. Gandhi permits violence, provided of course, that motive for violence is not anger but true love. Thus the moral content of Gandhi's doctrine of *Ahimsa*, which forms the fulcrum around which the entire doctrine of Sarvodaya ideology is based, has a higher significance than that of Tolstoy's. This is due to the fact that Gandhi was greatly influenced by the *Gita* ideal of *niskamakarma*, i.e. action without attachment.[23]

## Thoreau's Civil Disobedience

The American pacifist Thoreau was the champion of the free sprit and was repelled by the established political and economic routine of time. In him we discover an element of moral individualism culminating in his concept of 'civil disobedience'. Thoreau used the term in his speeches in 1849. It is obvious that Gandhi did not derive his idea of 'civil disobedience' from the writings of Thoreau. In fact, the resistance to authority in South Africa preceded before Gandhi got the essay of Thoreau on 'civil disobedience'. This movement was then known as 'passive resistance'. Gandhi was not satisfied with the term 'civil disobedience' because it failed to convey the full meaning of the struggle. Hence, he adopted the phrase 'civil resistance'.[24]

Thoreau did not believe in narrow sectarianism and felt that man is meant to experience God, not to theologies about him. Man according to Thoreau is a social being who is generally disposed to co-operation with fellow beings for social good. He felt that the moral institutions of the state supported by coercive authority hamper the individual's moral and spiritual freedom. He, therefore, visualised a society in which government will disappear. 'That Government is best which governs not at all', or, 'which governs least'. Like Thoreau, Gandhi also held that the democracy could be realized only in a stabiles society based on Truth and Non-violence. And Gandhi described it as Sarvodaya, which promotes not only social welfare but spiritual upliftment. Thus Gandhi heard an echo of his own thought in Thoreau.[25]

## The *Bhagavad Gita*

Gandhi drew his primary strength and inspiration from the *Bhagvad Gita*. To Gandhi, the *Gita* is the 'Eternal Mother'. According to him, the theme of *Gita* is self-realization. He says: "self-realization and its means is the theme of the *Gita*".[26] Again he affirms, "to one who reads the spirit of the *Gita*, it teaches the secret of non-violence the secret of realizing the self through the physical body."[27]

The sole aim of the *Gita* is to suppress unrighteousness and to establish *dharma*. It wants to bring prosperity and peace to all. It presents in concise form the Hindu view of life, which in turn stands for the universal brotherhood of all beings. It also highlights the importance of all selfless service for the promotion of the welfare of the whole creation since God and the creation is one. Through *Svadharma*, the *Gita* aims at '*Sarvabhutahita*' or the good of all beings.[28] In this way, *Gita* preaches the message of the welfare of all or Sarvodaya, which influenced Gandhi's thought, and action.

## *Isavayopanisad*

The first verse of *Isavayopanisad* deals with the ideology of Sarvodaya. The first part of the verse contains the principles of equality and fraternity. And the second part reveals the ideas of renunciation, non-acquisitiveness, non-exploitation and service to the society. According to Gandhi, since the entire universe is pervaded by God, the verse preaches the philosophy of equality and fraternity, which are the fundamental principles of the welfare of all. He confirms, "Universal brotherhood not only brotherhood of all human beings but of all living beings, I find in this mantra..."[29]

## Buddhism

According to Lord Buddha, all life is suffering. Suffering has to be extirepated in order to enjoy the bliss of *nirvana*, which is the highest goal in Buddhism. *Nirvana* is both individualistic and universal or cosmic. It may be realized in his life, here and there. It may also be known as full and perfect enlightenment for the sake of all beings. All can obtain *nirvana* if they meticulously follow the Noble Eight-Fold Path of Buddha. Gandhi was highly influenced and deeply impressed by the Buddhist philosophy, which preached universal love, non-injury to living beings, sacrifice and renunciation for the sake of promoting the welfare of all. The Buddha stressed on purity of means, which in turn influenced Gandhi who constantly maintained that there is indissoluble relationship between pure means and noble end.[30] Buddha preached about the middle path. Similarly, in Sarvodaya, it is understood that no one should take extreme step.

## Jainism

The ideal of the welfare of all forms is the corner stone of the Jainism. *Ahimsa* forms one of the five vows. The positive aspect of non-violence is the love for fellow beings, not only human but also all creatures. A Jain Tirthankara's duty is to devote his whole life for showering happiness on all the beings of the whole universe. About the place of Sarvodaya in Jainism, Benudhar Pradhan states: "The concept of welfare of all was so much an integral part of Jaina philosophy that the term 'Sarvodaya' was used by one Jaina teacher Samantabhadra even before the Christian era."[31] Further, Benudhar Pradhan argues that though the word 'Sarvodaya' is used by the Jaina Saint Samantabhadra for the first time, yet Gandhi's use of the word is completely his own. According to him, the term Sarvodaya came to Gandhi "as if in a flash."[32] Therefore he maintains that "the word Sarvodaya ... was purely his own coinage."[33]

## Islam

Gandhi had a great respect for Islam. He learnt the message of universal brotherhood from it. As for Islam, Gandhi declares that in his view, 'the point of brotherhood is manifested in no other religion as clearly as in Islam'. The reading of the holy Koran convinced Gandhi that the basis of Islam is not violence.[34] In fact, Gandhi shows remarkable catholicity and sympathetic and reverential attitude towards all religions of the world.

Apart from *Unto The Last, The Kingdom of God is Within You*, the *Upanishads*, the *Gita*, Buddhism, and Jainism, Gandhi's concept of Sarvodaya was also influenced by Vaishnavism, Zorostrianism and Christianity. The revival of the ancient teachings by Gandhi and incorporating them in his philosophy of Sarvodaya is perhaps his greatest contribution to the world of thought. Gandhi attempted the synthesis of the ideas of Vedanta, Buddhism, Jainism, Christianity and the teaching of prophets like Tulsidas, Tolstoy, Thoreau, Ruskin and national leaders of the Indian Renaissance movement. The philosophy of Sarvodaya takes up the Gandhian synthesis and tries to work out the implication of their ideas at more critical and analytical levels.[35]

## Ends and means in Sarvodaya

Morality is the essential means to achieve spirituality and good society or good ends. But communists like Machiavelli maintain that end justifies the means. This reveals that through any impure means like cunning, hypocrisy, hatred or violence one can get one's own desired end. To them, ends and means are watertight compartment. End is everything, no matter what or how the means are. Means become good if they serve the end. Jayaprakash Narayan observed impartially: "In Marxism any means are good means provided they serve the ends of the social revolution."[36]

For Gandhi means determine the end. He says, "As the means so the end".[37] Means are as important as the ends. In a way, his unique contribution to the world lies in his maintaining that the means are more important than the ends."[38] His emphasis on means rather than on the end is based on the doctrine of *niskamakarma* which holds that a person can have control over actions and not on their fruit. Gandhi is fully convinced that man can only strive but cannot command results. He maintains that "means are after all every thing. There is no wall of separation between means and ends. Indeed the creator gives us control over means, none over the end. Realization of the goal is in exact proportion to that of the means. This is a proportion that admits of no exception."[39] Gandhi stress on the strength of the means is based on the following reasons: (i) He believes in the progressive evolution of man; (ii) He fixes the end of man as self-perfection; (iii) He feels that the end is always out of man's grip till it is attained; and (iv) He is convinced that if means are subordinated to ends, the ends to which means are subordinated are likely to be less effective. All the above conviction made Gandhi to held the view that man must have complete control over means, despite both means and ends are various and contradictory.[40]

According to Gandhi, the end justifying the means is dangerous in practice and unsound ethically. If it is accepted, it permits resource to violence, fraud, untruth, opportunism etc. Gandhi viewed human beings as supreme. They are ends in themselves. If the means are pure, the end also becomes pure. When we take care of the means, the end will take care of itself.[41] By emphasizing only the means, Gandhi does not intend to give a secondary place to the ends. To him, means and ends are inseparably connected just like seed and trees are connected.[42]

By considering means and ends as a continuous process, Gandhi dissolved the age-old opinion of viewing both as water-tight compartments. The difference between them is imaginary.[43] Therefore he takes them as an organic whole. In a way, he proposes that both means and end must be homogeneous. He also holds that the extreme of means is itself the end. That is, the end progressively realizes itself through the means. The end can never result all of a sudden out of the means. In fact, when means slowly progresses, it turns itself into the end. The means apart from leading to an end shapes the end. In Gandhian philosophy, self-realization or spiritual freedom is the end of all human actions. Gandhi throughout his life tirelessly tried to use sarvodaya social order as the means to achieve spiritual freedom. Sarvodaya society guarantees moral freedom to every individual. This moral freedom, in turn, progresses itself into spiritual freedom, when it is followed meticulously placing faith in the supremacy of God. Moral freedom as means and spiritual freedom as end forms a continuous process or organic wholes. They cannot be divided into water-tight compartments. Their difference is only imaginary. Both are convertible terms. That is what Gandhi too reveals. What is needed is understanding and practicing ethics as god has given. Sarvodaya, as it enjoys ethico-spiritual basis, it can also be equitable both moral freedom and spiritual freedom. Thus, the problem of ends and means, as an organic whole, occupies a unique place in Gandhian thought, contributing to sarvodaya, moral freedom, spiritual freedom, political freedom, and spiritual economic freedom.

## Sarvodaya Social order

Gandhi with his many-sided personality had a clear vision and definite approach to the problems, which faced India of his time. Indian society was full with deep-rooted evils. It had totally degenerated itself socially, politically, economically and educationally.

Penury had further ruined India social conditions which were already corroded with caste-conflicts, child-marriages, untouchability, *Sati, Pardah*, negation of education to women, dowry, polygamy, corruption, exploitation, etc. Gandhi tried to find immediate solutions to all these problems.[44]

In sarvodaya society, there is no scope for exploitation, discrimination, inequality, and violence. Gandhi[45] envisaged that sarvodaya society should also be free from evils like 'politics without principle', 'wealth without work', 'knowledge without character', 'commerce without morals', 'science without mankind' and 'service without scarifies'. It should not be divided into water-tight compartments called social, political and religious where all these act and react upon one another. His aim of sarvodaya made him to establish a close correlation among these problems. The sarvodaya society is an indivisible whole. In order to establish a democratic and free society Gandhi suggested every individual to imbibe the spirit of love, tolerance, kindness, fearlessness, non-violence etc. A non-violent society, however small it is, is the strongest one. Non violence as the law of life includes individuals, societies and nations. To him, non-violence is both a personal and social virtue. A society built on the basis of complete *Ahimsa* is the purest anarchy.[46]

For Sarvodaya mentality, certain attributes are essential. Gandhi has offered the 'eleven vows' to discipline oneself so that a disciplined society could emerge. Self-scarifie is the essence of Sarvodaya social order. Every individual is to be ready and willing to sacrifice his happiness for the sake of others. Every one is to follow the policy of giving and not taking. He is to work for others and not expect anything in return for the same. Through Sarvodaya he wanted to rebuild the nation "from the bottom up-wards" and establish a new social order based on freedom, justice, equality and fraternity. Gandhi's ideal (Sarvodaya) society will be marked by following characteristics:[47]

- There should be no coercive state power in it and social cohesion should be maintained through the citizens' sense of social obligation like the obligations of Varnashram *dharma* in ancient India.
- It should consist of villages or rural agricultural settlements

in which wants are few and co-operation, conservation and decentralization are the governing norms of social, civil and economic activity.

- Besides agriculture, other production should be based on cottage industries and handicraft. Even education should be handicraft-centered.
- The ruling principles of decentralized and handicraft-centered production, three other economic norms should be maintained or practiced, namely, village self-sufficiency, bread labour (i.e. winning one's bread through work done by one's own body labour), and non-possession (acquiring or using the minimum possible articles of consumption). Heavy machines and heavy transport will have no place in this society.
- In such a society, disputes or conflict (generally arising out of the craze for power, property or possession) will be few and for between. But in order to deal with such disputes, as may possibly or occasionally arise, village panchayats should be organised. In the unlikely event of the failure of panchayats, recourse may be had to *Satyagraha*.

Gandhi had set up his first sarvodaya community on a farm near Durban and called it Phoenix (c. 1904), followed by another one (c. 1910) over Johannesburg named after Leo Tolstoy. The idea behind these two settlements was that the inmates had to perform all chores of running the farms, whatever is their avocation, on living wages, so that they become self-reliant and self-sufficient. In fact, through the pursuit of sarvodaya ideals, Gandhi wanted to chart out an alternative course. The ideas on sarvodaya social order find their fullest expression in his constructive work programme that began to unfold itself on his arrival in India from South Africa. Khadi, Communal amity, removal of untouchability, promotion of village industries, village sanitation, basic education, etc. came one after another and so did the supporting organization. Some of these organisations were: All India Spinners Association, All India Harijan Sewak Sangh, Hindustani Prachar Sabha, Hindustan Talimi Sangh and Akhil Bharat Sewa Sangh. The sarvodaya society is an ideal society and an ideal can not be fully realized. Gandhi also believed that an ideal is never fully realized in life."[48]

## Sarvodaya Political Order

Sarvodaya as a political doctrine is mildly anarchist. Infact the political ideal of Sarvodaya is an anarchism of its own variety. It concedes that a fully stateless society is beyond the reach of man, and the goal of human endeavour can only be to reduce the power and sphere of the state to the minimum. The politics of sarvodaya is politics of *lokniti* instead of *rajniti*. *Lokṇiti* is a comprehensive term, which denotes simultaneously a way of life a form of social order and a method. As a way of life, it stands for the self-regulation of individual conduct and for a habit to act on one's own initiatives. As a form of social order, it envisages a society in which police and military will have little to do and the law will interfere, least with life. A man will have the utmost freedom of action. As a method, it stands for social change in a manner that would maintain men's freedom of action.[49] The Sarvodaya Political order is based on certain fundamental political assumptions:

(i) All individuals are equally born.

(ii) People are the custodians of the supreme power in the State.

(iii) Political power should be decentralized both at individual and the village level.

(iv) All must train themselves for self-rule.

(v) All should believe in the divinity of every individual and strive for the welfare of all people.[50]

The ultimate goal for Gandhi is the greatest good of all people. Good, to him, means only the self-realization but not the material well being of the individuals or the society. A study on the nature of sarvodaya political order demands a brief survey of his view on State, Swaraj, *Satyagraha*, Democracy, Nationalism, Internationalism and *Ram Rajya*.[51]

According to Vinoba Bhave,[52] there are ten criteria of an ideal polity:

(i) International fraternity.

(ii) The conscious, spontaneous (as far as possible) and hearty co-operation of all the inhabitants of the country.

(iii) The identity of the good of the capable minority and the general majority.

(iv) The orientation towards the universal and equal development of all.

(v) The widest dispersion of political sovereignty.

(vi) The least amount of government.

(vii) The easiest availability of tantra or justice (?) – (Sulabhatama tantra).

(viii) The least possible expenditure.

(ix) The lowest degree of external protection.

(x) One universal, uninterrupted, and neutral or objective spread of knowledge.

## Sarvodaya Economic order

Gandhi adopted an integral approach to human problems. His basic aim was to reduce economics to terms of religion and spirituality. For him, ethics and economics are not two different entities. Economics that hurt the moral well-being of an individual or a nation are immoral and therefore sinful.[53] True economics, according to Gandhi "stands for social justice, it promotes the good of all equally including the weakest and is indispensable for decent life."[54] He mainly wants to formulate such an economic constitution to both India and the World that no one suffer from want of food, clothing and shelter. All necessities of life "should be freely available to all as God's air and water are or ought to be —— ".[55] Such an economic constitution, he aims at building not on material wealth but on spirituality. This is only possible when every one shows more truth than gold, greater fearlessness than pomp of power and wealth, greater charity than love of self.

The Gandhian Sarvodaya economic order is based on simplicity, decentralization, self-sufficiency, co-operation, equality, non-violence, sanctity of labour; human values, self-sufficient village units, nationalization of basic industries, swadeshi, and the theory of trusteeship. These, in turn, will solve the problems pertaining to labour, capital, production, distribution and profit etc.

In the Gandhian economic order, dependence on others is slavery and self-sufficiency is freedom. Regional self-sufficiency is must in Sarvodaya economic order. People should produce their own needs of life. Production must be in accordance with the need.

In the Sarvodaya economic order, man is totally free from material bondage. He never becomes a slave to material wants. He lives above his greed and amassing of riches. He views work as service. It is divine for him. He cherishes the principles of self-suffering, sacrifice, dedication and renunciation. His eating, clothing or dwelling shows no superiority or inferiority. He finds no difference between the rich and the poor. Really Sarvodaya economic system is practical, realistic and humane.

## Socialism, Communism and Sarvodaya

Gandhi called himself a socialist and even a communist but for him socialism and communism were transcendental forms of egalitarian social philosophy that find their fulfillment and culmination in Sarvodaya.[56] Although the situational background from which socialism and Sarvodaya have emerged is different, still their humanist idealism is almost similar.[57] According to Jayaprakash Narayan, Sarvodaya represents the highest socialist values. Socialism arose in the west as a philosophy of the industrial proletariat and challenged the pretensions of the contemporary state, which bolstered the interests of the capitalists.[58]

Socialism and communism are basically idealistic, ethical and humanitarian in nature. They are concerned with the illumination of the misery of the millions, elevation of the status of poor, unfortunate and downtrodden and founding a society based on the principle of economic equality and social justice. Sarvodaya stand for the just society free from all types of exploitation and human miseries. According to Rajendra Prasad,[59] Sarvodaya represents an aspiration "towards a society based on truth and non-violence in which there will be no distinction of caste or creed, no opportunity for exploitation and full scope for development both for individuals as well as groups." Jayaprakash Narayan[60] writes about Sarvodaya, "What we desire is the establishment of a society in which there will be no exploitation, there will be perfect equality and each individual will have equal opportunities for development."[61] Sarvodaya aims at a "classless, casteless and non-exploitative society."[62] Vinoba[63] said "There is no permanent conflict between the two ideologies—Marxism and Sarvodaya. Whatever differences there might be between Gandhism and communism, there are also points of similarity between these and these too are important. The cause of the have-nots is the basic sentiment running through both. Both Gandhism and communism regard the well-being of the poor and the oppressed with the intensely loving regard of the Mother." K.G. Mashruwala, prominent Gandhian observes, "the common point between Gandhi and Marx is the extreme concern of both for the suppressed and the oppressed, the resourceless and the ignorant, the dumb and starving section of humanity." Similarly, Jayaprakash Narayan[64] said "If we are true socialists, we would be true follower of sarvodaya as well."

Inspite of some fundamental similarities between socialism and sarvodaya, there is great differences between them on the question of means and methods. From the sarvodaya stand point; there are two shortcomings in the socialist philosophy. First the basic technique for effectuating socialism is supposed to be nationalization. But nationalization may entrench the control of the bureaucrats and may be another name for state capitalism. According to sarvodaya, the socialist belief in positive state action as the sovereign remedy for human ills is unfounded. Sarvodaya pleads for villagization while socialism believes in nationalization, sarvodaya accepts village ownership. Secondly, socialism adheres, at least in some cases, to the concept of violent revolution. But sarvodaya has no place for violence in its philosophy and technique.[65]

The difference between sarvodaya and communism are far more basic and fundamental. Communism advocates a violent technique for a change over in favour of egalitarian society, a society free form exploitation and privilege. Sarvodaya, to the contrary believes in persuasion and change of heart. Both Marx and Engels expressed their conviction that "violent overthrow of the bourgeoisie lays the foundation for the sway of the proletariat". Lenin and Mao used the technique of violence to bring about a change in the

Soviet Union and China respectively. While Gandhi has taught the ethics of self-suffering to convert the opponent because violence can never be the foundation of a just and equal society.[66] Violence breeds counter-violence. And on the basis of violence it is not possible to establish the just social order. In fact a new form of exploitation of man has come into existence and that is exploitation by the party bosses, bureaucrats and the state machine.

The Sarvodaya avoids the evils of legislative or legal coercion in democratic socialism and violence and physical coercion involved in communism. It relies on the technique of conversion for bringing about social transformation in the direction of a non-exploitative and egalitarian society. Gandhi was concerned with the welfare of all and hence rejected the view that the welfare of all can ever be attained by physical, intellectual and moral coercion perpetrated by a section of the people against the rest of the community. Gandhiji believed that sarvodaya could be realised only by the application of a moral and ethical method. Gandhi believed that through the application of the technique of persuasion and appeal to the innate good sense of the rich and the privileged, they might be made to renounce their privileges and apply their superfluous wealth for the welfare of the community. Such renunciation of wealth and privilege was to be for the good of the poor and the rich. "The essence of the revolution contemplated by sarvodaya is that it plans its faith on human approach, at the root of which stands the concept of revolution by human beings for the proliferation of human values and human virtues, and through a method that is strictly humane."[67]

The advocates of Sarvodaya also differ from the communists and socialists in respect of the role of the state. Both the communists and the socialists have their faith in the potency of the state to bring about equality in society. In the economic sphere, the communists and socialists advocate centralization and concentration of economic powers in the hands of the state and the proliferation of the economic activities of the state. To quote Jayaprakash Narayan:[68] "Democratic socialists, communists as well as welfarists are all statists." The concentration of both political and economic power in the hands of the state leads to too much of bureaucratisation, dehumanisation and loss of individual freedom.

To quote Jayaprakash Narayan:[69] "The democratic state remains a Leviathan that will sit heavily on the freedom of the people." The state is still worse under communism. It is true that the communists talk about the withering away of the state in the long run, but during the transitional period, the state is not only tolerated but also becomes more and more powerful. It devours the lofty ideals of classless society-liberty, equality, fraternity and fellowship. Jayaprakash Narayan writes, "The remedy is to create and develop forms of socialist living through the voluntary endeavour of the people rather than seek to establish socialism by the use of the power of the state. In other words, the remedy is to establish people's socialism, rather than state socialism."[70]

Considering from all angles, Sarvodaya is a far nobler, subtler, loftier, broader, deeper and transcendental concept than socialism or communism. According to Vinobaji, "Sarvodaya is a better word than 'socialist'; it is also our own native word, born from our own soil and carrying a noble meaning. We do not use the word because we are a little doubtful if we can live up to it. So we prefer the world 'socialist'. But our goal is in fact sarvodaya and our people are being prepared for absorption into the sea of sarvodaya". It is true that socialism and communism can realise their true meaning and fulfil their objective by merging their identity with sarvodaya. Jayaprakash Narayan[71] writes: "Socialism as we understand it today, cannot take mankind to the sublime goals of freedom, equality, brotherhood and peace. Socialism no doubt gives promise to bring mankind closer to those goals than any other competing social philosophy. But I am persuaded that unless socialism is transformed into sarvodaya, those goals would remain beyond its reach. Vinoba writes, "There is no permanent conflict between the two ideologies– Marxism and Sarvodaya. As the Ganges becomes wider and wider and moves on and finally merges in the ocean, I hope Marxism will merge in Sarvodaya one day."[72]

## Sarvodaya and Contemporary Crisis

The Sarvodaya principles are capable of meeting the greatest challenge of the age. The most urgent need of today is the abolition of human suffering as well as of war. Even Sarvodaya will be very important in 21st Century due to complexity of human behaviour.

Sarvodaya by laying stress on the goodness of human nature, unity of mankind, service of man, application of moral principles considered valid for individuals to group life and inter-state relations, the non-violent process of change, social and economic equality, economic and political decentralization, tries to resolve the various kinds of tensions that disturb domestic and international harmony. Sarvodaya is capable of strengthening the forces of love, creativeness and joy of life. Sarvodaya takes a whole view of man and emphasizes his spiritual nature. In modern context the concept of sarvodaya can be interpreted as the "awakening of one and all". Thus, in addition to the awakening of everyone, it refers to the awakening of the total human spirit and personality. Sarvodaya is also related to achieving the highest level of self-realization in which one sees one's manifestation in all others.

Our political, social and economic life has been sized with a malady. The malady of our times perhaps of all times, is mad quest for power, whether it is political, social or economic. Service is being given up in quest of personal aggrandizement. Humanity is undergoing almost a phase of moral collapse and ethical nihilism. In the era of the mad rush for power, the significance of Sarvodaya lies in stressing the permanent value of self-abnegation. Sarvodaya is giving expression to a moral principle of cardinal importance because it wants to enshrine the primacy of goodness and character in place of the skill of manipulation and self-assertion. Sarvodaya appeals to the mind and heart in terms of values and goals. The decadence and corruption, which in fact organized institutional mechanism, can be removed only by the reassertion of moral and spiritual values and their ever-growing incorporation in social, political and economic life. Sarvodaya is the only way to solve the problems of unemployment, unequal distribution of wealth, growing corruption in public life etc. The moral collapse and prostration of our world needs the revitalizing notion of ethical idealism and stress on the moral approach to social and economic problems, which sarvodaya envisages.

## Summing up

Sarvodaya philosophy, based on the insights and experiences of Gandhi, is a reassertion of the valuation and moral approach to the problems of mankind, which has been a part of ancient Indian culture for ages. Vinoba Bhave rightly said "Sarvodaya stands for not only making all happy by illuminating suffering from all but also for bringing a world state based on equality."[73] For Gandhi, sarvodaya stands for the merger of one in all with self-sacrifice and a selfless service. His Sarvodaya ideal, apart from standing for the meaning of the welfare of all, implies the meaning of the universal welfare and integrated development of all. As a universal ideal, it aims at not only fulfilling the minimum material needs but also developing the ethico-spiritual aspects of all people. The great contribution of Sarvodaya in the present century lies in the reassertion of the Gandhian moral approach to the problems of mankind and a vision that looks forward to the creation of a welfare state and society.

## Notes

1. V. P. Verma, *The Political Philosophy of Mahatma Gandhi and Sarvodaya,* Lakshmi Naryan Agarwal, Agra, 1980, 4th Edition, p. 279.
2. J.N. Mohanty, "Sarvodaya and Aurobindo–a Rapprochement", *Gandhi Marg,* Vol. 4, No. 30, July 1960, p. 211.
3. B.P. Pandey, *Gandhi, Sarvodaya and Organizations,* Chugh Publications, Allahabad, 1988, pp. 20-21.
4. Vishwanath Tandon, *The Social and Political Philosophy of Sarvodaya After Gandhi,* Sarva Seva Sangh Prakashan, Varanasi, 1965, p. 2.
5. Anil Dutta Mishra, *Fundamentals of Gandhism,* Mittal Publications, New Delhi, 1995, p.5.
6. Mahajan P. Mani and K.S. Bharathi, *Foundations of Gandhian Thought,* Dattsons, Nagpur, 1987 p. 68.
7. *The Collected works of Mahatama Gandhi*, Vol. 8., Publications Division, Government of India, New Delhi,1962, pp. 239-41.
8. K.M. Rathnam Chetty, *Sarvodaya and Freedom: A Gandhian Appraisal,* Discovery Publishing House, New Delhi, 1991, p. 46.
9. B.S. Sharma, "The Philosophical Basis of Sarvodaya", *Gandhi Marg,* Vol. 4, No. 3, July 1960, p. 259.
10. *Ibid.*
11. K.M. Rathnam Chetty, *op.cit.,* p. 47.
12. *Harijan,* 13.2.1949.
13. B. P. Pandey, *op. cit.*, p. 14.
14. Dada Dharmadhikari, *Sarvodaya Darshan*, Sarva Seva Sangh Prakashan, Varanasi, p. 18.

15. K.M. Rathnam Chetty, *op. cit.*, p. 48.
16. *Ibid.*, p. 38.
17. *Ibid.*
18. Benudhar Pradhan, *The Socialist Thought of Mahatma Gandhi*, G.D.K. Publications, Delhi, 1980, Vol. I, p. 284.
19. M.K. Gandhi, *An Autobiography The Story of my Experiments with Truth*, Navjivan Publishing House, Ahmdabad,1948, p. 365.
20. Benudhar Pradhan, *op.cit*, p. 285.
21. K.M. Rathnam Chetty, *op. cit.*, pp. 39-40.
22. *Ibid.*, p. 40.
23. *Ibid.*, pp. 40-41.
24. *Ibid.*, p. 41.
25. *Ibid.*
26. M.K. Gandhi, *Young India*, 12-11-1925.
27. *Ibid.*
28. K.M. Rathanam Chetty, *op.cit.*, pp. 42-43.
29. Anil Dutta Mishra, *op.cit.*, p. 11.
30. *Ibid.*, p. 11
31. Benudhar Pradhan, *op.cit.*, p.294.
32. *Ibid.*, p. 301.
33. *Ibid.*, p. 302
34. K.M. Rathnam Chetty, *op.cit.*, p. 45.
35. *Ibid.*
36. Jayaprakash Narayan, *Socialism, Sarvodaya and Communism*, A.P.H. Bombay, 1964, p. 149.
37. M.K. Gandhi, *Young India*, 12 November 1925, p. 364.
38. S. Gopalan, Means and ends: The Gandhian view, *Gandhi Centenary Volume*, 1969, p. 70.
39. *Young India*, 17.7.1924.
40. D.G. Tendulkar, *Mahatma*, Vol. II, New Delhi,Publications Division,1951, p. 299.
41. *Harijan*, 27.2.1949.
42. M.K.Gandhi, *Hind Swaraj or Indian Home Rule*, Ahmedabad, Navajivan Publishing House, 1946, p. 60.
43. *Harijan*, 27 February 19949.
44. Anil Dutta Mishra, *op.cit.*, p. 14.
45. *Ibid.*
46. *Ibid.*, p.15
47. S.C. Gangal, *Gandhian Thought and Techniques in the Modern World*, Criterion Publications, New Delhi, 1988, pp. 158-59.
48. *Ibid.*, p. 159.

49. Vishwanath Tandon, *op.cit.*, pp. 124-125.
50. K.M. Rathnam Chetty, *op.cit.*, p. 66.
51. Anil Dutta Mishra, *op.cit.*, pp. 16-17
52. V.P. Verma, *The Political Philosophy of Mahatma Gandhi and Sarvodaya*, Agra, Lakshmi Narayan Agarwal, 1980, p. 295.
53. N.K. Bose, *Selection from Gandhi,* Navjivan Publishing House, Ahmedabad, 1994, p.40.
54. *Harijan*, 9 October, 1937.
55. *Young India*, 15 July, 1928.
56. V.D. Mahajan, *Modern Indian Political Thought*, p.569.
57. Jayaprakash Narayan, *From Socialism to Sarvodaya,* Madras, Socialist Book Centre, 1956, p. 96.
58. V.P. Verma, *op.cit.*, p. 283.
59. V.D. Mahajan, *op.cit.* p. 569.
60. *Ibid.*
61. *Ibid.*, pp. 569-70.
62. *Ibid.* p. 570.
63. *Ibid.*
64. *Ibid.*
65. V.P. Verma, *op.cit.*, p. 285.
66. Vinoba Bhave, *Swarajya Shastra*, New Delhi, Sasta Sahitya Mandal,1953, pp. 58-68.
67. V.D. Majahan, *op.cit,* pp. 573-4.
68. Jayaprakash Narayan, *op.cit.*, p.33.
69. *Ibid.,* p. 34.
70. *Ibid.*, p. 34.
71. *Ibid.*, p. 21
72. V.D. Majahan, *op.cit.*, p. 574.
73. Anil Dutta Mishra, *op. cit.* p. 17.

# 7

# An Alternative Modernity with Reference to Hardiman

*– R. P. Misra*

The subject matter of this chapter is Mahatma Gandhi's contribution to debate on modern civilization and its derivative concept of modernity. Euro-centric thinkers treat the period between Enlightenment (seventeenth and eighteenth centuries) in Europe and the Second World War as 'modern' and all that happened in that period as the product of 'modernism'. Prior to 'modern' was a long stretch of an era designated as 're-modern' and the new thinking on progress that emerged in the West after the Second World War has been branded as 'post-modern'.

Gandhiji lived in the era called modern. It was the era, which witnessed a major shift in values that had charted the course of history from times immemorial. To distinguish the modern from the millennia bygone, the latter was designated as pre-modern. Europe and Anglo-America were declared modern; the rest of the world was pre-modern. Modern connoted and still connotes social, economic and technological advancement; a shift from agriculture to manufacturing, from rural to urban, and from experiential knowledge to scientific knowledge. The pre-modern was conceived to be archaic, backward looking and traditional. Each of these epithets conveys hidden meanings. It would, therefore, be pertinent to go deeper into what these terms mean.

## Pre-modernism

Pre-modern in the vocabulary of the modernists meant a social system that was collectively possessed by authority – all powerful kings, emperors, religious heads, village heads etc.; and wherein individuals were dominated by traditions and what the elders did. In pre-modern society all had to conform to the time honoured practices. Any questioning thereof amounted to heresay. Thus the pre-modernism relied on the authority of scriptures, traditions and conventions. Everyone was assigned a place in the society, which was immanent and fixed. It is not that things did not change. They did, but very slowly. Even the traditions changed; old ones were rejected and new ones introduced but no one knew when the old was out and the new was in. It was proclivity on the part of the people to adhere to what was customary was more important than the customs themselves.

In the pre-modern society, duties were more important than rights. Individuals were important but only as inseparable members of the family and community. The pre-modern society was essentially rural and agricultural; there were cities too but they served as centres of administration and business. Production, both agricultural and industrial was village based.

In the wake of the eighteenth century Enlightenment resulting from the discoveries of new lands; and a series of scientific breakthroughs, a belief set in Europe that progress was essentially linear direction and material in content. Anything that did not liberate the man to do what he considered best for himself was rejected. Religion, faith, and belief were branded as irrational and, therefore, unscientific. Given this paradigmatic shift, things that did not meet the standards of logic were rejected. And thus was born the concept of modernity.

## Modernism

As stated earlier, modernism is associated with European Enlightenment (Renaissance); it represents the rejection of tradition and authority in favour of reason and natural sciences. It takes the autonomous individual as the sole source of truth—the Cartesian cogito. History is linear and so also progress. It was associated with the Protestant mode of consciousness, which rejected authority in all spheres of life. It is also associated with industrialization, scientific and technological discoveries, scientific and technological discoveries, and capitalism. The fundamental act of modernity is to question the foundation of past knowledge brought forward through traditions, rituals and conventions.

Modernity seeks order out of chaos and believes that

rationality and rational behaviour alone can bring the order. It assumes that more rational a society is more ordered it would be and more ordered it is better it would function. Modern societies, therefore, reject things that generate disorder. Thus they tend to label everything that does not fit into the paradigm of modernity as disorder which in practical terms means 'the other'; something that is foreign. Thus anything non-white, non-male, non-heterosexual, non-hygienic, non-rational (etc.) becomes part of disorder, and has to be eliminated from the 'ordered, rational modern society'.

Modernism is based on the belief that reason is the ultimate judge of what is true and, therefore, in a world governed by reason 'truth, goodness and beautiful' (*Satyam, Shivam and Sundaram*) would have no meaning if they do not conform to the standards set by logic. It considers that there is stable, coherent knowable self, which is conscious, rational, autonomous and universal. The self knows itself and world through reason or rationality. The objective rational self knows the universal and eternal truth through science. The knowledge or truth produced by science would always lead to progress and perfection. Science is neutral and objective. Language or the mode of expression used in production and dissemination of knowledge must be rational too: it must represent the real/ perceivable world, which the rational mind observes.

Modern societies, by distinguishing 'order' from 'disorder' try to achieve stability and uniformity through grand or master narratives, which are a sort of meta-theories or meta-ideologies. For example, the grand narrative of the American culture is 'democracy' as the most rational and enlightened form of government. Democracy backed by capitalism is the best form of governance and social order; it alone can bring happiness to the whole world. Anything undemocratic must be rejected and ousted. The grand narrative of the USSR was, Marxism, which based on the theory that capitalism will collapse and a utopian socialist world will evolve. Clash of interests of the capitalists and the labour class would ultimately lead to the victory of the latter and thus a more ordered society would come into being.

The products and by-products of modernism has produced

reactions in many a thinkers. The violence, destructions, and negative ecological consequences produced by modernism has given rise to thinkers who challenge some of the very bases on which it is based. This reactive thinking became more pronounced after the Second World War although its roots go back to some of the nineteenth and early twentieth century thinkers. This paradigm is known as post-modernism.

## Post-modernism

According to the Oxford Dictionary, post-modernism is a philosophical stance, which claims that it is impossible to take grand statements – meta-narratives – about the structures of society or about historic causation, because everything we perceive, express and interpret, is influenced by our background in terms of let us say gender, class and culture. No one interpretation is, therefore, superior to other.

For example, the truth as perceived by a perpetrator of violence and the one who suffers the violence would be different. What is rational depends on the paradigm of our thinking and perceiving. As such even the grand narratives like democracy can be perceived differently. The ideal world is therefore one, which does not move linearly; which is not homogenous; and which protects the weaker sections of the society. Broadly speaking, post-modernism:

1. Rejects the rationality of the human action;
2. Respects heterogeneity and diversity;
3. Shuns the postulations of theories and meta-narratives;
4. Champions the cause of the poor, the weak, marginalized and downtrodden;
5. Challenges the concept of development as structural transformation of the national economy and calls for transmogrification of a society including sustainable development;
6. Calls for integration of time and space to reach the truth;
7. Believes in behavioural, experimental and participatory approaches rather than statistical and positivistic explanations;

8. Lays stress on micro as against macro;
9. Rejects the concept of sovereign autonomous individual and lays emphasis on anarchic collective anonymous experience, collage, diversity, the mystically unrepresentable Dionysian passion; and
10. Refers to the incipient or actual dissolution of the social norms and forms associated with modernity.

To begin, with it rejects master narratives on which modernity relies because they serve to mask the contradictions and instabilities that are inherent to any social organization or practice. In other world, every attempt to create 'order' always demands the creation of an equal amount of 'disorder'. It favours mini-narratives, stories that explain small practices, local events, rather than large-scale universal or global concepts. These 'mini-narrative' are situational, provisional, contingent and temporary making no claim to universality. This is a sarcastic playful parody of western modernity and 'John Wayne' individual and a radical, anarchist rejection of all attempts to define, reify or represent the human subject.

In post-modern societies knowledge is functional – you learn things not for knowledge sake; you learn to use that knowledge. Education in schools and colleges, therefore, should stress on skills and training more than on vague humanist ideals of education in general. The question is not how to get a degree; it is what is the use of the degree? The modes of production, storage, distribution and arrangement of information is ICT based. Thus the opposite of knowledge is not ignorance; it is the inability to convert the knowledge into digital formats.

There are lots of questions to be asked about post-modernism. Is the process of fragmentation, tentativeness and instability good for the man and his society? One of the consequences of post-modernism seems to be the rise of religious fundamentalism as a sort of reaction to the questioning of the grand narratives. Salman Rushdie's book the *Satanic Verses* was banned in Islamic countries and Taslima's novel was banned in Bangladesh because they deconstructed a grand Islamic narrative.

## Gandhian Alternative

Gandhi lived and worked in the so-called modern age. When

he wrote Hind Swaraj in 1908, modernism had swept all over Europe and America and had put the rest of the world in bondage. Gandhi challenged the notion of modernity on many counts. He blazed a trail that transcended even post-modernism and posed before humanity a challenge that it must meet squarely in order to survive and move towards its destiny.

Let me put before you the some of the postulates of Gandhi, which would help us to understand him better *vis-a-vis* the paradigms of modernism and post-modernism.

1. Gandhi did not subscribe to the dualism of man and nature; man is an inseparable part of nature. There is a Cosmic Law that keeps the universe in balance. This Law is immanent and hence should be adhered to by all including the humans.

2. Gandhi rejected Darwin's theory of evolution of species based as it was on survival of the fittest. He saw cooperation among the species more powerful a force than competition, that determined the evolutionary processes. At the same time he perceived cooperation and competition as two sides of the same coin. Modernism looks at the side of competition ignoring cooperation on the reverse. Thus it is the observer who differentiates between the two even if they together form a single whole.

3. Human body is not an assemblage of cells, tissues and organs. It has body, mind and soul and the three are inseparably linked to form a whole. Humans without mind would be animals and those without soul would be worst than animals.

4. Human progress is not the same thing as material progress. It means moral progress leading humans to higher levels of consciousness. Material progress is essential only so long as it enhances moral progress. And hence the concept of progress or development centering on material and technological developments as evolved in the West cannot be considered to be a goal towards which humanity must move. At best it is a means and hence it must be moderated

and tempered by the goal of real human progress. Further, it must be dispensed with when it comes in the way of moral progress.

5. Human Progress is not linear as perceived in the West nor is it circular as perceived in the East. It is helixical – a combination of linear and circular. And hence its division into pre-modern, modern and post-modern is arbitrary and unscientific.
6. History as written in the West is not a true history of human progress. It records only the deviations from the main currents of progress the humans have made through centuries and millennia. It is the history of wars and of kings and emperors; not the history of human society as such.
7. For the progress and survival of humanity, Swaraj must be its goal: swaraj of individuals, communities and societies, nation states included. Swaraj could be achieved only through Sarvodaya – the holistic development of all. Swaraj means self-control and Sarvodaya means moral and material development of all: from each according to his ability to each according to his need.

To a question as to what he thought about modern civilization, he replied 'it is a good idea'. He considered modern civilization to be one, which had put human beings on a high moral pedestal. And since it had not happened that far, it could at best be called an idea.

Commenting on what was berated as 'modern civilization' Gandhi called it a disease that ought to be cured. He considered the 'pre-modern Indian civilization' more modern than the twentieth century 'modern civilization' because it had the cure for the disease of modernity. He did not subscribe to the view that body welfare was the main object of life. And hence material advancement, which formed the core of modernity, could not be treated as the end all. At best it could be a means to fulfill the far higher ends of life. Similarly, scientific and technological development unmindful of its negative potentialities of destruction must be treated as a dangerous proposition. To quote him:

*"This civilization takes note neither of morality nor of religion. It votaries calmly state that their business is not to teach religion. Some even consider it a superstitious growth. Others put on the clock of religion, and prate about morality. But after twenty years of experience I have come to the conclusion that immorality is often taught in the name of morality. ...Civilization seeks to increase bodily comforts, and it fails miserably even in doing so.*[1]

*"This civilization is such that one has only to be patient and it will be self-destroyed. According to the teachings of Mohammad this would be considered a satanic civilization. Hinduism calls it the Black Age. ...It is eating into the vitals of the English nation. ...Civilization is not an incurable disease, but it should never be forgotten that the English people are at present afflicted by it."*[2]

*Gandhi made a frontal attack on the institutions that go with modernity. He makes special mention of parliament, railways, lawyers, doctors, machinery and education system. He uses un-parliamentary language to describe the proceedings of the House of Commons. His remarks are so apt to our parliament and state legislatures today. It is unfortunate indeed that despite Gandhi's forewarnings we threw away the British but kept the British institutions close to our heart."*[3]

Railways symbolized speed; they increased our mobility; cities grew in number and size and became exloitative; villages were impoverished and human touch that once constituted the soul of Indian civilization was lost in the wonder world of modernity. He was not against railways as such nor against speed either. He wanted the ill-effects of both to be countered by a constructive programme that brought people together. If the living conditions of the people were improved; self-government was strengthened, and institutions, which could bind the people together for cooperative action were strengthened, the necessary base for Swaraj would be established.

Gandhi's remarks on judiciary, medical practitioners, education, technology and many other instrumentalities of the so-called 'modern civilization' are as apt today as they were in 1908.

Look at what he said about lawyers and doctors.

*"My firm opinion is that the lawyers have enslaved India.... Those who want to perpetuate their power do so through the courts. ...Doctors have almost unhinged us. Sometime, I think that quacks are better than highly qualified doctors.... Hospitals are institutions for propagating sin."*[4]

*His views on education and machinery are equally unconventional, radical and relevant to this day. "Character building has the first place in it (education and that is primary education). A building erected on that foundation will last." Gandhi ji approvingly quotes the definition of liberal education as given by Professor Aldous Huxley.*[5]

"That man I think has had liberal education who has been so trained in youth that his body is the ready servant of his will and does with ease and pleasure all the work that as a mechanism it is capable of; whose intellect is clear, cold, logic engine with all its parts of equal strength and in smooth working order....whose mind is stored with knowledge of the fundamental truths of nature...whose passions are trained to come to heel by a vigorous will, the servant of a tender conscience...who has learnt to hate all vileness and to respect others as himself. Such a one and no other, I conceive, has had liberal education, for he is in harmony with nature. He will make the best of her and she the best of him."

Gandhi defined True Civilization in following words: *"Civilization is that mode of conduct which points out to man the path of duty. Performance of duty and observance of morality are convertible terms. To observe morality is to attain mastery over our mind and passions. So doing we know ourselves.*[6] *...the tendency of the Indian civilization is to elevate the moral being, that of the western civilization is to propagate immorality. ... it behooves every lover of India to cling to the old Indian civilization even as a child clings to the mother's breast."*[7]

## Was Gandhi a Post-modernist?

During Gandhi's time post-modernism had not emerged as a paradigm. Despite the dissenting voices here and there, the first half of the twentieth century marked the culmination of the final stage of modernism. The questions that Gandhi raised on the basic postulates of modernism were far more subtle than those raised by the post-modernists. His critique of modernity was devastating; he labelled it as retrogressive and unrepresentative of true modernity, which, he thought, was yet to emerge. He considered modern civilization retrogressive for it came in the way of real human progress, which was none other than moral progress. The so-called modern civilization empowered man to subjugate both nature and man and to deprive others of dignity, life support and basic human rights. Modernity to Gandhi was a deviation man has inadvertently taken from the road that led him to his ultimate destiny.

The world we are living in today is a world, which is full of violence, hatred, greed and selfishness. True, it is a world which lot of things at the disposal of man, which his ancestors could only dream of but behind the façade of material prosperity lie a shattered humanity and an uncertain future. It is a run away world: a world beyond man individually and collectively to manage. We admit that we have to adjust our lives to the new exigencies of the time as it moves from one crisis to the other. Gandhi challenged this helplessness and proved that post-modernism nothing but an extension of modernism, a devise to save modernism from total eclipse. He showed the way to recover humanity in man and to take it towards a new future – a future without violence, hate, inequality and exploitation. He not only showed the way but also demonstrated how to traverse it.

It would be pertinent to mention here that Gandhi did not reject western civilization. His attack centred on modern industrial civilization, which first emerged in the west (Europe) but it was not rooted in western civilization. He was appreciative of many of the traits of western civilization such as liberalism, democracy, dignity of the individual, etc. Gandhi was devastatingly critical of it because it deviated from its own principles when the question of its relations with other civilizations and peoples came. How else could it allow the wholesale destruction of many races, peoples and civilizations of what later became Latin America? How else could it sanction the subjugation of much of the world beyond Europe and Anglo-America and keep nations of rich cultural heritages under its feet for over two centuries? How else could it take away the rights of non-Europeans to govern themselves?

Post-modernism did not go far enough to undo the wrong perpetrated on much of humanity by the west. It was only a palliative; an apology; and an intellectual move in the face of the rise of the tormented people. It was not actualized to bring a semblance of equity, dignity, and righteousness. Gandhi had no interest in intellectual movements, which did not liberate the marginalized, downtrodden, and materially or spiritually poor. He went far beyond the post-modernist thinkers and gave a paradigm that could liberate not only the politically bonded non-Europeans but also the spiritually bonded Europeans.

Gandhi had two main complaints against western civilization as represented by the industrial civilization of his time. It was not modern in the true sense of the term. It represented a deviation from the real progress or evolution, which was none other than moral progress. Human beings to be so called must become better human beings morally and ethically. Secondly, it did not adhere to its own norms and principles while interacting with other peoples, races and cultures. In fact, it was known for the violations of its own norms more than for their adherence. Gandhi's paradigm of modernism rooted as it was in non-violence (*manasa-vacha-karmana*); sarvodaya i.e. rise of all in all respects; and swaraj i.e. self-control, was not only an idea but also a practical proposition, which he put into practice. In act, his domain was action, not intellectual debate. He went beyond what is rational and logical to what is rational and logical within a moral frame of reference. Tit for tat philosophy may be logical as a sensual response but not as a response of an enlightened human being. For Gandhi tit meant a moral, not physical, attack on tat. His was proactive philosophy designed to create a peaceful world order and to open up the route to real human progress.

In this connection let me refer to what David Hardiman in his recent book *Gandhi in His Time and Ours* (2003) has to say on Gandhian Critique of modernity.

"What is taken as Gandhi's 'critique of modernity' generally refers to his critique of the doctrines of materialism and instrumental rationality, the belief in scientific and technological progress, practices such as large-scale methods of production, rapid transportation, allopathic medicine, adversarial parliamentary system of democracy and so on, and the accompanying conviction that it was the duty of those who subscribed to such values to impose them on the rest of the world. Against this, he counterpoised his own definition of what entailed a genuine civilization that had, he argued, to be rooted in an alternative morality. His position in this respect is set out most clearly in Hind Swaraj."

We have now reached a stage in our discussion to reflect on some of the major challenges modern civilization has posed before us and see how Gandhian paradigm of alternate modernity could be used to face them successfully.

## New Dimensions of Modernism–Globalization

Globalization is one of the most popular terms in the world today. Every language has coined an equivalent of it. No matter what aspect life we take into account, the impacts and implications of globalization are very much there. It is, however, most prominently visible in two fields: information communication technology and international trade and associated financial transactions. ICT has converted the globe into a village. We are so close to each other; distance does not matter. Unfortunately, this gift of modern technology has been harnessed more negatively than positively. We are so close to each other physically yet so far away from each other spiritually. Technology is neutral to its use; it can be used constructively or destructively. Much depends on how advanced we are as human beings?

Then look at the speed with which the electronic communication moves today. Morse invented his system of dots and dashes to send messages to ships on the high seas in 1849 beamed its last message on first February 1999 "*Calling all. This is our last cry before our eternal silence.*" The new communication system has changed our lives no matter where we live. The other day when people were trying to rescue whatever was left after the devastating Tsunami disaster, I saw on the TV screen a lady who had lost everything including family members rescuing her television set and moving towards the relief camp with her two children. Electronic communication has become a part of our life. It brought down the 'closed' regime of the USSR and is threatening other regimes, democratic or undemocratic, which refuse to be transparent and people oriented. Globalization is not confined to economy; it has penetrated the innermost precincts of our houses and even hearts.

The level of world trade is much higher today than ever before. And so is the volume of global financial transactions. More than a trillion dollars are now exchanged daily on global currency market. To give an idea of what it means let me say that a billion (million million) dollars in currency notes of 1000 dollars each when stacked one on the other, it would be over 192 km high, 20 times higher than Mount Everest. It is this exchange that determines the value of the money we have in our pockets or bank accounts.

Globalization has yet another effect, which many of us fail to perceive. It pushes the better off up and pulls the worse off down. This happens because the two do not have level laying fields. As the nations become too small to solve global problems, they also become too large to solve the local problems. At the same time, globalization produces lateral effects and creates pockets of excellence and deprivation leading to widening of gaps between rich and poor individuals, groups and areas. While Bangalore becomes the Silicon Valley of India, just a few km from it, peasants commit suicide because agriculture is no longer remunerative to help farmers make their two ends meet. The share of poorest fifth of the world in global income has been secularly declining. It came down from 2.3 per cent in 1990 to 1.4 per cent in 2000. And it must be lower by a few points today.

According to the ILO, 120 million people are unemployed and about 700 million people are underemployed.1300 million people live in absolute poverty; they earn less than US $ 1 per day. More than half of the population of the world lives on less than US $ 2 per day. If we look at the data given in the recent Human Development Report, 46 countries of the world have become poorer since 1990. The poorest 20 per cent of people of the world account for only 1 percent of the world income; it was 1.4 per cent in 1990. At the same time the total assets of 358 billionaires of the world were more than the combined GDP of 2300 million people, i.e. more than 40 per cent of world population.

In India too the picture is highly disturbing. Number of distress suicides by farmers has gone up phenomenally. Rate of unemployment and underemployment has been increasing steadily and alarmingly and so also the number of people below the poverty line. At the same time, the number of billionaires has gone up from 71 in 1995 to 311 in 2005. On the social front, the situation is equally alarming. Half the population of India is functionally illiterate, the census data giving higher figures notwithstanding. In the land of world-class universities (IITs and IIMs), higher education in general is in shambles. It has little if any relevance to the problems of un- and underemployment the country faces. The health of the people of deteriorated as the number of doctors and hospitals has gone up. The control of major killers like plague, cholera, and smallpox has brought the mortality rates down but not the morbidity rates.

And add to these negative outcomes, the ecological and environmental risks the country faces have increased. It is not just the question of fast decreasing access to natural resources; even the resources the country had in abundance are being misused. The meaning of nature, nation, tradition, marriage, family, work etc. is changing giving rise to many unexpected setbacks. The *Panchbhootas* (land, water, air, energy and open space) are in distress. As globalization gets de-centralized, the risks accompanying it are being spread out uniformly all through the society and economy. We cannot handle these risks by the very means, which promote them. We do not have appropriate managerial instrumentalities to face them. The institutions that worked well in the past are now muted; they are no longer able to handle the emergent problems. They have become shell institutions; the appearance is shining and strong but the interior is muddy and rotten.

Our world is more hazardous today than ever before. Risks that accompany the natural hazard have been a part of life. If recent Tsunami that hit India, Sri Lanka, Indonesia, Malaysia and Thailand is any indicator, the risk of nature revenge has increased. In the days bygone, people worked with nature; they adapted themselves to the natural principle of symbiosis. When the hazards came, their fury was less devastating. People were prepared to face such hazards both psychologically and physically. When calamities came, people joined hands to help each other. No one blamed the government nor waited for the government to come forward with help. And hence the risks were lowered and community solidarity cemented.

'Modernization', changed much of old ways of handling the problems. Fate was ousted by an active engagement with the future. Man became the master of all he surveyed. He set upon to rule over nature. Armed as he was with science and technology, he tinkered with nature at will. A mad rush to tame the nature and to use it for industrialization, urbanization and locomotion was set in. Each step man took to control the nature enriched him materially in the short run but produced a series unexpected setbacks in the long run. So the apparent gains turned into real losses. We spend billions of dollars to undo the ill effects of what we considered a great step forward some years back.

Now the future appears to rebound forcing us to find new ways of handling it. We face a new type of risk - a risk that is self-inflicted; that is manufactured by us. These are ecological and environmental risks; risks attendant to poverty, inequity and loss of dignity. We are less interested in what nature can do to us and for us, and more about what we can do to nature so that it behaves the way we dictate. We just do not know what will be the risk of tinkering with nature, modifying genes, consuming fossil fuels, promoting large-scale urbanization, and proliferating nuclear arsenels, etc. We cannot depend on the scientists because scientific findings are never final. Further, many a times science has no answer for the problems we face.

The manufactured risks are not confined to ecology. We face equal or may be greater threat when we do away with family ties, marriage customs, and other traditions. Think of what has emerged from promiscuity in sexual relations? Science never warned us that AIDS would spread like wild fire? We just do not know, what else is there in store for our health? Many of the traditions are based on experiential knowledge derived from thousands of years of real life experience. Modern scientific knowledge is derived from controlled experiments in the laboratory. Both are importantt; they must cross-check each other and help man move up to the next higher level of consciousness.

Ours is a world where the manufactured hazards are as or even more threatening than those that come from nature. These manufactured risks are double edged; they affect us all no matter where we live in the form of ecological disasters like climatic change, nuclear hazards, terrorism and other forms of violence or widespread poverty and inequity in the midst of bourgeoning world economy. All these affect us individually too through the media of diet eat, medicine we consume, education we get, work we do.

## Loss of Human Values

We pride ourselves being non-traditional. It is abusive to call anyone a traditional person for it means a person who unquestioningly follows mysterious theology or ceremonies. Traditions provide a framework for action and for life and living too. There are people who guard traditions: wise men, elders, priests, sages and so on. It is they who had the privilege and also power to interpret traditions. All traditions were invented to meet a particular challenge. When the situation changed the traditions too changed even if very slowly. Traditions are thus invented and re-invented. Traditions provide a framework for human relations.

The eighteenth century Enlightenment in Europe gave tradition a bad name. It succeeded in weakening its hold but not in uprooting it. Even in Europe and America, there are traditions, which have persisted for centuries. It happened because modern civilization did not percolate down to the hearts of the people; it remained confined to various public institutions especially government, economy and politics. Traditions pertaining to family, gender and sexuality remained more or less as they were until the advent of the postmodern era i.e. in recent years.

Globalization has however changed the situation drastically. It has created a society, which is living not only at the end of nature but also at the end of tradition. A new global society, far more cosmopolitan than anyone known before, is on the rise. It is a society in which the old and the new and the tradition and the reason co-exist. In India many scientists are devout Hindus too. Look at the academic world. All disciplines work with a given tradition. But it is part of the academic life to explore new frontiers.

It is being increasingly realized that no man can live and be happy without faith. Gandhi demonstrated that faith and reason must co-exist. When his reason failed to give an answer to a problem he face, he called upon his inner self to guide him. If traditions reflective of the experiential knowledge, they should discarded only when we are armed with new and dependable knowledge. Even rituals have social meaning; if they are discarded new rituals would have to be created to prepare grounds for new traditions. Once the tradition retreats people live in a more open, reflective and autonomous way. But they find themselves lost in a world where nothing is fixed, there are no norms to go about. There is uncertainty all around.

The effect of this situation is anxiety and growth of addiction that is excessive attachment or inclination towards intoxicants, sex, work, food, and violence. Tradition was maintained by the collectivity; the addiction by the individual. Anxiety, anomy, and the need to reinvent oneself and find a place in a world where nothing is sure, produces sickness of the mind and therefore the need for psychopathic treatment.

Two of the glaring consequences of the clash between scientism and tradition are fundamentalism and terrorism. It points to the limitations of science on the one hand and acute sense of deprivation on the other. Fundamentalism need not be just religious. It could be anti-religious too. Think of the Red Guards of Mao's China. They were not religious zealots. I would assert that fundamentalism is a child of modernism and post-modernism. Look at the use of modern communication technology by Osama Bin Laden. Violence is inbuilt in fundamentalism. And we know that violence cannot be contained by violence. It forces us ask ourselves: Can we live in a world where nothing is sacred? Unless there are universal values, which guide our lives and that form the basis of the new institutions we have created, fundamentalism of one sort or the other will continue to raise its head.

Friends, it is here that Gandhi comes to forefront as the emancipator. We have rethink about traditions, science and technology, progress and development, civilization and the question of means and ends that Gandhi raised from time-to-time. 'All of us need moral commitments that stand above the petty concerns and squabbles of every day life. We should be prepared to mount an active defence of these values wherever they are poorly developed or threatened. None of us would have anything to live for, if we did not have something dying for.' Gandhi had a lot to die for and so he lives despite his death.

## Undemocratic Democracy

Let me now come one of the most or perhaps the most powerful energizing idea of the twentieth century. That is democracy. Leaving aside a few semi-feudal states such as Saudi Arabia, there hardly is a national state that does not call itself democratic. Even the USSR called itself people's democracy as does China today. Without going into the epistemological definitions, we can define democracy as a system of governance involving effective competition among political parties for position of power through regular and fair elections in which all adults can vote. This electoral process is accompanied by civil liberties like right to vote irrespective of sex, religion, economic status, freedom of holding opinion and expressing the same without any hindrance, freedom of forming and joining political parties, etc. It should be noted these freedoms. These rights did not come easily, they were fiercely resisted by the elites who held power during the nineteenth century.

For a long time, very few of the countries had democratic governments. Strangely, it were the democratic Europe, which suppressed democracy in Asia, Africa and Latin America until the 1940s. But even in Europe democracy was only partially developed. Before the First World War, women had right to vote only in Finland, Norway, Australia and New Zealand. They got this right in Switzerland only in 1974. Some countries like Germany, Italy, Austria, Spain and Portugal moved back from democracy to authoritarian rule. Since the 1970s, democracy has spread all over the world, a few military dictatorships and semi-feudal monarchies notwithstanding.

This gives some hopes but there are disturbing signs emerging from even the so-called mature democracies. The people are getting disillusioned with their governments. In a world based on modern information communication technology, power that comes from the top to the bottom loses its sharpness. The orthodox form of democracy confined to the top becomes insensitive to the change sweeping through people's lives at the bottom. People lose a good deal of trust they earlier re-posed in politicians and political institutions. Yet they support democracy as the only means of governance acceptable to them. So, democracy is continues to the choice of the people but the politicians are becoming increasingly unpopular. Politics has now become a corrupt business and politicians self-interested rather than having the good of the citizens in their view. The younger generation especially is disillusioned with the way the governments are handling the global economic issues and local ecological, gender and human rights issues. The current wave of terrorism has further alienated the people from their governments.

The global sweep of ICT has both positive and negative effects on democracy. On the one hand it has made the government more porous than ever before; on the other, the hold on multinationals on information channels has given them more control over the minds of the people than politicians have. Countering them needs democratization of democracy. The sovereign nation states have lost part of their sovereignty to global forces. Environmental risks, fluctuations in global economy and global technological changes do not respect national boundaries. At the same a new space has been created between the global and national institutions, which needs to be filled up by new multinational entities like European Union apart from the transnational corporations. In the same way the space between the individuals and the nation has to be filled by mini-democratic institutions. In popular parlance, it is known as decentralization. In the context of India, it would be Gandhi's Gram Swaraj. Then and then alone democracy will take deeper roots.

## Breaking Down of Family Solidarity

Another institution that is under tremendous pressure of modernization is family. Hardly there is a country, except of course the ones governed by fundamentalist and authoritarian governments, where the future of the family is not one of the major social concerns. The old family ties were based on certain emotional and economic interdependencies As these dependencies weaken the family structure is falling apart. Marriage was not sexually driven contract. The inequality of men and women was built in the system. Women and children did not have many of the human rights people demand today. Children were cared because they would keep the family going till eternity. They had a role to play. Sexuality was therefore dominated by reproduction. Sexual promiscuity among the males was considered a sign of masculinity but the same trait among the females was treated as a crime. Homosexuality too was almost invariably considered not only unnatural but also perverse, even if it was tolerated as an act of a small minority.

In the traditional family the married couple was just one and often a minor part of the family. Whether it should continue to live together or not did not depend on its own decision; decision had to be taken by the whole family. Today the married couple is the core of the family. The family ties are based on emotional and sexual satisfaction at least in the early stages and decision on whether they should live together or not depends on them and them alone.

In the new family culture, it is the equality among the sexes and transparency that keeps it together. Conflicts are sorted out by discussion and dialogue. Thus the good relationship depends on how equal they are and how honest they are to each other. In other words, how democratic the family is. This applies to ties with children too. Parents must have some authority over children but this authority must be based on certain democratic principles so that the child as he grows understands the logic behind how and why his parents treat him in a particular way.

The traditional family is on the way out but a family based on equality of sexes is still a far cry. The equality of sexes based on equality of promiscuity, violence and hatred is not the answer. As the family breaks and anomy grips the young and old alike, demand for new policies on family life, check on divorce, and regulations on sexual expression, are on the card. Family without love and sacrifice can never be enduring. And where there is love and sacrifice, there is democracy too. This is what Gandhi said as early as 1908.

## David Hardiman on 'an Alternative Modernity'[8]

Gandhi is believed to be against modernity in all its forms. His Hind Swaraj is quoted as an evidence of this. But, actually a deeper analysis of Gandhi's thoughts and actions shows that he was not against all the aspects of modernity. In fact, several key aspects of modernity like equality, democratic representation, governance through persuasion etc. were accepted by Gandhi.

He was not totally against the modernity but was critical of some aspects of it. He was against the belief that only western modernity was the best way of life and everyone wishing to become civilized must accept/follow it. He presented his own definition of a genuine civilization, based on a different kind of morality. He discussed this in his Hind Swaraj.

### Hind Swaraj

This book by Gandhi was written in 1909 in Gujarati, then translated into English in 1910. It is in a dialogue form as is the *Bhagwat Gita*. Gandhi presented his views on the uselessness of violence in it.

He was also very critical of equating a civilization's progress with material achievements. So, railways, machines, press, weapons, new technology brought in India by the British have not benefited India but harmed it. It actually helped the British gain control over India.

Gandhi used a Gujarati term for civilization "sudharo" meaning 'good way of life'. To him, civilizational progress should be seen in terms of moral achievements. Having control over our own desires and greed would be the best sign of civilized life. He maintained that the pre British Indian civilization was like that and each Indian must try to go back to those values.

The British government reacted by banning Hind Swaraj. Gandhi stuck to this view till 1914. In 1914, he changed the tone of his comments and made it clear that in Hind Swaraj he has not criticized the British as such but the present day modern European civilization.

In his later years, Gandhi accepted quite practically that some aspects of modern civilization were indispensable like railways, hospitals, mills, etc. What could be done, however, was to not let these elements rule us. These should be used as a utility and not as an object of enjoyment.

He was not against the western culture as such but was critical of the modern ways of life. He was equally against the British when they used it, as he was against the Indian nationalists who favoured violence as a means to the end.

Although Gandhi was severely criticized for his stand against modernity, later on it proved to be a valid stand. His views were very strong but they left their mark and proved to be true as time went by.

## A Gandhian Civilization

Gandhi's criticism of modern civilization was directed at its consumerism, competitiveness, slavery of desires and subjugation to technology.

Gandhi preferred a civilization that would use technology and science, for the benefit of the human beings, and not for satisfying the greed of a few rich capitalists.

Donald Worster has explained this divide in terms of two types of thinking prevalent. One an imperialist science and two, an Arcadian sensibility. In simple words, the former stands for an aggressive control over nature, with a completely material understanding of the world of life; the latter believes in a harmonious coexistence within nature, an ethical, spiritual understanding of nature, world and people.

Gandhi stood for the latter position. His understanding of the concept of nature shows this attitude. His notion of nature was determined by the concept of *'prakruti'* it is not just a material from but a manifestation of God. He did not, like others, see a divide between 'nature' and 'culture'. For him *prakruti* or nature stood for 'the original, natural form of anything'. So in this sense, no divide exists between material force and divine force, between nature and culture.

Gandhi found the modernist scientific attitude misplaced when it showed an arrogance of having conquered nature. He believed that to think so is to challenge the unlimited powers of God and nature. He promoted a scientific attitude that would be humble, that would not dream of conquering nature, that would take from nature only as much as is required. He suggested that if human beings stopped exploiting nature for their greed there would be enough for everyone on the earth.

Gandhi disliked the modern city with its noise, rush, smoke etc. His ideal was that of a small-scale agricultural community, cultivating common land in a sustainable, self-sufficient way. He tried to have this sort of life in his ashramas. He was in the favour of rational of scientific approaches so long as they stayed under the guidance of moral principles.

## The Constructive Programme

This programme of incorporating technology in a people friendly manner comprised of three principles — *Swadeshi* (home-based production); Sarvodaya (aim of public welfare) and *Aparigraha* (non-possessiveness). This programme was inaugurated during 1920-21 and was very close to Gandhi's heart.

A technology appropriate for the majority of people's needs was to be encouraged. India required labour intensive technology as there were many hands available which would be unemployed if labour-saving technology was used. Self-reliance through labour was also considered important for the Indians. The spinning wheel was a key example of this approach. This campaign was launched in 1919. A small, portable design of spinning wheel was popularized. People were encouraged to make khadi, for themselves and for the markets. Economically, however, khadi did not prove to be a very profitable venture. It was expensive as compared to mill-produced cloth. It led to some criticism of Gandhi's economic theory. He was accused of promoting time-consuming, back-breaking devices instead of labour-saving devices. Actually, to an extent this criticism was not wrong because technology had made people's life easier in many ways and which were beneficial. For example improved *chulha* (stoves), gobar gas plant, hand pumps, new designs of ploughs, new varieties of seeds, improved breeding programmes, new techniques of water harvesting, water storage etc. proved hugely beneficial for the people.

Even khadi could have been a success but the problem was that khadi weaving was put on a very high symbolic from while the equally important aspect of sustainable cotton-growing economy was neglected.

An open-minded, clear, investigative approach is equally important for a noble cause to survive and make an impact.

Gandhi realized the importance of this method and following the example of the great Victorian investigators of British, he sought to know about the problems of the people through fieldwork, data and local investigation.

This interest in the problems of the local people of various districts indirectly popularized the nationalistic sentiment of Gandhi.

## Gandhi's View on Socialism

Gandhi's picture of an ideal civilization did not give much significance to Marxian School of Socialism. It did support the views like equality, eradication of poverty but the essential importance of struggle for it in Marxian theory was not appreciated by Gandhi.

More and more leaders in India's freedom struggle were getting influenced by socialism. Gandhi entered into a dialogue with them. He respected the basic aims of socialism like right of all to a livelihood, elimination of poverty etc., but he claimed that the method of the socialists was flawed. It was a very political method, gave importance to violence, believed in destroying the capitalist for attaining its aims. Gandhi subscribed to an entirely different approach. His method was driven by compassion not just for the poor but also for the capitalist. He maintained that the enemy was not the capitalist but capitalism. Cooperation of the capitalists should be sought in order to eradicate the ills of modern capitalism.

Violence, he said, would only increase hatred. Instead of class struggle he gave the solution in the form of '*Satyagraha*'.

Both the capitalist and the worker should be made to realize that without each other's help they would be destroyed. In fact the capitalist should be encouraged to behave like a trustee of social property. Gandhi argued that it was possible to appeal to the good in every person, however oppressive they might appear to be.

Everyone should practice '*aparigraha*' i.e. an attitude of non-possessiveness. Each should hold whatever assets they have for the good of the society. Owners should not take more than what is required for a comfortable life. The workers should be treated as the members of a family.

This view of Gandhi's was criticized by socialists for downplaying the class struggle. But it is true that although Gandhi was against the use of violence, he was very deeply, strongly dedicated to the cause of the upliftment of the poor.

It is sad that except for a few industrialists (like Jamnalal Bajaj, JRD Tata) none respected this spirit of social good.

Gandhi's views on class struggle are similar to those of Paul Ricoeur who maintains that there are various factors like language, culture, nationality that cut across the class boundaries and can act as integrating forces. The effort should not be towards destroying the enemy but towards integrating.

## Gandhi's Influence Beyond India

The Gandhian way of resolving socio-economic problems is being emulated outside India also. The trend was started by E.F. Schumacher (1911-77), a German economist who has been an advisor to the British Government during the 1940s and the 50s. He felt that the so-called 'developing' countries were moving on an economic strategy that would ruin their resources and economy. The local conditions in these regions were not compatible with the demands of the capital-intensive economic models. These regions needed a technology suited to their circumstances. In most cases, it meant labour-intensive, small scale, low investment technology.

He stood for a Gandhian attitude favouring an appropriate technology, an intermediate technology. Intermediate in the sense that it should be superior to the primitive technology but at the same time, much simpler, cheaper and freer than the super technology of the modern times.

He differentiated, using Gandhi's views, between mass production and production by the masses. The system of mass production is highly capital-intensive, consumes high energy, is violent, ecologically damaging. The production by the masses, on the other hand, uses human resources like creativity, skillful hands etc.; it encourages production activities compatible with local resources, is eco-friendly and frees the human beings from the servitude of machines. Technologies should not be copied or aped but should be tailor made for each socio-economic context. This requires much higher level of innovation, creativity.

Another propagator of an alternative economic order was Ivan Illich (1926). He was an Austrian who worked as a catholic priest in the 1950s. During 1970 to 1975 he wrote four books, one of which talked of decentralization and the importance of knowing the limits of growth. He was critical, like Gandhi, of the Western medicine. He found that the western style doctors did nothing to really cure the patients. They never advised any control over appetite or prescribed discipline over self.

He was also against rapid transport. He saw more ill in it than good. Such a system not only consumed a lot of energy and caused severe pollution but also enslaved human beings because in order to have them and use them people needed to slog for hours.

Another international agency to be influenced by Gandhi's ideology on economics was Oxfam, a non-government organization working for the betterment of poor countries. In 1966-67, Oxfam's relief workers working in Bihar came in contact with some Gandhian workers. For the first time, it is commented, that a truly authentic and inspirational Indian ideology was seen at work. Through that interaction, the Oxfam directors realized that the Green Revolution which they thought was benefiting the poor countries was in fact not all that beneficial. It emphasized on the use of high-yielding plant hybrids developed by multinational agencies, which needed lots of water, fertilizers, pesticides etc. which increased the dependency of the farmers on the multinational companies. From a Gandhian perspective the Green Revolution increased the gap between the rich farmers and the poor farmers. This could not be good for rural development.

During the 1970s Oxfam became known for its criticism of such big plans, unsuitable for the poor, developing countries. It started focusing on working with local people, tried to be sensitive to local methods and requirements. Appropriate technology was encouraged with the emphasis on maximum village self-sufficiency.

Gandhi saw these problems basically rooted in a lack of morality, lack of principles. He blamed materialism and consumerism for most of the ills of the present day society.

## Concluding Remarks

In conclusion, we can say that Gandhi was a traditionalist and yet at the same time a modernist too. He extolled traditions that took man to the path of morality seen in its broadest perspectives. He was a modernist because he stood for reason, rationality and search for truth. At the same time he was not a modernist because all through his life he fought against all that modernity had created in his time: colonialism, inequality, exploitation of nature and man by man, gender inequality, and war. Gandhi was postmodernist, because he refused to take any scripture as the words of God and therefore final, because he questioned the rationality of science and its power to solve all human problems, because he worked for gender equality, and because he worked for peace and harmony. But he was not post-modernist because he rejected the sovereignty of individual; because he did not accept material progress as the goal of humanity and because he did not reject God even if it meant Truth. His life was a personification of the Vedic verse chanted at his funeral pier:

> Lead me from Unreal to Real
> From Darkness to Light
> From Death to Immortality

## Gandhi became Immortal in his Death

So what Gandhi was? Gandhi belonged to a genre of his own. He transcended all classifications of time and space based on scientific reasoning. His was a universe that was essentially human and spiritual and scientific at the same time. If the human spirit is one, Gandhi cannot be bound in any artificial division and classifications.

## Notes

1. M.K. Gandhi, *Hind Swaraj or Indian Home Rule*, Ahmedabad, Navajiwan Publishing House, 1938, pp. 32-33.
2. *Ibid.*, p. 33.
3. *Ibid.*, p. 27.
4. *Ibid.*, pp. 47-50.
5. *Ibid.*, p. 51
6. *Ibid.*, p. 53
7. *Ibid.*, p. 55
8. Parapharased version from David Hardiman's book, *Gandhi in His Time and Ours*, New Delhi, Permanent Block, 2003.

# 8
# Trusteeship : Moral and Spiritual Approach to Economics

*– Neeru Kapoor*

Gandhi formulated his economic ideas and principles in the context of his design, of an ideal social order, a non-violent, non-exploitative humanistic and egalitarian society. This social order embodied the fundamental philosophy of his life. He approached all facets of his social order – its economics, its politics from the philosophical premises – truth and non-violence – that governed his entire life. He was not willing to draw any sharp distinction between economics and ethics. "I must confess that I do not draw a sharp or any distinction between economics and ethics. That economics is untrue which ignores or disregards moral value. The extension of the law of non-violence in economics means nothing less than the introduction of moral values as a factor to be considered in regulating international commerce".[1]

The Mahatma rejected the Marxist solution to the most important and controversial issue of economic philosophy i.e. the right to private property, because he believed it be based on violence and tyranny. He also rejected the capitalistic solution because he considered it to be based on exploitation, competition and tyranny. The question of property relations assumed a great significance for him and he was of the confirmed belief that instead of changing the property relations, if we change the uses to which property is put we can have the desired results.

For this he advocated trusteeship as a relevant choice between the existing but unacceptable system of capitalist organization and its 'inevitable' throw by violence. He believed that as for as the present owners of wealth are concerned they have to make a choice between war and voluntary converting themselves into the trustees of their wealth. Thus he seeks to harmonize the economic relations and to conciliate the ultimate values into a state of equilibrium through trusteeship. Mahatma does not ignore the divinity of man which is epitomized in the great maxim that 'a jiva is always shiva': a man is by and large, divine. And in this respect, it is difficult to distinguish between a man and a man. It is from this deep feeling of spirituality and divinity of man that Gandhi derived his ethico-economic theory of trusteeship and inheritance.

He wrote, "Everything belonged to God and was from God. Therefore, it was for his people as a whole, not for a particular individual. When an individual has more than his proportionate portion, be became a trustee of that portion for God's people".[2] That is why he talked of equality of distribution of national wealth.

## Sources of Trusteeship

Trusteeship was not just an economic expedient for Gandhi. It was a way of life. In his own words, "My theory of trusteeship is no makeshift, I am confident that it will survive all others theories. It has the sanction of philosophy and religion behind it."[3] Indian philosophy, religion and morals are replete with this. The ancient Indian concept of rulers or King was that of a real trustee. *Ramarajya* bears testimony of the fact that under the Indian cultural heritage the rulers wielded power not for their own sake but for the sake of their subject. Bharat reigned over Ayodhya during Ramachandra's absence as the latter's trustee. Lord Krishna acted as the Charioteer of Arjuna in the battle of *Mahabharta*, not with any ulterior motive or expectation of any gain from the battle, he asked as a trustee of Arjuna to give satisfaction to the latter.

The heads of Hindu joint families in those days used to live the life of true trustees. According to K.M. Munshi, "He held the family property and was expected to manage and administer it for the welfare of the family. He was expected to watch with care the advancement of his younger members belonging even to collateral branches and had to give asylum to the orphans, widows, destitute in the family,"[4] writing specifically about the property, Dr. S. Radhakrishnan has pointed out, "property according to the Hindu view, is a mandate held by its possessors for the common use and benefit of the commonwealth. The *Bhagvata* tells us that we have acclaim only to so much as would satisfy our hunger. If any one desires more, he is thief deserving punishment."[5]

Thus the concept of trusteeship should be viewed in the context of the values it stood for. The doctrine is as old as the ages. But it was the Mahatma who tried to apply this philosophical teaching to the concrete realities of life for the solution of the existing economic problems.

Pyare Lal mentioned, "Gandhi based his trusteeship doctrine on a celebrated verse in the ancient Hindu philosophical scripture. '*Ishopanishad*' which says: "All that is in the universe is pervaded by God, renounce first, therefore, in order to enjoy, covet not any body's riches."[6]

The words like, *aparigraha* (non-possession) and '*samabhava*' (equality) had gripped him.[7] He now came to realize that the principles of non-possession and renunciation of one's property or possession or assets as advocated in the *Gita* can be given effect to by way of trusteeship whereby the propertied people while retaining their property can still divest themselves of such possessions by holding the property in form of trust for the real beneficiaries. His study of English Law also came to his help in deciding upon his divesting himself of all possessions. To quote from his *Autobiography*, "My study of English Law came to my help. Snell's discussion of the maxims of Equity came to my memory. I understood more clearly in the light of *Gita,* teaching the implication of the world trustee... I understood *Gita* teaching of non-possession to mean that those who desired solution should act like trustees who, though having control over great possessions, regards not an iota of them as his own."[8]

In a letter to Polok on October 14, 1909, who was at that time in India, Gandhi employed the word 'trustee' for the first time. He wrote, "then the British rulers will be servants and not masters. They will be trustees and not tyrants and they will live in perfect peace with the whole of the inhabitants of India."[9] Laying his heart bare before the august audience assembled on the occasion of the opening of the Banaras Hindu University on February 4, 1916, he appealed to the 'richly bedecked nobleman present on dias to strip themselves of the jeweller and 'hold it in trust' for their countrymen in India.[10]

Gandhi divided property in two parts; gifts of nature and product of social living. The gifts of nature include land, mines, natural resources etc. The second parts deals with man made property. "सर्व भूमि गोपाल की". All land belong to Gopal where there is the boundary line? He asked?[11] Land, mines and other natural resources are the gifts of nature. No individual has made them. God created these not far any particular individual or group of individuals. Man has only occupied a piece of land and demarcated it. He is only the maker of a boundary line. He cannot be called the real owner of that property.

Same is the case with man-made property. A capitalist has accumulated huge wealth and established several industries. He alone can not make that. There may be so many persons who helped that capitalist in accumulating that wealth. Since the poor have helped the capitalist in accumulating the wealth they have their share in that also. None has a right to acquire more than what is needed to satisfy his absolute and immediate needs, particularly, when millions are unable to satisfy their most basic requirement.

He accepted trusteeship as a practical proposition which shall liberate the wealthy and the possessing class of their sin of acquisitiveness and greed and effect a change over in favour of egalitarian society.

## Origin of Trusteeship

The trusteeship formula was evolved by Kishorilal Mashruwala, Narahari Parikh and others. Professor Dantwala from Bombay had sent the draft of simple, practical trusteeship formula which he had prepared. It was placed before Gandhiji, who made few changes in it.[12]

The amended final six-point draft contains the basic ideals of trusteeship as follows:

1. Trusteeship provides a means of transforming the present capitalist order of society into an egalitarian one. It gives no quarters to capitalism, but gives the present owning class a chance of reforming itself. It is based on the faith that human nature is never beyond redemption.

2. It does not recognize any right of private ownership of property except so far as it may be permitted by society for its own welfare.
3. It does not exclude legislative regulation of ownership and use of wealth.
4. Thus, under state-regulated trusteeship, an individual will not be free to hold or use his wealth for selfish satisfaction or in disregard of the interest of society.
5. Just as it is proposed to fix a decent minimum living wage, even so a limit should be fixed for the maximum income that could be allowed to any person in society. The difference between such minimum and maximum incomes should be reasonable, equitable and variable from time-to-time so much so that the tendency would be towards obliteration of the difference.
6. Under the Gandhian economic order the character of production will be determined by social necessity and not by personal whim or greed.

## Basis of Trusteeship

According to J.D. Sethi, a well known economist, the theory of trusteeship is based on three Gandhian concepts: Non-violence, Swaraj and Equality which are inter-linked with one another. Broadly speaking, Truth (*Satya*), Non-violence (*Ahimsa*), Bread Labour and Non-Profession (*Aparigraha*) led Gandhi to the concept of Trusteeship. Let us discuss briefly their relationship with the concept of Trusteeship.

## Truth

To Gandhi, truth occupies the first place and *Ahimsa* the second. In the course of his pursuit of truth, he discovered *Ahimsa*. His goal was truth. He wanted to realise truth through *Ahimsa*. To him truth is harmony of thoughts with words and of words with actions. To Gandhi, the statement, 'God is Truth' is only partial. The statement 'Truth is God' is all inclusive and pervasive. The social workers is in search for Truth by way of his service; the craftsman is in search of truth by way of his craftsmanship; the philosopher searches truth by way of the prime cause and the scientist is in quest of truth by way of empirical experimentation.

Thus each and every one would be serving God, according to Gandhi's definition – Truth is God. To him, truth stands above everything in this universe. He is ready to sacrifice everything including man to uphold truth. Gandhi says, "wife, children, friends, possessions – should be held subservient to truth. Each one of these should be sacrificed in search of truth."[13]

## Non-Violence

Gandhi saw that the idea of Trusteeship was inherent in the ideology of *Ahimsa*, "Non-violence is the law of the human race and is infinitely greater than and superior to brute force".[14] For him trusteeship was an inescapable stage in the methodology of a non-violent revolution. It was not transitional. It is a stage that yields the result that one was seeking. In that sense, therefore, it was both a 'means' and on 'end'. Hence, Gandhi claimed "no other theory is compatible with non-violence".[15] While acquisition stands for violence, non-violence stands for non-acquisition. A votary of non-violence keeps away from possession. Every kind of possession is based on exploitation which is a form of violence. A non-violent society is a non-exploitative society. It can be non-violent only when it assumes economic equality. Equal distribution is the ideal.

## Bread Labour

"The law, that to live man must work first came home to me", Gandhi says, "upon reading Tolostoy's writing on Bread Labour".[16] Gandhi was very much influenced by this concept. For Gandhi, labour is the root of the entire creation. That too "to people furnishing and idle, the only acceptable form in which God can dare appear is work and promise of food as wages". Therefore work is God. Everyone can see God through his own work. He believes that no body should eat his bread without performing sufficient labour. The idea is that every healthy individual must labour enough for his food, and the one who performs labour acquires legitimate right to get his bread. Nobody should acquire more than his absolute need. In other words, need based acquisition is the root to establish egalitarian society.

A silent revolution in the structure of the society can be brought by the law of bread-labour. Compulsory obedience to it only breeds poverty, disease and discontent. It is a state of slavery, willing obedience alone brings contentment health and wealth. In fact, Gandhian concept of bread-labour epitomizes, "from each according to his ability, to each according to his need". When everyone works and become trustees of their labour, there will not be either rich or poor".[17]

## *Aparigraha*

*Aparigraha* is the ethical ideal of non-possession; of the renunciation of ownership, of liberation from the subtle as well as the coarse bonds that possessions forge for one. It is a hoary ideal sanctified by every religion.[18] In a pithy verse, the *Isopanishad* exhorts:

Tena Tyaktena Bhunjeethah: Ma Gridha Kasyaswiddhanam? (enjoy by renouncing donot covet or cling or to possessions, for, whose is wealth?)[19]

According to Gandhiji "Non-possession means non-dependence on material things. It implies total abolition of private property in all kinds of belongings, a view more radical that of extreme communists". To Gandhi, stealing lies in possessing something which is not at all needed now. Non-possession is the result of non-stealing. He says: "I suggest that we are thieves in the way. If I take anything that I don't need for my own immediate use and keep it, I thieve it from somebody else. I suggest it is the fundamental law of nature, without exception that nature produces enough for our wants from day-to-day and if only everyone took enough for himself and nothing more, there would.be no pauperism in this world".[20]

Absolute non-possession is an abstraction. It is unattainable in its fullness. Non-possession does not mean remaining satisfied with poverty. Already Indian masses are suffering with hunger and poverty. They need not practice voluntary poverty. They have to work and get sufficient food. What Gandhi wanted was to avoid unnecessary possession by which individual and society are deprived of legitimate enjoyment.

Non-possession makes a man to keep everything open,

trusteeship gets life. In trusteeship nothing is hidden. Everything that is excess from everyone joins the trust and is readily available to every needy.

Gandhi cited five reasons to explain why man should practice non-possession as follow:[21]

1. Possession is not present in nature. God creates everything in accordance with the need of the hour. So possessing more than the need reveals man's thief mentality.
2. By birth man depends upon the things created by both nature and society. Using these without replacing them, depicts him a thief. Moreover, he stands as a debtor both to nature and society. So his duty lies in not indicating anything. Every when he uses anything he should replace them though his labour – physical, mental and spiritual.
3. Hoarding for future deprives the real needy.
4. The attitude of possessing loads to the multiplication of wants. Consequently, it results in the lack of peace both in the individual and in the society.
5. Possession implies all kinds of troubles. It is always accomplished by force. A man of faith in non-violence never resorts either to possession or to force; he prefers non-possession.

The concept of non-possession commands certain social implications which leads to trusteeship.

1. In a society where non-possession is in practice wealth is not the mark of respect.
2. Multiplication of wants is not the measure of civilization.
3. As every need is to be fulfilled by work, work is the medium of self-expression and existence.
4. A man of work possesses a right to honourable livelihood.
5. As all work has equal value all receive equal remuneration.
6. The means adopted is always based on truth and non-violence.
7. Such an ethical life leads everyone to attain self-realisation.

Non-possession to Gandhi is a noble idea. No doubt,

practically he himself renounced his wealth. But possession grants a sense of satisfaction and security to man. So, Gandhi wisely offered a solution. Accordingly, he asked to shed possessiveness, if not possession, and greed for wealth, if not wealth itself. The rich may keep their wealth by considering their excess of wealth as the property of the community. They become the trustees of such wealth and use it for the welfare of all. As total dispossession is a remote possibility, Gandhi suggests: "I accept the proposition that it is better not to desire wealth, than to acquire it and become its trustees. But what am I to advise those who are already wealthy or who would not shed their desire for wealth? I can only say to them that they should use their wealth for service".[22] In this way Gandhi offered trusteeship as a realistic solution to set right the lopsided development of both individual and society.

## Meaning of Trusteeship

The concept of trusteeship is not Gandhi's creation it traced to *Isavasya Upanishad*. In Indian context, 'trustee' is used in connection with temples and mutts. 'Trustee' means any individual who manages the temple property without any self-interest. According to Devadatta Dabholkar, "voluntary surrender of privileges, power and prestige without expecting anything in return (even by way of appreciation or recognition) is trusteeship".[23] According to K. Arunachalam, "trusteeship means confidence reposed in a person with respect to property of which he has possession and over which he can exercise power for the benefit of some other person or object."[24] V.K.R.V. Rao found in 1970 Gandhi's vision of trusteeship "prophetic for the world" and, according to J.D. Sethi "in trusteeship, Gandhi produced a grand alternative to the prevailing economic organizations whether in the communist or capitalist countries."

The concept of trusteeship implies several meanings. A brief analysis of such meanings is given below:

## Trusteeship as an Attitude

Trusteeship as an attitude involves everyone's identification with the entire humanity. According to G.S. Shroff, "trusteeship is an attitude. It has to come from within. It cannot be forced from outside. It can never be imposed on people for long. It should not be done.[25]

H. K. Paranjape clarifies trusteeship as an attitude as follows: "To say that trusteeship is a matter of an attitude of the mind is in effect to say that there are certain ethical values which have always been, at least formally, endorsed by humanity. Truth, non-exploitation of others, honesty and helpfulness–even generosity towards others have been such values."[26]

In fact as an attitude trusteeship ensures a balanced relationship among productive elements. The kind of relationship between those who work and those direct the work is always dependent upon their attitude. Trusteeship involves a certain responsive attitude by different elements in the economic system towards each other. Through trusteeship Gandhi was emphasizing a basic moral attitude on the part of all.[27]

Arvind A. Deshpande says, "the Gandhian concept of trusteeship expresses enterprise to its workers, share-holders, consumers and the community and the mutual responsibilities of each to the other. This is the price of democracy. Without virtue in the individual and in the organ of society, democracy cannot survive.[28]

## Trusteeship as a Method

Trusteeship is a method for the socialization of wealth. Wealth belongs to all. As God is the supreme and only owner of everything, to hold it exclusively with love alone, is a sin. Trusteeship as a method also stands for socializing everything. As a trustee, the capitalist becomes a co-sharer. At that moment all are joined as trustees for everything. There is no place for unnecessary personal claims. It drives every individual to achieve Sarvodaya.

## Trusteeship as a Movement

Trusteeship is not a choice, either to a capitalist or to a selfish bureaucrat. It is a movement towards social self management of industry. As a movement, it aims at a socio-economic and political arrangement in the society. At personal level, trusteeship as a movement makes man strengthen himself. At inter-personal level, trusteeship as a movement always tries to establish cordial relationship. It streamlines and strengthens the relations between the individual. At the institutional level, trusteeship's role is laudable. As institution it stands for serving a common purpose. Trusteeship as a movement, goes against every kind of authority – economic, political and social etc. It is against the monopoly of decision making. In fact, trusteeship provides ample opportunity to human beings in all spheres.

## Trusteeship as a Legal Institution

Gandhi was ready to make trusteeship a legalized institution. He wants to give it a statutory form through the legislative channel. He mentioned the following series of measures to bring about the change in the heart of the rich:

1. Appeal to the better instincts in the rich,
2. Persuasion,
3. Education regarding inevitability of change,
4. The greater unattractiveness of the alternative of change by violence,
5. Non-violent, non-cooperation by the exploited that would make the exploiters functioning impossible, and
6. Legislative action.

Trusteeship Law should guard the following:

1. Non-production if good or services are of anti-social character.
2. Non-production of goods or services which contribute to modern degeneration.
3. Non-production of goods or services which prevent attempts at spiritual development.
4. Non-production of goods or services which prevent the development of the best in the individual consumer.

Trusteeship Law should provide scope for modern technology and methods of production. This should be in tune with natural harmony and ecological balance. Further it should safeguard the interests of coming generations.

Trusteeship Law should be for promoting cultural and

aesthetic values in production and distribution. Work should be a thing of joy and self-fulfillment. No where pain or frustration or boredom be seen. Trusteeship law should provide for the separate registration of all economic activities.

Trusteeship system should be given privileges and incentives on par with co-operative institutions and philanthropic foundations.

Separate departments of trusteeship should be opened at both the centre and the state, separate ministers should be allotted.

The report of the ministers should be presented before the public and the legislations for free discussions and development.

Special recognition need to be given to trustee enterprises which contribute to the growth of the individual and the spiritual awakening.

An enterprise need not be registered under the trusteeship law with compulsion.[29]

Without proper registration, no enterprise is entitled to special privileges. Gandhi's opinion was to see trusteeship as legalized institution. Accordingly the state has the following functions:

1. It has to give a statutory recognition to the institution of trusteeship,
2. It has to determine the rate of commission for the trusteeship,
3. It has to supervise the fulfillment of conditions of trusteeship,
4. Depending upon the end, it has to regulate and approve the appointment of a successor trustee, and
5. It has to disapprove a trustee, who fails to act in accordance with the basic features of trusteeship.

The constitution of trusteeship need not be governed by laws, as every law carries with it some violence. But Gandhi admits laws, sanctioned by public opinion. U.N. Dhebar views Gandhian approach as follows: "The basic approach to the concept of the trusteeship which is a part and parcel of the law of property, is merely to ensure proper use of property for the benefit of its owner – subject to certain social obligations". In fact, the purpose of Gandhian trusteeship is much wider and more fundamental than the narrow legal conception.[30]

## Trusteeship as a Theory

Theory of trusteeship no doubt is present in our epics and well practiced by our kings. In the modern world, life is becoming highly polluted because of his greedy nature. Gandhi has no other alternative than to bring trusteeship into human life. Gandhi's trusteeship is accepted by one and all in theory. But nobody is coming forward to put it in practice. Everyone wants freedom but no responsibility. As freedom is responsibility, no one prefers it. Freedom lies in self-ruling. In every field, the problem of master-slave exists.Economic field is not exception Gandhi found a way out to this problem. It is trusteeship that relates labour or work, directly to production but not to its price or to consumption. Every man has some talent. He has to go on producing the excess of his talents and pool it in the trust. His primary duty lies in production. At no time be should value it by attaching a rate. At the same time he should not produce anything with the view of self-consuming. This is well illustrated by the work done in our families. The mother prepares food for everyone in the family. It is produced not on the basis of equality, but according to the need of each person.[31]

## Trusteeship as an Ideal

Every right thinking man has to put before him some goals or deals either as primary or secondary. Accordingly, he has to travel to fulfill them. Trusteeship as an ideal is there to perfect the human life of every individual here, on earth. It brings discipline, devotion and dedication, of a man's body and mind. A well trained personality is bound to realize himself which is the ultimate goal of every man. Thus, trusteeship is the best secondary ideal to push and place man as the fittest person for self-realisation.

## Nature of Trust

When a group of individuals join together and pour their excess of faith, a trust is born. The excess of either talent or property or wealth is put together for the proper utilization by the need in the society. The trust is a boon to the whole mankind. A trust contributor is above caste, creed, colour, age and sex. Trust belongs to no one.

It is everybody's treasure. There is a need to look after the trust, which is a deposit of all the excess of the genuine needy. He is called a 'trustee'. He is selfless service-oriented personality. Without trust, any human transaction on this earth is impossible.

Gandhi said, "the most practical, the most dignified way of going on in the world is to take people at their word when you have no positive reason to the contrary".[32] He further said, "I believe in trusting. Trust begets trust. Suspicion is fortid and only stinks. He who trusts has never yet lost in the world."[33] He is so cautious that he has never broken a promise. To him, a breach in promise is a serious issue because it happens to our trust in others.

## Qualities of a Trustee

A trustee is one who self-consciously assumes responsibility for upholding, protecting and putting to good use whatever he possesses, acquires or earns.[34] He is always a moral giant. A trustee has no heir but the public.

Raghavan Iyer[35] describes the following as the essential characters of a trustee:

(a) He is self-governing.

(b) He is morally sensitive.

(c) He always knows the unmet needs of others.

(d) He has the capacity to control and transmit his own tendencies.

(e) He always improves his generous feelings and altruistic hopes for others.

(f) He consciously keeps away all exploitative attitudes and relationships.

(g) He always strives to become self-regulating, reliable and sacrificial.

(h) He learns to think altruistically.

(i) He behaves with utmost purity and solicitousness, in his speech, touch and act. He is always alert to all situations both inner and outer. He holds that everything belongs to

God, mankind and to future generations.

(j) He never exhibits the fear of multiplying his possessions talents and gifts.

(k) He never exhibits selfish indifference.

(l) He never hoards anything.

(m) He trains himself as a servant to the whole mankind.

(n) He enjoys inward moral balance.

(o) He lives with detachment.

(p) He reposes unshakable confidence in the ontological plenty of nature and in the inexhaustible resourcefulness of man.

(q) He has a benevolent and self-sustaining motive.

R.B. Upadhyaya also brilliantly enumerates twenty-four qualities of a trustee "which may work as general directions for the trustees to mould their personality traits accordingly."[36] These qualities are given below:

1. A trustee should be a man of high character, complete honesty on his part is presumed.
2. He should always act in good faith with the best of intentions for the benefit of the party that has reposed confidence in him.
3. His action should be taintless.
4. If there is even the slightest doubt he should always be ready to submit himself to the strictest of public scrutiny.
5. He must maintain accurate and correct accounts of receipts and payments, assets and liabilities of the trust. He should be prepared to get them audited and examined by independent and impartial authority.
6. He must practice, utmost frugality in regard to trust and money.
7. He should never use trust money and property for his personal work.

8. He should not believe in conspicuous consumption and vulgar display of wealth and must led to a simple life not very much different from the living standards of the society.
9. He should possess business acumen and managerial talent.
10. By nature and conviction he should believe in the dignity of physical labour and should himself put in some physical labour daily.
11. He should try to eschew snobbery, high-brow and 'ivory tower' mentality and should not have fake airs about himself. He should be attracted towards the ideal of self enforcement.
12. He should know that he is more of a servant of the cooperation and not a boss.
13. He should be straight forward, simple and considerate but firm in his manners and behaviour.
14. He should behave like a leader of the group.
15. He should be a firm believer in individual dignity and freedom and should abhor flattery.
16. He should be committed to a sense of social responsibility and growth of his business within the bounds of fair trade practices.
17. He should belong to a higher level of need-hierarchy so that he is motivated more by social and self-realisation needs.
18. He should believe in building upon egalitarian society and should possess a judicial bent of mind in his behaviour towards all, particularly towards his opponents.
19. Though he may have material ambitions, he considers material prosperity as a means to an end rather than an end in itself. He should have a balanced view of life as a whole.
20. He should take philosophical view of life and should avoid excessive greed in his behaviour.

21. He should be a man of firm conviction in regard to basic and fundamental principles of life but at the same time he should know that in relation to the numbers of the society a compromising temper in regard to details is a great asset.
22. He should be a man of drive and dynamism, active and dedicated to work.
23. Real understanding requires empathy – an attempt by one person to put himself in the position of another and then viewing the situation accordingly.
24. He should believe in the dictum, 'service first and profit second'.

## Criticism of the Concept of Trusteeship

The principle of trusteeship has been subject to much misconceived criticism. It has been described as a 'make-shift', as an 'eye wash' as a shelter for the rich an as 'merely appealing to the more fortunate ones to show a little more charity. It has been generally objected to, on the ground that as a means of affecting social transformation this theory, its ethical content notwithstanding is ineffective. Professor M.L.Dantwala in his, 'Gandhism Reconsidered' quotes a Marxist appraisal of the doctrine.' The division of the society into the property owning and the property-less classes, which is the characteristics of capitalism, is sought to be retained in Gandhism also. The only difference in Gandhism is that the erstwhile capitalist, property owning classes will consider itself trustee on behalf of the proletariat. The change is purely on the subjective sphere. The objective conditions of production will continue by remaining as they were in capitalism. Production will continue by unplanned private competition among the individual trustees. These conditions of production have a compelling logic of their own which will lead to the same contradictions as are witnessed under capitalism today. The class appropriation of surplus value, which trust production will continue in a pious guise, will mean larger and larger accumulations of the capital on the one hand and pauperization of the masses on the other… These evils cannot be banished by wishing a change in the hearts and minds of the owners of property.[37]

E.M.S. Namboodiripad has attacked not only his philosophy but his intentions also. In his own words, "Not only in relation to the rural poor, but also in relation to the working class and other sections of the working people his was an approach which, in actual practice, helped the bourgeoisie. His theory of trusteeship, his insistence on certain moral values as the guiding line for any political activity, the skillful way in which he combined his own extra-parliamentary activities (constructive programme and *satyagraha*) with the parliamentary activities of his lieutenants, the characteristically Gandhian way of combining negotiations with the enemy even while carrying on mass direct action against him – all these proved in actual practice to be of enormous help to the bourgeoisie in (a) rousing the masses in action against imperialism and (b) preventing them from resorting to revolutionary mass action. This ability of his to rouse the masses and yet to check them, to launch anti-imperialist direct action and yet to go on negotiating with the imperialist rulers made him the undisputed leader of the bourgeoisie".[38]

The criticism of theory has not been levelled only from the Marxist quarters. Even a sympathetic reviewer of Gandhian economics like Professor J.J. Anjaria doubts its validity as a long-term solution, "as a short-term measure, this is excellent, coercion is ethically bad, on any large scale, it is also not expedient. But the run away from the problem by merely appealing to the more fortunate ones to show a little more charity—awful word—is no solution".[39]

Even Pandit Jawahrlal Nehru, Gandhi's political heir and most trusted disciple, wrote in his autobiography, "Again I think of the paradox that is Gandhiji. With all his keen intellect and passion for bettering the down trodden and oppressed, why does he support a system and a system which is obviously decaying, which creates this misery and the wastes? He seeks a way out, it is true, but is not that way to the past barred and bolted? And meanwhile he blesses all the relics of the old order which stands as obstacles in the way of advance—the feudal states, the big zamindaris and taluqdaris, the present capitalist system. Is it reasonable to believe in the theory of trusteeship to give unchecked power and wealth to an individual and to expect him to use it entirely for the public good? Are the best of us so perfect to be trusted in this way? And is it good for the others to have even these benevolent superman over them."[40]

The main thrust of trusteeship is very broad and deep and is thus not easy to comprehend. There is no historical example of it to go by. Besides full trusteeship cases has not been experimented anywhere. The problem with this doctrine is that either it has been bitterly criticized or eulogized but not experimented Gandhi had a way of prescribing sugar coated quinine for the maladies of the society. He would administer the bitterest of truth under a thick coating of a *ahimsa*. But his followers have developed a way of lapping up the sugar and spitting out the quinine. The theory of trusteeship has been dealt in the same manner. That is why the country has not yet been able to enact a statue on trusteeship through several efforts have been done for this.

The late Dr. Ram Manohar Lohia had given notice of his intention to move an 'Indian Trusteeship Bill' in the Lok Sabha in March 1967. It was supposed to provide for the voluntary conversion into trust corporations of concerns owing industries, plantations, banks, trade, transport etc. The Bill made detailed provisions for efficient management of trust corporations in the light of Gandhi's views on trusteeship. The President of India withheld sanction to the introduction of this Bill in Lok Sabha on the ground that aforesaid provision made it a Money Bill. Dr. Lohia had appealed to the President for reconsideration, but death snatched him away before he could pursue the matter.[41]

On November 21, 1969 George Fernandes introduced the same 'The Indian Trusteeship Bill' in the Lok Sabha but it lapsed without discussion. Picking up the thread Atal Behari Vajpayee introduced the same on 18th April, 1975 but it also lapsed with the dissolution of the Lok Sabha in 1977. The Janta Trusteeship Bill by Professor Ramjee Singh of April 20, 1978 also met the same fate.[42]

Gandhi had hoped that statutory trusteeship would be India's gift to the world but up till now we have not yet been able to fulfil this moral responsibility. "The mantra of trusteeship" writes Gadre, can influx life into the skelton of Gandhism which, if revived, will swallow us along with our comfortable arm chairs.[43] Because of this fear we always try to find out some scapegoat here or there in its implementation. It will snatch away from our rulers, leaders, industrialists, bureaucrats, and other elites their luxuries and comforts and will distribute them into the masses. We will be able to realize Gandhi's dream only if in the pursuit of Truth, we prefer self-sacrifice to self-preservation.

It is heartening to note that recently some eminent social scientists have shown some renewed interest in the theory of trusteeship. Professor S.L. Malhotra, Professor Ramjee Singh, Professor N. Radha Krishnan and Dr. J.D. Sethi have shown particular interest in this field. Dr. J.D. Sethi in his 'Gandhi Today' have termed 'Trusteeship—The Grand Alternative'.

In the present day India, the theory has become more relevant. Here we have mixed economy model with a large public sector and a very large private sectors. But the distribution of resources is highly skewed in both, much more sharply in industry than in agriculture. The one hundred largest industrials firms control the Lion share of the economy. What is more frightening here is that the concentration of economic power in these houses keep on increasing. The process of nationalization has resulted in the creation of a new bureaucratic class in whose hands all kinds of power get compounded. The workers lose their elementary right to struggle for higher wages, status, unions, etc.

Trusteeship provides an alternative mechanism for reducing the concentration of economic power. Prof. J.D. Sethi has suggested three steps for this.

Firstly, a certain percentage of the assets of large houses will have to be transformed to a set of trustees.

Secondly, all other new industries and firms will have to follow the principle of trusteeship.

Thirdly, some basic principles with respect of price 'distribution, wages, profits will have to be laid down for trusteeship firms'.

Critics may view that trusteeship in utopian in their nature. It is true that every idea looks like an utopia in the beginning. But given a proper attention and careful practice, nothing is beyond the human capacities. Every solution is always to solve a problem. Gandhi have studied the grave situation in human societies, where there is an increasing gulf between 'have' and 'have nots' aimed at establishing a classes society. As a great psychologist he thought that every solution which is based on faith alone can serve and save mankind. He realized that human faith tied with truth and non-violence alone is the most powerful one to bind the whole humanity into one, despite its dissensions and disparities. In this respect Gandhi is a great visionary in trying to establish 'Vasundhi Kakutam Bakem' (one would family).

Thus every individual by becoming a trustee for himself and for others can cater to the needs of the society. This may dispel all the disparities both in the individual and social levels and contribute to the welfare of all. Except this solution, there is no other alternative to the modern melodies of the mankind. This noble cause of saving the whole mankind made Gandhi to choose trusteeship. Here lies the greatness of Gandhi.

## Notes

1. *Young India*, 13.10.1921, p. 325.
2. *Harijan*, 23.2.1947, p. 39.
3. *Harijan*, 16.12.1939, p. 376.
4. K.M. Munshi, *Reconstitution of Society Through Trusteeship*, Bombay, Bhartiya Vidya Bhawan, pp. 15-16.
5. S. Radhakrishnan's article "The Individual and the Social order in Hinduism in Hughes, E.R. (ed.) *The Individual in East and West*, London, Oxford University Press, 1937, p. 127.
6. Pyare Lal, *Mahatama Gandhi: The Last Phase*, Vol. 2, Ahmedabad, Navajivan Publishing House, 1958, p. 624.
7. M.K. Gandhi, *An Autobiography, op. cit.*, p. 221.
8. *Ibid.*
9. CWMG, Vol. IX, p. 481.
10. *Ibid*, Vol. XIII, pp. 210-16.
11. S.C. Biswas (ed.), *Gandhi: Theory and Practice, Social Impact and Contemporary Relevance*, Shimla, IIAS, 1969, pp. 124.25.
12. M.L. Dantwala, "Trusteeship Its Value Implications", *Gandhi Marg*, Vol. 7 No. 8 and 9, Nov. Dec., 1988, p. 504.
13. *Harijan*, 22.2.1942.
14. *Harijan*, 5.9.1936.

15. Ravindra Varma, "Gandhi's Theory of Trusteeship": An essay in Understanding", *Gandhi Marg*, Vol. 7, No. 8 and 9, Nov. Dec., 1985, p. 518.
16. M.K. Gandhi, *From Yeravade Mandir*, Ahmedabad, Navjivan, 1935, p. 50.
17. Surineni Indira, *Gandhian Doctrine of Trusteeship*, New Delhi, Discovery, 1991 p. 47.
18. Ravindra Varma, *op.cit.*, p. 510.
19. *Ibid.*
20. Surineni Indira, *op.cit.*, pp. 47-48.
21. *Ibid.*, p. 50-51.
22. *Ibid.*, p.59.
23. Devdatta Dokhalkar, "Trustees – A Blind Alley or Break Through", *Gandhi Marg*, Vol. 7, No. 8 and 9, p. 588.
24. K. Arunachalam, 'Applied Trusteeship', *Gandhi Marg*, Vol.7, No. 8 and 9, p. 621.
25. S.K. Deshmukh (ed.), *op.cit.*, p. 230.
26. *Ibid*, p. 239.
27. Surineni Indira, *op. cit.*, p. 68.
28. S.K. Deshmukh (ed.), *op.cit.*, p. 259.
29. *Ibid.*, p. 259.
30. Surineni Indira, *op.cit.*, p. 73.
31. *Ibid.*, pp. 76-77.
32. *Young India*, 26.12.1924.
33. *Ibid.*, 4.6.1925.
34. *Harijan*, 22.4.1939.
35. R.B. Upadhyaya, *Social Responsibility of Business and the Trusteeship Theory of Mahatma Gandhi*, New Delhi, Starling, 1976, p. 253.
36. M.L. Dantwala, *Gandhism Reconsidered Bombay* Padma Publications Ltd., 1945, pp. 55-55.
37. E.M.S. Namboodiripad, *The Mahatma and the I & m,* New Delhi, People Publishing House, 1959, p. 115.
38. J.J. Anjaria, *An Essay on Gandhian Economics* Bombay, Vora and Co., 1944, p. 31.
39. Jawaharlal Nehru, *An Autobiography,* London, Bodley Head, 1936, p. 528.
40. Ganesh D. Gadre's in S.C. Biswas, *op. cit.*, pp. 128-29.
41. Jai Narain, *Gandhi's Theory of Trusteeship*, paper III, Lesson No.6, Post-graduate Diploma Course in Gandhian Studies Through Correspondence, Department of Gandhism Studies, Panjab University, Chandigarh.
42. Ganesh D. Gadre, *op. cit.*, pp. 122-23.
43. J.D. Sethi, *Gandhi Today,* New Delhi, Vikas Publishing House Pvt. Ltd., 1978, p. 168.
44. *Ibid.*

# 9

# Nationalism

– *R.S. Yadav*

## What is Nationalism?

Nationalism is a peculiarly modern phenomenon, and had its origin in the 18th century. It was only during this period that state first begins to become the focal point of political activity. Consequently, nationalism originated from the assumption that nations are the primary focus of political allegiance – an assumption that has been accepted widely. However, the spread of nationalism on a global scale has been the result of Europeanization and modernization of non-western and pre-modern societies. Its rise is linked to numerous phenomena, important among these are: "origins of popular sovereignty; the theory of government by the active 'consent' of the governed; the growth of secularism; the lessening of the older religious, tribal, clannish, or feudal loyalties; and the spread of urbanization, industrialization and improved communications".[1]

Nationalism is thus, defined as "a political creed that underlies the cohesion of modern societies and legitimizes their claim to authority. Nationalism centres the supreme loyalty of the overwhelming majority of the people upon the nation-state, either existing or desired. The nation-state is regarded not only as the ideal, 'natural', or 'normal' form of political organization but also as the indispensable framework for all social cultural and economic activities".[2] In the context of European nationalism it is generally considered that it encompasses certain specific characteristics such as organic unity in terms of population, distinct territory, a single economy, common language, common psychological orientation and a common culture. To put things in a more succinct manner E.H. Carr has described the major traits of nationalism as under:

(a) The idea of a common government whether as a reality in the present or past, or as an as aspiration of the future;

(b) A certain size and closeness of contact between all its individual members;

(c) A more or less defined territory;

(d) Certain characteristics (of which most frequent is language) clearly distinguishing the nation from the other nations and non-national groups;

(e) Certain interests common to the individual members; and

(f) A certain degree of common feeling or will associated with a picture of the nation in the mind of the individual members.[3]

However, it is also true that these traits are not available in later kind of nationalism that spread in the Third World countries. Moreover, nationalism is sometimes associated with states whose identity as a political unit is already established. But simultaneously it can also spring up in ethnic, social or cultural communities that do not exist as independent political units but are under the domination of other states.

Nationalism progressed from 18th century to the present times in different modes and with diverse characteristics. During its *first phase*, from late 18th century and early 19th century, it was more liberal and internationalist in character. It generally accepted and embraced national differences, which led them to view each other as participating in common struggle. Except some regimes general acceptance of common traits were there in most of the Europe. In the *second phase*, from early 19th century to the end of World War II, nationalist movements began to lose some of their internationalism and became more conservative and even reactionary. This tendency started intensifying between the two world war era. Even the communist movements, which were originally cosmopolitan and anti-nationalistic in character, began to acquire national flavour.*Final phase* started with the independence of newly liberated states of Asia, Africa and Latin America in the post-second World War era. Now nationalist movements shifted from Europe to Third World. It arose mainly as a result of their struggle against the colonial masters. Even after independence it worked in the form of third world solidarity (through non-aligned movement) as bulwarks against domination of major powers in international arena. Recent developments like end of cold war and beginning of globalization might again develop a liberal kind a nationalism linking all the economies irrespective of their political affiliations. But this will be dependent upon numerous domestic and external imponderables both at national and international levels.

## Indian Nationalism

Indian nationalism has its own peculiarities. Therefore, before Gandhi's views on this theme are analysed at the outset two important clarifications becomes essential regarding the origin of Indian nationalism. In the debate on nationalism, these are not only inevitable, but are likely to help in the better understanding of the whole process.

(i) It must be admitted that Indian nationalism has not developed in the format and stages of nationalism as that has been developed in Europe. Because the very nature and context of Indian nationalism has been quite different from that of the Europe. Consequently, its scope do not encompasses those parameters as are usually found in the classical/European type of nationalism. In the European context generally a nation is considered to be composed of certain specific characteristics such as organic unity in population, district territory, a single economy, common languages, common psychological orientation and a common culture.[4] But Indian nationalism has grown and developed in a peculiar complex socio-economic and political background, hence it is different from that of the classical tradition of European nationalism.

(ii) Indian nationalism is also not the by-product of certain revolutionary ideology or product of certain social transformation due to different stages of growth in the economic system. Rather, it has been based on certain unorthodox experiences linked to the growth of anti-imperialistic thrust of the movement. It was in no way the planned growth of society to move in a particular direction.

> The challenges of colonial period, along with the sufferings caused to its people due to colonial rules, made its leaders to devise strategies to handle that crisis. Moreover, as a result of the prevailing foreign rule the main objective of this struggle has been towards the independence of India. Consequently, Indian nationalism was the by-product of this struggle for freedom. Therefore, the changing contours in the way of achieving the goal to free the country from colonial yoke, has also changed the verv nature and scope of Indian nationalism.

The above explanations absolve the study of Indian nationalism from the charges of Western sociologist that Indian nationalism is "Nationalism without a Nation"[5] or Cambridge historians' view that here nationalism emerged more as the by-product of skillful game to be played for fame, status, survival, self-interest and advancement of personal interests, rather giving importance to certain ideals, ideas and ideological thinking.[6] Rather, like other Third World countries, Indian nationalism be considered "primarily a form of politics" manifested in the form of anti-colonial struggle.[7]

## Gandhian Perspective

Gandhi did not elaborated much about his idea of nationalism; rather it was part of his overall philosophy from which interpretation of nationalism could be discerned.[8] It was linked to his struggle for the freedom of India. But before such broad concerns could be deciphered from his philosophical moorings, two things much be acknowledged at the outset: *firstly*, it was in South Africa, not in India, that Gandhi first acquired his vision of Indian nationalism, a fact which differentiates his nationalism from those of the other Indian nationalists. *Secondly*, it was in the politics of the Transvaal, not Champaran and Bardoli, that Gandhi first developed his unique political philosophy and political techniques.[9]

As Gandhi has not explained his views on nationalism at one place, his ideas could be understood by his total readings. From the study of Gandhi following features of nationalism emerge:

1. Gandhi's nationalism was "incorporative" forging a nationalist harmony between different kinds of groups in India.[10] His ideas of composite nationalism included not

only religious groups but castes and communities in general. That is why Ravinder Kumar has rightly observed that, "Because Gandhi had a realistic picture of India as a loose constellation of classes, communities and religious groups, he was able to activate the peoples of the subcontinent in a way no one had done before, or has since".[11] He, in building the alliances that would remove the British, sought to bind together various ethnic, caste, religious and regional groups, all of which were enjoined to work out their destinies through the cleansing fire of nationalist activism. This was done by him not on the basis of establishment of hegemony and dominance by any of the group. Rather an effort had been made that each group would respect the beliefs, and even prejudices, of its fellows from the good of the whole country.

2. Though Gandhian nationalism was pursuit of emancipation from the colonial yoke, yet in terms of methods used for this purpose had been different from that of the West. He was against the use of any sort of violent and aggressive means for this objective as it was used in the West. Rather he emphatically rejected a nationalism that sought freedom through violence. He was in favour of use of the method of *ahimsa* or non-violence for this end. Because he felt that; "the force of arms is powerless when matched against the force of love or the soul".[12] Besides, he felt that violence not only had a tendency to escalate violence, but will also precluded dialogue. In the Indian context he visualized that the aim should be to seek to persuade the British of the wrongness of their ways and bring about a change of heart through *satyagraha*. Therefore, violence has no place in his scheme of getting liberation for country.

3. His nationalism has been the collective assertion of all communities, including the deprived strata of the society. He was against any sectarian outlook in term of caste or class. Theoretically, he was against the caste hierarchies and practically he made serious efforts to end untouchability from India. So he was always for a nation based on the plurality of population from different strata of the society.

In his practical life he took numerous measures for the end of untouchability from India. While in South Africa, Gandhi's associates belonged to all castes and communities. In his first ashram at Ahmedabad, which he founded after his return to India in 1915, he welcomed an untouchable family despite the protests from rich merchants. He gave them the name '*Harijan*' (Children of God) and started publication of a weekly by this name to highlight their problems and ameliorate their condition. After his release from jail in 1932, he embarked on a tour, which covered 12,500 miles, to purge Hinduism of the evil of untouchability. He also established a 'Harijan Fund' for this purpose. Thus, Gandhi with utmost seriousness was not only opposed to untouchability, but had also made sincere efforts for the removal of the same. It is because he did not with it to become an instrumentality in the hands of Britishers for dividing the country further as they had been successful in doing so between Hindu-Muslims through the Act of 1909. Hence, for the sake of national unity and integrity Gandhi was opposed to all obnoxious activities of the Britishers which may weaken Indian nationalism.

4. Gandhian nationalism has secular outlook, despite his being attached to religion. Though Gandhi's outlook towards India was that of a pluralistic state having creative synthesis of different religious, linguistic and ethnic group, yet when it comes to articulating the nature of synthesis and the manner of their co-existence, "he unwittingly fell back on Hinduism".[13] Most of the time confusion about Gandhi's ideas about religion arise out of the use of word religion by him. His concept of religion had little in common with what commonly perceived idea about organized religion: dogmas, rituals, superstitions and bigotry. Shorn of these accretions, Gandhi's religion in case of individual was simply an ethical framework for the conduct of daily life and secular and cosmopolitan in the context of nation. Similar kind of observations has been made by other scholars about Gandhi. For instance, M.N. Roy also observed that in the beginning he was critical about Gandhi's

"religious approach to politics" but he later realized that beneath the religious terminology his message had been "moral, humanist and cosmopolitan".[14]

India on the basis of religion could be nation was contested issue at the time of writing of *Hind Swaraj* by Gandhi. At that time he used the word *Praja* for nation, as this world already existed in pre-Islamic period. He felt that the traditional notion of *Praja* offers a basis upon which new edifice of a modern, composite Indian nation-state could be built.[15] That is why, in *Hind Swaraj* he pleaded for the development of moderate, liberal nationalism based on the concept of *Praja*. In an effort to free religion of the evil of sectarianism, Gandhi introduced his famous distinction between religion as organization and religion as ethnic and spirituality which teaches the unconditional love for God and the neighbour. Simultaneously religion as organization serves as a convenient means of maintaining a certain type of pre-political identity and as a means of reaching certain, much yearned for spiritual ends. As such, every organized religion has legitimacy. It follows that organized religions ought to practice tolerance towards each other. Thus, despite Gandhi's leaning towards a Hindu framework, he was not at all thinking in terms of sectarian or fundamentalist overtones, rather very liberal and secular outlook has been the hallmark of his thinking when talking in terms of religion as basis of nationalism. No doubt, there is evidence to indicate that Gandhi did not rule out the importance of secular ideals and approaches, but this aspect of his idea was not militant in nature. Rather he sought to resolve communal differences mainly by exhorting each of the communities to be better religionists.[16] He was building nationalism on the basis of harmonious co-existence and reconciliation, rather than on assimilation, amalgamation and fusions.[17] Even some scholars are of the view that during his last days his religious pluralism went beyond the permissions of a 'plural' Hinduism into considerably wider multi-religious interpellations, and also moved his position towards a wholly secular universalism.[18]

5. Gandhian nationalism had internationalistic overtones. He felt that both could coexist with each other. It is because he considered 'state' and 'nation' different from each other. According to him 'nation' is a meaningful combination of individuals, each with a distinct potentiality of his own to fulfill a common mission. Whereas, 'state' is a mechanical arrangement super-imposed on a nation. For Gandhi, nation stands for creativity and vitally, while state is an archetype of convention and conservation.[19] Gandhi wants to make sure that the social potentiality of nationhood should not be overshadowed by an overwhelming concern of the state. Hence, he viewed that state should not crippled the creativity of the people as a so-called controller of the destiny of a nation.[20]

However, Gandhi rarely used the term 'nation' except when forced to do so by such antagonists as Jinnah. Here also he referred that India was not a motley collection of groups but consisted of people sharing common aspiration and interests and a vague but nonetheless real commitment to the kind of spiritual civilization. In this context, Bhikhu Parekh has rightly observed that when he occasionally used the term 'nationalism' he largely meant 'love of one's country'. For the most part he preferred ideas of collective pride, ancestral loyalty, mutual responsibility and intellectual and moral openness.[21] Thus, his idea of nationalism could supplement and compliment internationalism as well. As he himself has candidly said that:

It is impossible for one to be internationalist without being a nationalist. Internationalism is possible only when nationalism becomes a fact, i.e. when peoples belonging to different countries have organized themselves and are able to act as one man. It is not nationalism that is evil; it is the narrowness, selfishness, exclusiveness which is the bane of modern nations which is evil. Each wants to profit at the expense of, and rises on the ruin of, the other. Indian nationalism has struck a different path. It wants to organize itself or to find full self-expression for the benefit and service of humanity at large.[22]

6. Gandhi was also not in favour of communitarian approach rather used civilizational context in terms of plurality and synthesis. It becomes all the more evident during the time of Jinnah's demand for separate nationhood on the basis of muslim as separate community. Gandhi viewed that unlike the European countries India was not a nation but a civilization which had over the centuries been benefited from the contributions of different races and religions and was distinguished by its plurality, diversity and tolerance. It was "community of communities", each enjoying considerable autonomy within a larger and shared framework.

   He added further that Indian muslims are Indian not merely in a territorial but also in cultural sense, and co-heirs with the Hindus to Indian civilization. Though they did have several distinct customs and social practices, yet this was equally true of every other community and could not prevent them from living peacefully within a single state. To him India represented a monolithic religio-cultural community having the same cultural and social characteristic everywhere. He was attuned to the unifying aspects of Indian culture only, while diversification was to an extent considered an aberration.

   Thus, by talking in terms of civilization, rather as different communities, Gandhi tried to develop an Indian nationalism based on plurality and synthesis which not only tolerated and respected but positively cherished diversity and differences. It had provided a hospitable framework within which different communities, culture and religion had lived side by side and made their distinctive contributions. Therefore Gandhi's nationalism is akin to civic distinctive humanism[23] and since Gandhi considered the community as collection of individuals, so the conflicts among people will be resolved like those solved among friends or members of a family.

   His nationalistic thrust was based on the total mobilization of the masses. That is why with the arrival of Gandhi on the scene of Indian freedom movement has brought about a qualitative difference in the emergence of nationalism. His period is understandably seen as an era in which nationalist movement became multi-class and mass-based, gained politico-moral legitimacy and achieved enormous power due to its indigenous tone and style. At social level, pre-Gandhian political awakening was not only interest-based but also a reflection of horizontal cleavage between the upper castes and lower caste masses in general, a cleavage that had widened as a result of colonial politics and practices. Seeds of communal division had also been introduced. But through Gandhi's efforts with "experiments in isolated place like Champaran, Kaira, Bardoli, the country wide mobilizations around Rowlatt Acts, Khilafat and Salt tax and the overt mass flexing of political muscles during Non-cooperation, Civil disobedience and Quit India Movements were to transform politics, which were limited to a microscopic minority till the First (World) War, into a mass movement".[24]

At this time, Congress was dominated by Gandhi, hence all the efforts of the Congress reflected mainly his ideological orientations. All programmes of the Congress were based on the ideology of 'pragmatic dynamism'. In this context, Bipan Chandra has succinctly remarked that, "The anti-colonial ideology, combined with the vision of a civil libertarian, democratic, secular, socially radical, economically developing, independent and united polity, and the pro-poor radical orientation enabled the Congress to base the national movement on the masses and mass mobilization and to give it the character of a popular, people's movement.[25] However, Gandhi was aware that such mass movement could not be continued for longer duration. This is why, period of rest and 'breathing time' is also inevitable to consolidate, recuperate and gather strength for the next round of struggle. Hence, Gandhi adopted the strategy of "struggle-truce-struggle (S-T-S)"[26] for the sustenance and continuation of this movement.

To give practical shape to the above movement Gandhi

enumerated a thirteen-point agenda of constructive programme.[27] These programmes included: communal unity, removal of untouchability, prohibition, education, upliftment of women, health and hygiene, rastrye bhabha, love of one's own languages, economic equality through trusteeship. But Aloysius is of the view that out of the above programmes only three programmes–Hindu-Muslim unity, removal of untouchability and Khadi–could acquire all-India popularity.[28] Chronology wise Hindi-Muslim unity was important during Khilaft Movement, later efforts for the popularization of Khadi was made and finally removal of untouchability became his obsession. Though Hindu-Muslim unity was again revived in the last days of India's independence followed by partition of the country. Though there have been controversies regarding Gandhi's contribution to made it a mass movement and relations to his success to achieve the desired goals, yet one thing has been certain that last phase of Indian struggle for nationalism was dominated by Gandhian ideas and strategies.

Thus Gandhian nationalism was beyond sectarian and narrow outlook coordinating all castes and classes together. It even pleaded for the upliftment of downtrodden and backward classes so that an egalitarian and harmonious social system could be evolved. Though his approach of secularism is very much debatable, yet he was above the narrow and petty confines of religion. He not only distinguished religion in terms of individual's code of conduct, as well as, at an organizational level. It must also be admitted that his outlook has been to a greater degree influenced by his Hindu overtones. But it was not dogmatic and ritualistic, rather imbibed in the larger framework of civilizational context preserving Hindu-Muslim unity. Gandhi, at the same time, was not a conservative nationalist rather internationalist in his approach. His nationalism was woven in the all embracing concerns for humanity. He also did not approve of 'communitarian' nationalistic frame, but he was in favour of 'civic humanism'. Since in India nationalism is closely linked with its struggle against colonial yoke, so Gandhi made this feeling of nationalism a movement for the masses. To mobilize the huge masses he not only preached and practiced non-violence movements but also introduced constructive programmes for the national unity and integrity. Therefore, Gandhian nationalism could be well understood by understanding his philosophy and broad ideological moorings which not only worked towards the independence of India but also integrated it in the form of a nation.

## Critical Appraisal

Gandhian perspective has been criticized by different scholars both in terms of his ideological contradictions and practical approach followed by him.

1. First and foremost criticism of Gandhi has been made on the basis of his mixing of religion with politics. The main agenda of nationalism revolve around the paradigm of Hindu-Muslim unity started with Gandhian support for Khilaft Movement. But it has been observed that, "Khilaft and Non-Cooperation, though ostensibly intended to bring about Hindu-Muslim unity, prevented the maturing of the masses into a whole in terms of secular politics......."[29] Rather it has been alleged that Gandhi has shifted the course of political development in the wrong direction, because the Gandhian pursuit of Hindu-Muslim unity "shifted the unity discourse from the realm of interest-based politics to religion and community-based mobilization......."[30] That is why, some scholars do not consider his thinking as secular as it has made use of religion in one sense or the other. It has also been felt that it degenerated both religion and politics. It is commented that this has led to disastrous fallout as an instrument as hypothetical use of religion to cover up power pursuits, *degrading both religion and politics*.[31] Thus, justification/support to the use of religion for political activities has question marked his secular credentials.

2. Second criticism is also related to the above context of religion and politics. It is true that Gandhi cared to provide equal respect for all religions. It is also true that unlike Tilak, Aurbindo and Savarkar for whom Hinduism was to be the basis of Indian Unity, Gandhi took a genuinely plural

view of India. Though in his argument with Jinnah, he used some harsh words for Muslims as "ex-Hindus", "converts", "basically Hindus", yet he was supporting it in a broader cultural sense of common Indian civilization. But still some analyst viewed that despite his liberal, plural and broad outlook, his Hindu biasness could be easily noticed. That is why, Bhikhu Parekh has rightly observed that, "when it came to articulating the nature of the synthesis and the manner of their coexistence, he *unwitting fell back on Hinduism*"[32] thus, it has been viewed that the "Gandhian vision of national synthesis was basically communal".[33]

3. Third problem with Gandhi's idea of nationalism has been his misunderstanding regarding Hindu-Muslim Unity. It is alleged that Gandhi failed to make an appropriate assessment about the nature of differences between Hindus and Muslims in India. As Gandhi remained convinced until the end of his life that since the two communities shared common civilizational, ethnic and other bonds, nothing substantial divided them save the British policy of 'divide and rule' and 'small' misunderstandings. He could not apprehend the deeper economic and historical roots of conflict either, and attributed it to narrow hearts and emotional insensitivity. This may have been either due to his experiences and generalizations in South Africa or due to like many of his predecessors' wrong understanding about centuries old Muslim rule in India. But both the context of India and South Africa were different and finding any commonalities between them was erroneous on the part of Gandhi.[34]

In this context, some scholars went to the extent that because of the misperceptions regarding the Hindu-Muslim unity the issue was enlarged and got disproportionate importance. Aloysius pointed out that the Hindu-Muslim communal problems was basically a regional problem of Punjab, Bengal and the United Provinces where the Muslim masses were near equal or in majority.[35] It has been further alleged that within the new structure of politics, when numbers became politically significant, the caste Hindus there could not bring themselves to accept their own reduced political significance. Therefore, instead of solving this problem by containing it, Gandhi enlarged and nationalized it and further complicated it through mystification.[36]

4. Gandhi's contribution to mass mobilization was even considered "ambiguous both in intent as well as content".[37] It is because the mobilization of masses against colonial regime was neither carrying out the agenda nor for the all round involvement of masses. Rather people were called into arena purely for their demonstrative effect. Their role in the programme was passive, to add the elite, to follow them, to boost them whenever required.[38] In Marxist terms, the masses agenda to participate in anti-imperialist movement was mainly anti-feudal. But the elite anti imperialist posture were of dubious nature in view of their strong pro-feudal social base. Therefore, Gandhian mobilization was vertical in nature rather than horizontal. It took the endogamous and hierarchical structure of the communities as it was and the traditionally dominant individuals and groups within this hierarchy were expected to organize and lead the traditionally subservient classes. It may be because for Gandhi primary aim was nation's freedom and social transformation could be taken care of later on. But if looked into his overall philosophical moorings it seems that he was mobilizing the masses for the political end but not for making this end to serve the purpose or agenda of masses in general.

5. Finally, removal of untouchablity and uplifment of the Harijan did not fare any better way within the Gandhian programme.[39] Though Gandhi started this programme with more pump and shows, yet he could not continue it with more seriousness due to his priority of national independence and political expediency at domestic level. It has been alleged by some scholars that Gandhi adopted an tribal family to live in his ashram, but soon had to succumb to the pressure of his financiers and say goodbye to the unfortunate family.[40] Even some critics are of the

view that similarly the establishment of Harijan Sevak Sangh was an agency for congress propaganda and not designed to ameliorate the condition of Harijans in the society.[41] Even on the issue of temple entry Ambedkar felt that Gandhi adopted a very tardy, reluctant and half hearted approach while implementing the programme.[42] This ambivalent attitude of Gandhi led to the political demand by the oppressed castes in the form of share in political representation. Their demands before the Simon Commission and at the time of Round Table Conference were explicit exposition of their thinking. Even here Gandhi adopted a strong action in the form of 'fast unto death' which prevented the final fallout. Gandhi's action on this issue may be justified on the basis of his outlook in the context of country's freedom. But this has definitely created a wedge between upper and lower castes in the social set up. Instead of creating national unity some sort of caste dissension has been created by Gandhian programmes. This has to a great extent influenced the perceptions of political elites from depressed classes while participating and working in the freedom struggle of the country.

All the above criticism on Gandhian perspectives may not be true as some of these misperceptions arised due to the shifting attitude of Gandhi on number of issues. Besides, all his ideas are looked into the broader framework of his struggle for independence. Changed context of freedom movement also forced him to make deviations and retaining all other issues at secondary levels. However, to a great extent his ideas about religion were liberal and secular but definitely in the overall Hindu frame of reference. Similarly sometime extraneous factors led the thing go astray despite his best efforts. The question of Hindu-Muslim unity is one such example. His attached importance to the ultimate goal of the freedom of the country, did allow him to make compromises with all other problems of the time.

## Conclusion

From the above analysis it could be discerned that to

understand Gandhian perspective on nationalism is a very difficult task. This problem has arisen due to both complexity of Gandhian philosophy and changing situational context of India's struggle for freedom from colonial yoke. Gandhi's views have been changing, if not paradoxical, during the last three decades of freedom struggle. Similarly the socio-political dynamics of India's struggle for independence has changed the contours of Hindu-Muslim amity and coexistence. This has also to a great extent influenced the views of leadership in the Indian National Congress, including Gandhi. Despite these entire limitations one could agree with the fundamental parameters of Gandhian ideology in this context. With all reservations, Gandhian nationalism was above the sectarian outlooks perceived in terms of caste, class or other such considerations. Even in terms of nation, he was not strictly adhering to the territorial limits, rather he considered both nationalism and internationalism as supplementary and complementary to each other. Though in the broader sense of the term, he was very much secular in his approach, yet his perceptions regarding Hindu-Muslim unity kept on changing. He also did not justified Muslims to be an independent and separate community outside the Indian civilization. Though at one point of time he did not consider the justification for the support of the Khilafat Movement, yet at other time he could not justified the use of religion in politics as it will led to the establishment of separate state for Muslims. This kind of contradictory approach has been justified by some scholars because of Gandhi's wrong understating about Muslims support for Gandhian struggle in South Africa, whereas others felt that this was due to continuous change in Gandhi's views. However, to achieve the final goal of India's independence, Gandhi was successful in term of great mass mobilizer. He has also chalked out certain constructive strategies for the success of such activities. Finally, one could only comment that whatsoever is the limitation of his idea on this theme, but one been certain that he has taken a holistic view of the existing socio-political and socio-religious plurality existed in India. Hence he visualized them in a greater civilizational context, rather than narrow framework of Hindu ideology. And above all country's struggle for independence was core to his heart. That is why some apparent deviation in his ideas might have crept in due to these factors.

## Notes

1. Hans Kohn, "Nationalism", *International Encyclopaedia of Social Sciences*, Chicago, 1976, Vol. 11, p. 64.
2. *Ibid.*, p. 63. Also see *The New Encyclopaedia Britannica*, Chicago, 1987, Vol. 8, p. 552.
3. E.H. Carr, *Nationalism*, 1939, p. xx.
4. *Ibid.*
5. G. Aloysius, *Nationalism Without a Nation in India*, Delhi, Oxford, 1997.
6. Important Cambridge Historians among them are: Percival Spear, Duncan Forbes, John Gallagher, C.A. Bayly, Judith Brown, Francis Robinson, Anil Seal, Richard Gordon, David Wash Brook, C.J. Baker, Sir Valentine Chirol etc. For details see, V.N. Datta, "Interpreting Indian Nationalism", *Indian History Congress*, Bodh Gaya, 1981, pp. 15-22 (Presidential Address in Forty Second Session on Modern India).
7. John Breuilly, *Nationalism and the State*, Manchester, 1982, p. 1.
8. R.S. Yadav, "Gandhian Perspectives on Indian Nationalism", *Journal of Gandhian Studies*, Vol. 3, No. 3, 2005, pp. 1-15.
9. Anthony J. Parel, (ed.), *Gandhi-Hind Swaraj and Other Writings*, Cambridge University Press, London, 1997, p. xxi.
10. David Hardiman, *Gandhi in His Times and Ours*, Permanent Block, New Delhi, 2003, pp. 12-38.
11. Ravinder Kumar, "Caste, Community or Nation? Gandhi's Quest for a Popular Consensus in India" in his ed., *Essays in the Social History of Modern India*, New Delhi, 1983, p. 51.
12. M.K. Gandhi, *Hind Swaraj*, CWMG, Vol. 10, p. 290.
13. Bhikhu Parekh, *Gandhi's Political Philosophy: A Critical Examination*, Delhi, Ajanta, 1995, p. 189.
14. See Dennis Dalton, "Gandhi and Roy: The Interaction of Ideologies in India", in Sibnarayan Ray (ed.), *Gandhi, India and World*, Melborne, 1970, p. 166 cited in B.R. Nanda, *Gandhi and His Critics*, Delhi, OPU, 1998, p. 75. Also see, Louis Fisher, *Life of Mahatama Gandhi*, London, 1951, p. 430.
15. Parel, No. 9, p. liii.
16. Dev Dutt, "Indian Nationalism and Gandhi", *Gandhi Marg*, 13(3), July 1969.
17. *Harijan*, 5 October 1947.
18. For details see, Kumkum Sangari, "A Narrative of Restoration: Gandhi's Last Years and Nehruvian Secularism", *Social Scientist*, Vol. 30, Nos. 3-4, March-April 2002, pp. 3-33.
19. Nalin Anadkat, *International Political Thought of Gandhi, Nehru and Lohia*, New Delhi, Bhartiya Kala, 2000, p. 53.
20. For details see, R. Chakrabarti, "Gandhian View of the Nation-State as a Constituent of International Community", in V.T. Patil, ed., *Study in Gandhi*, New Delhi, Sterling, 1984, pp. 155-162.
21. Parekh, No. 13, p. 194.
22. *Young India*, 18 June 1925, cited in M.K. Gandhi, *India of My Dream*, Ahmedabad, Navjivan, 2003, p. 14 (compiled by R.K.Prabhu).

23. Parel, No. 9, p. xvi.
24. Aloysius, No. 5, pp. 201-202.
25. Bipan Chandra, *Indian National Movement: The Long Term Dynamics*, New Delhi, Vikas, 1988, pp. 14-15.
26. *Ibid.*, pp. 28-29.
27. M.K. Gandhi, *Constructive Programme: Its Meaning and Place*, Amhedabad, Navjivan, 1941.
28. Aloysius, No. 5, p. 188.
29. *Ibid.*, p. 184.
30. S. Natrajan, *A Century of Social Reform*, Bombay, Asia, 1959, p. 133; Dhananjay Keer, *Mahatma Gandhi*, Bombay, Popular, 1973, p. 312; and Ravinder Kumar, *Nationalism and Social Change*, New Delhi, NMML, 1983, p. 28 (Occasional paper).
31. Arvind N. Das, *Agrarian Unrest and Socio-Economic Change in Bihar, 1900-1980*, Delhi, Manohar, 1983, pp. 90-100.
32. Parekh, No. 13, p. 189 (emphasis added).
33. Aloysius, No. 5, p. 101.
34. Parekh, No. 13, pp. 185-188.
35. Aloysius, No. 5, p. 191.
36. For details see, Sasadhar Sinha, *Indian Independence in Perspective*, Bombay, Asia, 1963, pp. 150 ff; and B.B. Misra, *The Indian Political Poetics*, Delhi, Oxford, 1976, pp. 162 and 250-251.
37. Judith Brown, *Gandhi's Rise to Power*, London, Cambridge University Press, 1972, p. 345.
38. Suniti Kumar Ghosh, *India and the Raj*, Culcutta, Prachi, 1989, pp. 23 & 210; Sinha, No. 36, pp. 158 and 161; Judith Brown, *Gandhi and Civil Disobedience*, Cambridge, 1977, p. 340; Bipin Chandra, *Nationalism and Colonialism in Modern India*, Delhi, Orient Longman, 1979, p. 128; and Bhiku Parekh, *Colonaialism, Tradition and Reform*, New Delhi, Sage, p. 211.
39. Aloysius, No. 5, pp. 192-194.
40. Keer, No. 30, pp. 224 ff.
41. B.R. Ambedkar, *What Congress and Gandhi have done to Untouchables*, Bombay, Thacker and Co., 1945, p. 143; Brown, No. 38, p. 357; and Swami Shradhan, at al, *Inside Congress*, Bombay, Phoenix, 1946, p. 190.
42. Ambedkar, *Ibid.*, pp. 107 and 125.

# 10
# Gandhi and Women

*– S.K. Jolly*

Gandhi wanted build a society based on justice, peace and equality. In order to achieve these three cardinal principles it was very essential to grant equality to the two builders of the society, men and women. This gender equality is a prerequisite for peace and development of the nation. Gandhi addressed women is glorifying terms, "women are the noblest of God's creation," "she is anyway superior to man in her religious devotion," and she is "an incarnation of *ahimsa.*"

Now the question arises, how could Gandhi understand women so deeply and respect them so greatly. One has to go back right to Gandhiji's childhood to study and appreciate the role of various women who took care of him during his lifetime. To begin with, his mother and sister impressed him. Gandhi talks a lot about his mother in his writings and speeches. His first lessons in *satyagraha* were taught by his mother. After marriage, his wife Kasturba influenced him as did other women in the *ashrama*, especially Meeraben and Amrit Kaur, whose sincerity and commitment impressed him deeply.

According to Barbara Southard, Gandhian feminism stands two major pillars: gender equality in all respects and at every level and gender specific role-differentiation.[1] Gandhi once said, "The man should look to the maintenance of the family, the woman to household management, the two thus supplementing and complementing each other's labours. Gandhian philosophy on gender emphasizes that social expectations from men and women differ and in turn their responses and responsibilities in the public and private sphere are also different from each other. Commenting on gender equality, he quotes widely from Hindu *shastras* (texts) and asks that if every soul originates from *Braham*, then *where* do differences between men and women arise? He stresses that it is not the gender, but the individual's soul that matters. Commenting on the role of scriptures, Gandhi said that all written in *Smritis* is not divine as there are false interpolations.[2] If religion and religious scriptures teach unethical codes then they ought to be disobeyed. Gandhi went on to say, "Hinduism leaves the individual absolutely free to do what he or she likes for the sake of self-realization for which and which alone he or she is born."[3] Gandhi rightly observed that the degenerated position of women resulted from historical circumstances and said, "the soul in both is the same. Each is a complement of the other…But somehow or other man has dominates woman from ages past, and woman has developed an inferiority complex. She has believed in the truth of man's interested teaching that she is inferior to him. But the seers among men have recognized her equal status."[4] There is no difference in the basic mental faculties of man and woman, and she too deserves the same liberty and freedom.

As early as 1921, writing in '*Young India*', Gandhi said, "of all the evils for which man has made himself responsible, none is so degrading, so shocking or so brutal as his abuse of the better half of humanity to me, the female sex, not the weaker sex." Discerning the cause of the inequalities and injustice to women in general, he firmly believed that, "if I were born a woman, I would rise in rebellion against any pretension on the part of the man."[5]

As far as men and women's sphere of activity in concerned, Gandhi advocates the theory of separate spheres. While on the one hand the man is the breadwinner, on the other the woman is responsible for tending to home and children. Gandhi's vision of women was one of nurturance and he believed that "woman is essentially the mistress of the house…she is the keeper and distributor of the bread…the art of bringing up the infants of the race is her special and sole prerogative. Without her care, the race must become extinct."[6] He did not regard marriage as an absolute essential for women.

Even though he does not advocate an "active role" for women in the public sphere, however when the issue of women's suffrage was first raised in 1921, Gandhi supported it and even felt that the success of the *satyagraha* movement and the *Dandi March* was inextricably linked with the active participation of women. Picketing liquor shops and sellers of foreign cloth were activities, which were predominantly undertaken by women. By 1939, Gandhi was thoroughly convinced that if the national movement had to be escalated to the level of a mass movement, then women would definitely have to be included as active participants. He said, "I would love to find that my future army contained a vast preponderance of women over men. If the fight came, I should then face it with greater confidence, than if men predominated. I would dread the latter's violence. Women would be my guarantee against such an outbreak."[7] According to Southard, Gandhi did not see his advocacy of women's participation in non-violent resistance campaigns as contradictory to his basic concept of women as nurturer and caretaker of the home. On the contrary, the participation of women in *satyagraha* was seen as an extension of her special mission as the caretaker of humanity.[8]

Gandhi often observed that religion could be safeguarded only in the hands of women and not in those of men or religious Brahmins. He saw religion as a way of life and as an indicator of one's character or true nature. Addressing a women's meeting in Kaithal, Gandhi said, "the foundation of which society rests is the home and *dharma* is to cultivated in the home. The fragrance in the home will spread all over the society."[9] He was highly impressed by the simplicity of dress and attitude of the Indian women. He repeatedly writes that he was impressed by the white sari of Madurai, the red-bordered sari of Bengal and the simplicity of the Punjabi women's dress. He stressed that a woman's real ornaments were her noble qualities, talents, her purity and chastity and therefore it was the soul that was important and should be the focus of self-improvement, rather than external beauty, which is skin-deep.

Today the world speaks of pure love, one family, and one husband and wife in a monogamous and faithful relationship, thus echoing Gandhi's teachings concerning the family. He considers the cohesive family to be the building block of a healthy society. Gandhi said that providing healthy, intelligent and well brought-up children to the country is in itself a great service rendered by women. He also believed that the Hindu Law of Inheritance required changes and improvement. Women must be given equal rights where family property is concerned because the disinheritance of women from family property is responsible for male dominance and women's subordination. Gandhi opined that women should not suffer from any legal disability. He said, I should treat daughters and sons on a footing of perfect equality.[10]

The All India Women's Conference made a declaration to this effect in 1931, "This conference places on record its opinion that there should be complete equality between the sexes in the matter of inheritance and property."[11]

Moving on, *purdah*, another evil which still affects women's lives in certain sections of society, has also been decried by Gandhi with the help of historical examples. Giving the evidence of ancient Indian history, he writes that women's lives during that period were less secluded and insular. They participated in public debates and discourses and their lives were much fuller and less restricted when *purdah* was unknown. He raised pertinent questions, "Why do our women not enjoy the same freedom that men do? Why should they not be able to walk out and have fresh air?" Women's organization also took up this issue and protested strongly against it. Mrinalini Sen went as far as saying that women in modern India were asking for a freedom that was actually their birth right. Gandhi denounced *purdah* as a "barbarous custom" which had incurred incalculable harm to the country. In 1928 the All India Women's Social Conference that met in Calcutta passed a resolution against *purdah*.

Like other social reformers, Gandhi was against the custom of forcing a marriage without the consent of the boy and girl. He also opposed child marriage and when the Children's Protection Act was brought up, Gandhi supported it whole-heartedly. In 1925 he said that the issue was not just raising the marriageable age for girls from 14 to 16, but rather not forcing marriage on any individual without their prior consent. Being a strong supporter of widow remarriage, he wrote, "I have repeatedly said that every widow has as much right to remarry as every widower. Voluntary widowhood is a priceless boon in Hinduism, enforced widowhood is a curse."[12] Hence Gandhi's belief in equality and justice guided his stance on widow remarriage. Addressing people from various communities, he wrote, "If any child widow wants to remarry do not despise or outcast them."[13]

One of Gandhi's foremost interpretations of *swaraj* or self-rule concerned his regard for women and their emancipation. Commenting on prostitution, one of the most derogatory conditions of women's existence and in the words of Gandhi, "a social disease," he often said that women are forced to sell their body due to sexual and economic exploitation and because of men this problem will continue to persist. He emphasizes that if no one comes forward to help these women then they themselves need to become agents of change and fight their exploitation at the hands of men. Similarly, speaking against the *devadasi* tradition, Gandhi said that while "it is good to swim in the waters of tradition but to sink in them is suicide." Labeling the *devadasi* tradition as "moral leprosy," and "an insult to god," Gandhi was trying to break the decadent socio-cultural customs and rituals that had held women in a subordinate position for centuries.

Dowry system has been another social evil, which has plagued the lives of women in India. Gandhi saw this as a hateful practice and termed marriages involving dowry as "marriage by purchase." He wrote that in marriages where wives and daughters-in-law are purchased there couldn't be any harmonious relationship. In 1929 Gandhi astounded his contemporary society by saying that "if I had a girl under my charge, I would rather keep her a maiden all her life than give her away to one who expected a single pie for taking her for his wife."[14] Gandhi advised people to boycott young men who expected dowry from their prospective bride's family. He saw inter-caste and inter-community marriages as a solution to this social evil. Urging young people, especially young men to give up this decadent practice, Gandhi envisioned his anti-dowry belief to take on the stature of a youth movement.

Today we are dealing with the problems resulting from population explosion, however, this problem was recognized as early as 1932-33. The All India Women's Conference passed a resolution that centres for dispensing information on birth control measures should be opened at the municipal and local levels. This resolution was passed by a thundering majority of 99 votes as opposed to just 7 votes against it. Although Gandhi expressed his admiration for this resolution and the feeling behind it, but he strongly believed that self-control is the only legitimate means of birth control.[15]

Gandhi did not like the use of contraceptives or other artificial means of birth control. According to him, "birth control by contraceptives no doubt, regulates to a certain extent, the number of newcomers, and enable persons of moderate means to keep the wolf from the door. But the moral harm it does to the individual and society is incalculable. For one thing, the outlook upon life of those to satisfy the sexual appetite for the sake of it is wholly changed. Marriage ceases to be a sacrament for them."[16] Gandhi believed that women had more self-restraint and therefore he gave the responsibility of birth control through abstinence to women. In his pursuit of attributing greatness to women, Gandhi also, although sometimes unjustly so placed more than their share of responsibility on women. This was especially so in the case of family planning and Gandhi's insistence on abstinence amongst women, when in reality this is a male problem and they are the ones to be held responsible for it.

Gandhi supported education for both boys and girls. In his Basic National Education Scheme, in 1937, Gandhi proposed free and compulsory education for children of both sexes from ages 7 to 14.[17] As far as the curriculum of the syllabus was concerned, in his early years, in 1918 Gandhi had different ideas about girls' education and he suggested that girls' educational programme should be planned in a such a way so as to meet the special needs of girls in order to prepare them to be mothers and homemakers. However by 1937, his views had undergone a change and he proposed that till the 4th or 5th standard girls and boys ought to have the same curriculum and then 6th standard onwards girls should also be taught courses such as domestic or home science. It is interesting to note that for purposes of girls' higher education, Lady Irwin Home Science College was established in 1932 by the efforts of the All India Women's Conference. Gandhi preferred women as teachers and in 1931 the All India Women's Conference passed a resolution to this effect that as far as possible women teachers should be engaged in the earlier stages of education for both boys and girls, in fact they emphasized that the earliest stages should be wholly the concern of women.

Gandhi believed that economic freedom could indirectly play a vital role in the empowerment of women. In the course of his speeches and writings, he was inspiring and motivating women for spinning yarn and weaving cloth. Addressing women at Nadiad in 1919, he emphasized, "You have two or three hours when you do nothing. You spend them in temples. Telling the beads in the temple is *dharma*, but at the present time real *bhakti* consists in this work for cloth.... women in rich families should spin two or three hours everyday and pass it on to the store here or gift it.... Anyone who spins for money will get 3 *annas* a pound (of yarn) every pie earned is useful. With the money so earned you can buy your needs. The more you earn the more you gain. This is an excellent means of earning."[18]

In fact Gandhi realized that the success of the *Swadheshi* Movement was possible only if women spun yarn and wove cloth in large numbers, at the same time he also saw that this would enable them to be economically independent. He writes in Young *India* that while spinning yarn can add to the resources of the middle class, it can infact become a major source, sometimes even the sole source of subsistence for lower class families.

In conclusion, it is very interesting to see how Gandhi viewed women as victims of social and cultural exploitation and at the same time he also saw them as instigators of social change at grass root levels as mothers, wives, teachers and activists picketing at liquor and foreign cloth stores. He was an astute observer of women's social role in the family and society and vested in them the responsibility to change lives at the level of the family and that of the nation by placing them at the vanguard of the *Swadeshi* Movement as the producers of precious homespun yarn and cloth which was an essential prerequisite for the boycott of foreign cloth. His programmes of *Swadheshi* and Non-cooperation Movement are both inspired by women's traditional roles and attitudes. Historically speaking, women have universally been responsible for spinning and weaving cloth for household use and their main forms of protest in a male dominated world have been silent and non-violent. Amazingly, Gandhi adopted these two traits integral to women's culture and transferred the arena of activity from the family to the nation where metaphorically speaking Indians took on the female person and the British colonial rulers took on the male persona and these two main female responsibilities and attributes were transferred on to the nationalist struggle. He thus gave importance to the so called 'women's work and labour', which usually went unseen and made it an important tool of the Indian National Movement.

## Notes

1. Barbara Southard, "Feminism of Mahatma Gandhi," *Gandhi Marg*,Vol. 3, No.71, October 1981, p. 403.
2. "Women in Smritis," *Harijan*, 28 November 1936.
3. "The Hindu Wife," *Young India*, 3 October 1929.
4. "What is Woman's Role?" *Harijan*, 24 February 1940.
5. *Young India*, 9th December 1927.
6. *Harijan*, 24th February, 1940.
7. "Swaraj Through Women," *Hariijan*, 2 December, 1939.
8. Barbara Southard, "Feminism of Mahatma Gandhi," *Gandhi Marg*, Vol. 3, No.71, October 1981, pp. 405.
9. Navjiivan, 8 May, 1921, *CWMG*. Vol. XX. p. 63.
10. "Position of Women," *Young India*, 14 October 1929.
11. Report of the All India Women's Conference, Seventh Session, p. 134.
12. "Helpless Widows," *Harijan*, 22 August, 1935.
13. Gujrati Navjivan, 12 October 1919.
14. *Young India* 14 February, 1929.
15. "Birth Control-1," *Harijan*, 14th March 1936.
16. "Birth Control-2," *Harijan* 21st March 1936.
17. M.S. Patel, *The Educational Philosophy of Mahatma Gandhi*, Navjivan Publishing House, Ahmedabad, 1953, p. 109.
18. Pushpa Joshi, *Gandhi on Women*, Navjivan Publishing House, Ahmedabad, 1988, pp. 30-31.

# 11

# Gandhi and Untouchablity

*– Sushma Yadav*

Untouchability is the worst feature of the Caste system[1] which is so deeply embedded in the minds of the Hindu society that our entire outlook on life and politics is coloured by it[2]. It has erected a powerful barrier against the emotional integration of the people of India. It has divided them into numerous small and hierarchically arranged closed groups. It has also divided Indian society into high-born and low-born caste compartments. Since caste remains one of those social institutions, which have always exercised a predominant hold on the public and social life of Indian society, untouchability has also remained a social concern for all those who have occupied any significant space in the Indian public domain.

Gandhi beyond doubt occupied the largest public space as a great leader, a saint and a great social reformer. He believed in simple living and high thinking which deeply influenced almost everyone who came in direct contact with him. Gandhi's ultimate search was for righteous conduct. For him, the means were more important than the end, and he believed that with the right means, desired ends were bound to follow. In time, he was proven right-almost always. Gandhi showed India, as well as the World, the path of truth and non-violence. He believed that it was truth alone that prevailed in the end. According to him, India's real emancipation depended on *Swadeshi* i.e. boycott of foreign goods and removal of untouchability and he worked all through his life for seeking solution to the most fundamental problems facing Indian society: Hindu-Muslim Unity and the abolition of untouchability. He worked hard for the upliftment of the Harijans, the name given by him to the untouchables. Besides, Gandhi regarded untouchability a sin against God and Man.

There are very few things that are more needed today than a

careful, concrete, comprehensive and consistent study of Gandhi as he fought for the removal of untouchability, a blot on Indian humanity. His fight was unique. He stressed, in the main, that the conscience of the so-called 'higher' castes in Hindu society had to be roused against the crime or the practice of untouchability, which has tarnished their image. A sensible and scientific study can help to heighten the democratic content and character of the fight he initiated, a fight still to be won, against untouchability and all that it connotes. The study must be undertaken not in a detached academic fashion with mechanical objectivity but with a certain insight accompanied by a certain 'passion' and a feeling for our own long-suffering, often nearly demented but somehow still unvanquished people. Only then can one ascertain the 'truth' and can put purposeful and perceptive effort to carry forward and synthesise to the extent possible, our healthy forward-looking heritage/legacy left by Gandhi in modern times. Moreover, the study remains necessary because the fact even today is that despite being 'abolished' by our Constitution and in spite of the statute book calling it an offence attracting punishment, 'untouchability' with its myriad miserable implications remains a sheer sickening shame. The present chapter is a modest attempt in that direction.

Gandhi desired to deliver the untouchables, who he called Harijans, from the slavery of centuries by means of changing the hearts of the Caste Hindus. This desire was as strong as his desire for freedom/independence was. He had said that freedom would be meaningless if untouchability was not removed. He also said that attainment of *Swaraj* was a must, but that would not be complete unless a social order based on equality and fraternity was established.

This year, 137th Gandhi Jayanti (2006) happens to coincide with the seventy second anniversary of the conclusion of Gandhi's historic campaign against untouchability which, though less than a total success immediately, had shaken the fundamental structure of Hindu society as nothing else had done either before or during the entire span of the century that has just come to a close.

Gandhi always held caste Hindus responsible for the plight of the untouchables and he also asserted that the Hindus would have no right to claim *Swaraj*, as long as freedom, was not restored to the exploited classes. He believed that the political bondage of Indians was a well-deserved punishment meted out to them for observing untouchability. Therefore, at times it is alleged what Gandhi categorically proclaimed that his *Harijan Seva* (upliftment) movement was not intended for upliftment of Harijans, but for the salvation of Caste Hindus as penance for the crime they perpetrated against the *Harijans*[3].

Gandhi aroused the people's attention more widely than anyone had done before in history, to the evils of social injustice. He took it upon himself to awaken the conscience of the human race. He could realize the astonishing phenomenon of a revolution led by a saint. He had struggled successfully to liquidate the system of indentured labour in South Africa. Similarly, he sought to fight against the horrors of untouchability and the other social wrongs, which he found humiliating and shameful for Indian society. In 1925, he wrote, "untouchability is our greatest shame the humiliation of it is sinking deeper".

Gandhi's influence over the masses was tremendous. The people of India had unflinching faith in him. The most remarkable feature of his leadership was that he was able to lead and direct the movement without holding any position of power of any high office. He was able to command the respectful obedience of millions though there was nothing divine about Gandhi. However, he was also accepted as a great emancipated saviour and *Messiah* for the socially downtrodden and the victims of socio-economic exploitation. It can be easily claimed that Gandhi had spoken and written more on untouchability than any other subject. He had publicly put abolition of untouchability as the essential prerequisite for India's independence[4].

One frequently comes across the word '*Harijan*' or '*Harijans*' in Gandhian literature–a word used by him for the *Shudras*, the *Chandalas* or the *untouchables*. Distinguishing between a Harijan and Durjan, Gandhi wrote; "the 'untouchable: to me, is, compared to us, really a *Harijan* (a man of God), and we are *Durjan* (men of evil). For while the untouchable has toiled and moiled and dirties his hands so that we may live in comfort and cleanliness, we have delighted in suppressing him. We are solely responsible for all the shortcomings and faults that we lay at the door of these 'untouchables': it is still open to us to be *Harijan* ourselves but we can only do so by heartily repenting for our sin against them[5]."

Therefore, Gandhi sought to change the hearts of the caste Hindus by moral pressure. He strived hard to force on the Indian conscience the problem of untouchability as an issue of national concern. Although the measures of legally abolishing untouchability were adopted in the Constituent Assembly with the slogans of "Mahatma Gandhi ki jai", Gandhi never advocated legal measures. He did feel that all changes must come voluntarily from the heart. The only visible effect on the Hindu-mind is that the practice of untouchability is now being considered as wrong and the upliftment of the untouchables as good.

Gandhi, no doubt, anathematized 'untouchability' with all the force of his spirit. His crystal earnestness was proved by the life he lived and the works he did. Work was worship for him "I am an 'untouchable' by adoption" said Gandhi to Ambedkar during the crucial talks before the Poona Pact of 1932 over the representation of Scheduled Castes and Scheduled Tribes in the legislatures then to come under the Government of India Act, 1935. "My greatest worry", he said then, as he had said repeatedly before and since "is the ignorance and poverty of the masses of India and the way in which they have been neglected by the classes, especially the neglect of the *Harijans* by the Hindus. We are custodians of a great religion and yet have been guilty of a crime, which constitutes our greatest shame. Had I not been a believer in the inscrutable ways of providence, a sensitive man like me would have been a raving maniac[6]." It was with this conviction that Gandhi could say unconventional things, such as, a '*Bhangi* does for society what a mother does for a baby'. He could also match such words with action, as he did when he adopted an 'untouchable' girl as his daughter. From time-to-time, he used to express his desire that independent India should have an 'untouchable' woman as its President, a desire yet to be fulfilled.

Gandhi was strongly committed to a social philosophy which consolidated his faith in persuasion and he opposed what he called "reform by compulsion". He insisted that the "*satyagrahis* must stoop to conquer" and wanted "to set even the most orthodox and the most bigoted at ease" during the Travencore Movement 1924-25 for unfettered use of roads to the temple by the 'untouchables'. It was Gandhi's idea of "the beauty of compromise" that led to a settlement, hailed by Gandhi himself as a 'miracle' adding only eight furlongs or so to roads free for all (including untouchables) which led to the creation of a new and more promising atmosphere for social change.

Gandhi believed in the traditional concept of *Varna* system cleansed of untouchability, in which untouchables would be '*Harijans*' and their unclean work would be accepted as honourable. Eleanor Zeiliot has called it accommodative style of leadership.[77]

It is because, though an ardent champion for removing untouchability, he sought to do so within the Hindu Chaturvarna framework. Naming the Untouchable 'Harijan' i.e. man of God (first in 1931) to avoid conflict with Ambedkar on the issue of separate electorate for *Dalits*/Depressed classes, he primarily appealed to the caste Hindus to use to them *Harijan* instead of *Antyaja*.

The period 1932-34 marked an important crossroad both in Gandhi's own life as well as in the annals of the national movement. After his frustrating experience at the second Round Table Conference (R.T.C) in London, Gandhi had understood most deeply with what handicaps, in the form of the many fissures and fragmentations in our society, India had to wage her battle confronting the foreign power[8]. In addition to the communal divide, the deep division between the *Savarnas* and the *Avarnas* had shown up fully.

In the context of the scramble for power (or rather for imperial favours) in the aftermath of the second R.T.C., the traditionally antagonistic relations between the untouchables and the upper-caste Hindus had reached an acute confrontational stage. On top of that, the proposal of the British Prime Minister Ramsay MacDonald to grant separate electorate to the Scheduled Castes population was a means to ensure that the very thin educated and comparatively well-to-do elite stratum of the scheduled caste population should be able to elect their representatives to the Councils or Assemblies (soon to come into existence) *proportionate to the total Scheduled caste population.* This prospect of separating the Scheduled Castes not only from the general electorate but also from the Hindu society at large rang the alarm bell for Gandhi, the Congress, and the Hindu nationalists generally. Separate electorates were not a new move in British India. Muslims were granted that in 1909 (and Lord Minto, the then Viceroy, had gloated over this adroit step that would keep almost a quarter of the population away from the nationalists)[9]. Then, the Sikhs too were granted separate electorate in 1919.

But when British Prime Minister MacDonald proposed separate electrorate for the Untouchables at the R.T.C., Gandhi put a firm resistance. He argued endlessly that Muslims, Sikhs or Christians will remain so for all times, but why would the Untouchables remain untouchables in the future too, or should they? His suggestion was to grant them adequate concessions to ameliorate their condition and even reservations to ensure their representation in the Councils and other elected bodies but no separation from the general electorate, which if decided, he would oppose with his life, Gandhi had warned.

In a few months when the proposal for separate electorate for the untouchable Scheduled Castes was moved in MacDonald's Communal Award, Gandhi announced his decision to undertake a fast till death, unless this provision was changed. He explained that his primary concern was not merely to oppose this particular administrative-cum-constitutional measure that the British Government was going to introduce in India[10]. His principal concern was the inhuman odium of the practice of untouchability which cried for its immediate abolition, together with other reforms in Hindu society, on the one hand, and the excuse and the justification it provided to the colonial power to play its game of disrupting and fragmenting Hindu society, on the other.

He was for granting whatever concessions the Depressed Classes leaders wanted provided they strengthened the integration of Hindu society in general rather than weakening it. With the fast continuing and the Mahatma's life at stake, there was a tidal wave of public opinion, which battered against hard-core Hindu Conservatism; hundreds of temples were opened to the untouchables and a large number of Hindu leaders pledged to do away with the centuries-old discriminations practiced against the untouchables[11]. In the bargain the Scheduled Castes were offered almost double the number of reserved seats than that promised in the British White Paper. In the event the agreement was clinched, the British Government agreed to make the necessary amendments in the White Paper if the Scheduled Castes and the Hindu sides were mutually satisfied on their agreement. It was then that the Mahatma broke his fast on 25 September, 1932 the seventh day of his fast unto death. Of all the large number of Indian leaders who had expressed their anguish at the impending threat to the Mahatma's life, it was Rabindranath Tagore who said that untouchability was a serious enough blemish on the face of Hinduism which justified even putting to risk the Mahatma's precious life for its removal[12].

Parallel with the signing of the accord on the issue of representation of the Scheduled Castes and modalities of elections (popularly known as the Poona Pact), Gandhi insisted from his Yeravda prison that the Congress, Liberals, and the Hindu Mahasabha leaders also publicly announce their acceptance of another declaration, the text of which he drafted himself[13]. This was adopted on 25 September 1932 at a joint public meeting held in Bombay. The text was as follows:

"This Conference resolves that henceforth, amongst Hindus, no one shall be regarded as an untouchable by reason of his birth, and that those who have been so regarded hitherto will have the same right as other Hindus in regard to the use of public wells, public schools, roads and all other public institutions. This right shall have statutory recognition at the first opportunity and shall be one of the earliest Acts of the Swaraj Parliament, if it shall not have received such recognition before that time.

It is further agreed that it shall be the duty of all Hindu leaders to secure, by every legitimate and peaceful means, an early removal of all social disabilities now imposed by custom upon the so-called untouchable classes, including the bar in respect of admission to temples"[14].

It is to be noted that Gandhi himself considered this declaration of historic significance and on several occasions in the course of the following decade and a half (till the transfer of power, that is) he reminded his fellow Hindus that this was a standing commitment[15]. Regrettably, however, neither any broad convention of Hindu society nor the Congress-led Ministries that were in office from 1937 to 1939 took any formal or legal step to implement the essence of this declaration.

Although the British Government, honouring the compromise agreement, withdrew its original proposal and accepted what came to be commonly known as the Poona Accord, there were all-round murmurings of perceived grievances on a large scale. In Bengal specially, the grumbling against the Communal Award generally as also against those aspects that emerged as a result of the Poona Accord, was particularly vociferous and organized. It was at this stage that the orthodox Hindu campaign went on a general offensive on the need to preserve the traditional customs of Hindu society on the one hand, and on the other, in its fight to ensure that the Hindus received their hitherto unquestioned lion's share of the concessions the British were about to grant in India.

It was in this post-Poona Pact situation of general dissatisfaction, when the effervescence of the national movement was rather at a low ebb, flowing as it did at a much lower level as compared to the high-water mark of the Salt *Satyagraha* of only a couple of year ago, that Gandhi was searching for a new path, seeking the guidance of his inner voice[16]. He sought to evolve a new strategy and a new slogan that would enable him to mobilize the people, first of all the Hindu majority in their entirety. That would not only fully overcome the *Savarna-Avarna* divide but having done so would so integrate them, breaking down the hierarchical division of high and low in the Hindu society, that it would clear the path for communal unity too, so believed Gandhi. He watched the situation: the depressed classes movement was making very slow progress, but the orthodox camp's propaganda was becoming increasingly bold and offensive.

Meanwhile there was an unofficial bill before the Central Assembly demanding the withdrawal of government recognition of the 'Scheduled Castes' right of entry to a large number of Hindu temples. What should be the attitude of the various non-governmental public bodies (otherwise well disposed towards the SCs' temple entry) towards the bill, that too was among the questions before Gandhi. Gandhi observed the situation for almost a whole year. In view of his prison sentence and the government ban on the civil disobedience movement which had led to the arrest of almost all the other Congress leaders, Gandhi devised a social reform campaign that the government would be unable to prohibit, yet which would be so dynamic that in fact it would tantamount to the most direct and sharpest confrontation between the deeply entrenched conservative vested interests on the one hand and a reformatory movement in support of the starkly oppressed and the exploited on the other[17].

More than a year passed (14 months) between the Poona Pact and the start of the campaign during which Gandhi, apart from speaking at some meetings and talking to innumerable colleagues and other leaders, wrote every frequently on the untouchability question. In fact he declared several times that this was the one issue that was then commanding all his attention[18]. He started new journals reflective of the new campaign-Harijan—first in English (February 1993) followed by other editions in Gujarati, Hindi, Bengali, Tamil, and other, all at short intervals.

Meanwhile, colonial government had issued a general order asking for the most detailed reports of Gandhi's campaign and of its assessment and requested the Viceroy and the Governors to make sure that this was done as ably and efficiently as possible. The reports were notably comprehensive, mostly finalized by the Chief Secretary of the Province concerned. Other more detailed reports were by the Deputy Commissioner or the Superintendent of Police of the district concerned and vetted by the Home Department. In this way week by week the file grew in bulk at the Whitehall. A similar file must have made up its bulk in New Delhi too but no such material has been handed over to the National Archives of India for scholarly inspection. As may be imagined, such top intelligence reports were all top secret material and the contents of the file were for the eyes of the India Committee members only. As was to be expected, the reports were very rich in information, not of the sort that could be gleaned from the press but contained a great deal of intra-Congress and inner-party goings-on in all the relevant parties and groups. In fact the reports are a revelation of how far-reaching and penetrating were the tentacles of the government agents gathering information. The collection of documents consists entirely of British intelligence reports on Gandhi's intense and passionate campaign against untouchability in which he engaged himself from November 1933 to August 1934 and which took him not only to almost all parts of British India but also to a large number of the adjoining Princely states. The Gandhi campaign was a great social-historical event in India. It represented a great social turmoil. This campaign, therefore, revealed and manifested all the contradictions of our social reality:

## Sufferings of Untouchables

Gandhi used to say often: 'I do not want to be re-born. But if I have to be re-born, I should be born an untouchable, so that I may share their sorrows, sufferings, and the affronts levelled at them, in order that I may endeavour to free myself and them from that miserable condition. I, therefore, pray that if I should be born again I should do so not as a Brahmin, Kshatriya, Vaishya, or Shudra, but as an Atishudra'[19].

## No Sanction for Untouchability

Gandhi said time and again that untouchability is the sin of the Hindus and they must purify themselves by paying the debt they owe to their suppressed brothers and sister. Hinduism has sinned in giving sanction to untouchability. It has degraded us, made us pariahs. Even the Mussalmans have caught the sinful contagion form us"[20].

He sought to emphasize that in Hinduism there is no sanction for treating a single human being as untouchable. In the estimation of a Brahmin, knowing and living his religion, a Shudra is as good as himself. The *Bhagavad-Gita* has nowhere taught that a *Chandala* is in any way inferior to a Brahmin. A Brahmin ceases to be a Brahmin immediately he becomes insolent and considers himself a superior being. India owes a deep debt to the Brahmins who voluntarily sacrificed themselves for the betterment of all. It was Brahmins who have called God Servant of Servants, the Purifier of the Fallen. It was Brahmins who taught that the prostitute and the *Chandala* could attain *moksha* if she or he only purified her or his heart[21].

It was, therefore, Gandhi believed, the moral duty of all Hindus to see that the 'untouchables' do not feel that they are despised or looked down upon. Let them not be offered leavings from our plates for their subsistence, he exhorted the Hindus and questioned them as to how could one accord differential treatment to any person, be he a Brahmin or *Bhangi*, who worships the same God and keeps his body and soul pure and clean? He warned them that one would have to regard himself as having sinned if one gave to a *Bhangi* unclean food from the leavings from the kitchen or failed to render him personal assistance when he was in need.

Gandhi argued that, "Untouchability is a snake with a thousand mouths through each of which it shows its poisonous fangs.It needs no sanction from Manu or the other ancient law-givers. It has its own local Smriti. Thus in Almora a whole class of people, whose occupation is, even according to the *Sanatana Dharma* so-called, innocent, are untouchables.They are all cultivators owning their own holdings. They are called *Shilpi*, i.e. farmers. Another similar class of people called Boras suffer in the same manner although they do not even eat carrion or take liquor and observe all the rules of sanitation as well as any others. Tradition has condemned them as untouchables."[22]

He further proclaimed that, "Hinduism that refuses to think and accepts the tradition unquestioningly, exposes itself to merited ridicule and worse. Reformers are trying to cope with the evil. I feel, however, that much more drastic methods are needed than are employed to rid Hinduism of the blot. We are needlessly afraid to wound the susceptibilities of orthodoxy. We have to shed the fear, if we expect to end the evil in our own generation. This untouchability naturally recoils on the heads of those who are responsible for it".[23]

The difference, therefore, between the caste system and untouchability is not one of degree, but of kind. An 'untouchable' is outside the pale of respectable society. He is hardly treated as a human being. He is an outcaste hurled into an abyss by his fellow-beings occupying the same platform. The difference, therefore, is somewhat analogous to the difference between heaven and hell.

Gandhi was of the view that Untouchability as it was practiced in Hinduism was a sin against God and man and was, therefore, like a poison slowly eating into the very vitals of Hinduism. He wrote, "In my opinion, it has no sanction whatsoever in the Hindu *Shastras* taken as a whole. Untouchability of a healthy kind is undoubtedly to be found in the *Shastras* and it is universal in all religions. It is a rule of sanitation. That will exist to the end of time; but untouchability as we are observing today in India is a hideous thing and wears various forms in various provinces, even in districts. It has degraded both the untouchables and the touchable. It has stunted the growth of nearly 40 million human beings. They are denied even the ordinary amenities of life. The sooner, therefore, it is ended, the better for Hinduism, the better for India, and perhaps better for mankind in general".[24]

Gandhi further elaborated his views saying that it may not be denied that untouchability is an old institution. But if it is an evil, it cannot be defended on the ground of its antiquity. If the untouchables are outcastes of the Aryan society, so much the worse for that society. And if the Aryans at some stage in their progress regarded a certain class of people as outcastes by way of punishment, there is no reason why that punishment should descend upon their progeny irrespective of the causes for which their ancestors were punished. It merely demonstrates that the evil cannot be confined and that its deadening effect is all-pervading. He felt that the existence of untouchability amongst untouchables is an additional reason for cultured Hindu society to rid itself of the curse with the quickest dispatch.

In attacking untouchability, Gandhi had gone to the very root of the matter and, therefore, it was an issue of transcendental value, far surpassing *Swaraj* in terms of political constitutions and he said such a constitution would be a dead-weight if it was not backed by a moral basis in the shape of the present hope engendered in the hearts of the down-trodden millions that the weight is going to be lifted from their shoulders[25].

However, Gandhi did not believe the caste system, even as

distinguished from Varnashrama, to be an odious and vicious dogma. It has its limitations and its defects but there is nothing sinful about it, as there is about untouchability, and if it is a by-product of the caste system, it is only in the same sense that an ugly growth is of a body, or weeds of a crop. It is as wrong to destroy caste because of the outcaste, as it would be to destroy a body because of an ugly growth in it or a crop because of the weeds. The outcasteness, in the sense we understand it, has therefore to be destroyed altogether. It is an abscess to be removed, if the whole system is not to perish. Untouchability is the product, therefore, not of the caste system, but of the distinction of high and low that has crept into Hinduism and is corroding it. The attack on untouchability is thus an attack upon this 'high' and 'low'-ness. The moment untouchability goes, the caste system itself will be purified, that is to say, according to Gandhi's dream, it will resolve itself into true *Varnadharma*, the four divisions of society, each complementary of the other and none inferior or superior to any other[26].

Gandhi regarded untouchability as the greatest blot on Hinduism. The idea was not brought home to him by bitter experiences during the South African struggle. It is equally wrong to think—as some people do—that he had taken his view from his study of Christian religious literature. These views of his date as far back as the time when he was neither enamoured of, nor was acquainted with the Bible or the followers of the Bible.

Gandhi was of the firm view that the removal of untouchability is much more than building a temple of brick and mortar. Hindus must bleed for it, must pay for it. They must be prepared to forsake wife, children and all for the sake of removing the curse.[27]

He believed that to remove untouchability is a penance that caste Hindus owe to Hinduism and to themselves. The purification required is not of 'untouchables' but of the so-called superior castes. There is no vice that is special to the 'untouchables', not even dirt and insanitation. It is our arrogance which blinds us, superior Hindus, to our own blemishes and magnifies those of our down-trodden brethren whom we have suppressed and whom we keep under suppression. Religions like nations are being weighed in balance.

Gandhi further emphasized, God's grace and revelation are the monopoly of no race or nation. They descend equally upon all who wait upon God. That religion and that nation will be blotted out of the face of the earth, which pins its faith to injustice, untruth or violence. God is light, not darkness, God is Love, not hate, God is Truth, not untruth. God alone is great. We, His creatures are but dust. Let us be humble and recognize the place of the lowliest of His creatures. Krishna honoured Sudama in his rags as he honoured no one else. Love is the root of religion'.[28]

Gandhi told congressmen that by making removal of untouchability a plank in our platform, we assert our belief that untouchability is not only not a part and parcel of Hinduism but a corroding and sinful superstition-which has infected Hinduism, and that it is the bounden duty of every Hindu to strive for its abolition. Every Hindu, therefore, who considers it a sin, should atone for it by fraternizing with untouchables, touching them in a spirit of love and service; deeming himself purified by that touch, redressing their grievances, helping them patiently to overcome ignorance and other evils due to the slavery of ages and inspiring other Hindus to do likewise. When one visualizes the removal of untouchability from this spiritual standpoint, its material and political results sink into insignificance in his eyes, and one befriends the so-called untouchables regardless of such results[29]. Seekers after truth will never waste a thought on the material consequences of their quest, which is not a matter of policy with them but something interwoven with the very texture of their lives. This is equally true of the removal of untouchability. Removal of untouchability spelt for Gandhi the breaking down of barriers between man and man and between the various orders of being. Such barriers can be found erected everywhere in the world, but Gandhi was mainly concerned with the untouchability which had received religious sanction in India and reduced lakhs and crores of human beings to a state bordering on slavery.[30]

Gandhi also believed that the cause of *Harijans* and Hinduism will not be served by the methods of rabble. He found the exercise to be perhaps the biggest religious reform movement in India, if not in the world, involving as it did the well-being of nearly forty million human beings living in serfdom. One had to win them by love, by self-sacrifice, by perfect self-restraint, by letting the purity of One's life produce its own silent effect upon their hearts. It could be done by having faith in truth and love converting the opponents to one's own way.

Untouchability, Gandhi was convinced, could not be removed by the force even of law. It could only be removed when the majority of Hindus realize that this is a crime against God and man and feel ashamed of it. In other words, it was to be a process of conversion, i.e. purification, of the Hindu heart. The aid of law has to be invoked when it hinders or interferes with the progress of the reform as when, in spite of the willingness of the trustees and the temple-going public, the law prohibits the opening of a particular temple, felt Gandhi.[31]

Gandhi maintained that the spirit of untouchability must have been a product of our lowest ebb. He called it a curse for society. So long as this curse prevails in the society, people will be committing crimes. Further, one finds that according to Gandhi, the idea of untouchability does not have any religious sanction. Religion did not provide any room for this. He reinforced and emphasized, "Untouchability is not a sanction of religion, it is a device of Satan."[32] He often said and wrote, "I regard untouchability as the greatest blot of Hinduism".[33] He further emphasized, "It is against the *Shastras*".[34]

Gandhi tried to preach the gospel of love to the whole world. According to him, all men, irrespective of their caste affiliations, belong to one God and were his expressions. He said and believed that removal of this great sin of untouchability meant, "love for, and service of, the whole world, and thus merges into *Ahimsa*. Removal of untouchability spells the breaking down of barriers between man and man and between the various orders of Being. We find such barriers erected everywhere in the world".[35]

Gandhians like Baran Ray feel that there is an evident propaganda and misrepresentation against Gandhi as if the abolition of caste system as a whole-lock, stock and barrel-was quite possible and ready at hand, and Gandhi alone stood in the way insisting on abolishing untouchability only and retaining the rest of the system.[36] He did believe *earlier* that *varnashram* and the caste system had in ancient India served Hindu society well to integrate a wide range of ethnic entities and as a practicable system of social division of labour. Gandhi's ideas and understanding and interpretation of Indian history held before the 1930s cannot and must not be critiqued today in the light of subsequent archaeological or anthropological discoveries made or scientific analyses done in the decades, long after independence.

Gandhi is believed to have advocated that people should continue in their ancestral occupations and it is also alleged that he advised the *Dalits* to nurture a relationship with the upper castes analogous to that of the black Uncle Tom towards the latter's former white masters[37]. Nothing could be farther from truth and from what Gandhi really stood and campaigned for.

The fact is that together with all other nationalist leaders, Gandhi too had, at times, glorified past history as a necessary input in the independence struggle. But what is remarkable about him is that instead of falsely glorifying the past, Gandhi in fact infused the past with his very modern ideas of truth, justice, fearlessness, fraternity, absence of hierarchy, and dignity of the individual values which he thought were essential for the revivification of our ancient but also decadent society. Thus, he was most unsparing in condemning all that was reactionary, oppressive and exploitative in our traditional customs, characterizing them as the excretions of the historical process, and called for their absolute elimination. There he stood not behind but far a head of all his other contemporaries.

Thus, Gandhi coined a new term for articulating his vision of Indian society and the way he wanted to transform it in accordance with his vision and imagination. This overall term was "Sarvodaya", literally the "Welfare of All". A term that called forth a series of other terms all along the line of an effort towards a total reconstruction and transformation of the Indian society in context of the contemporary world situation. Sarvodaya, *Swaraj*, *Ahimsa*, *Satyagraha*, *Gramodaya*, *Sampattidana*, *Samya-yoga*, *Harijan*, Civil Resistance, *Asahayoga* or Non-Cooperation, Campaign for Removal of Untouchability, and similar other terms that he used, are all indicative of a new paradigm and a new vision. Quite a few of them were older and commoner terms, without doubt, but he imparted new meanings, as well as new connotations to them and sharpened their edges so as to make themselves usable as weapons of effective action towards realizing his vision of a totally non-violent and just society inhabited by true '*vaishanav jana*'—people who could feel and share the pain of others.

## Notes

1. A.P. Barnabas, and Subhash C. Mehta, *Caste in Changing India*, New Delhi, IIPA, 1965, p.15.
2. *Ibid.*, p.2. For detailed analysis, see J.H. Hutton, *Caste in India*, Oxford, Oxford University Press, 1961 and S.V. Ketkar, *A History of Caste in India*, Taylor & Carpenter, Ithaca, 1909.
3. See M.K. Gandhi, "Anit Untouchability – A Movement of Self-Purification", *Young India*, 26-12-1924, pp. 423-24 and also *Harijan*, 28.9.1934, pp. 257-258.
4. See, *Harijan*, February 11, 1933.
5. See for details, *Young India*, 6.8.1931.
6. Tendulkar, D.G., *The Mahatma*, Vol. IV, pp. 125-26.
7. Zeiiliot, Eleanor, 'Gandhi and Ambedkar. A study in leadership' in Mahar, J.M. (ed.) (1972). *The Untouchable in Contemporary India*, Universiity of Ariizona, p. 70.
8. *Young India*, 5.5 1930, p.7.
9. See M.K. Gandhi, (1957) *From Yervada Mandir*, p.66.
10. See for details, *Speeches and Writings of Mahatma Gandhi*, Vol. II, pp. 336-44.
11. *Harijan*, 9.10.1937, p.292.
12. See Iyer, Raghvan (1973), *Political and Moral Thoughts of Mahatma Gandhi*, New York: Oxford University.
13. See for details, *Speeches and Writings of Mahatma Gandhi*, Vol. II, pp. 340-54.
14. *Ibid.*, p. 345.
15. *Ibid.*, p.346.
16. Tendulkar, D.G., (1953) *Mahatma*, Vol. VI, pp. 357-58.
17. Acharya Shri Tulsi (1968), *Speeches on Non-Violence*, Anuvrat Vishva Bharti Rahsamad (mimeograph).
18. *Writings and Speeches of Mahatma Gandhi*, p., 340.
19. *Young India*, May 4, 1921.
20. *Young India*, April 27, 1921, p.135.
21. *Young India*, May 11, 1921, p.151.
22. See for details, *Young India*, July 11, 1929.
23. *Ibid.*
24. *Writings and Speeches of Mahatma Gandhi*, pp.351-356.
25. Swami Ranganathananda, *Eternal Values for a Changing Society*, Bombay: Bhartiya Vidhya Bhawan, Vol. IV, pp. 281-82.
26. *Harijan*, February 11, 1933.

27. *Young India*, May 1, 1924.
28. *Young India*, December 26, 1924, pp. 423-24.
29. See for details, *Harijan*, June 2, 1946.
30. See for details, *Young India*, September 18, 1930.
31. See for details, *Harijan*, September 23, 1939.
32. *Young India*, January 19, 1921, p.22.
33. *Young India*, January 21, 1926, p.30.
34. *Writings and Speeches of Mahatma Gandhi*, p. 501.
35. Gandhi, M.K., *Removal of Untouchability*, p. 25.
36. Baren Ray, "Gandhi Against Untouchability: An Introductory Essay", in *Gandhi's Campaign Against Untouchability*, 1933-34, Edited by Baren Ray, New Delhi, Gandhi Peace Foundation, 1996, p.1.
37. *Ibid.*, Also see, Jagjivan Ram, "Mahatma Gandhi and Social Change" in S. Radhakrishnan (Ed.), *Mahatma Gandhi* – 100 Years, Gandhi Peace Foundation, New Delhi, 1968, pp. 156-160.

# 12

# Gandhi's View of Swraj

*– Ashu Pasricha*

In ancient Indian political thought the notion of the self-government as applied to the collectivity of members of a polity was closely related to the conception of self-rule as applied to the moral growth of every human being.[1]

The maturity and development of a polity were regarded as a reflection as well as an index of the degree of moral maturity and self cultivation of an elite or a generality of individuals. At the centre of the ancient Indian political thought lay the concept of *swaraj* or self-rule connected with the notion of *Swarajya* which referred to a particular mode of securing self-determination in a polity comprised of several distinct sectors. In modern India the term *swaraj* was exclusively identified by Dadabhai Naoroji, B.G. Tilak and Sri Aurbindo with the goal of national independence. The emphasis was wholly shifted from the positive to the negative connotation of the term and its application entirely transferred from its individual to collective scope. Toward the end of the nineteenth century – even before the term *swaraj*, in its new sense, acquired common currency in the nationalist movement – the Bengali militants sought to justify their doctrine of boycott of British goods in the name of *Swadeshi* or patriotism.[2]

When Mahatma Gandhi entered the Indian scene, he was able to restore to the term *swaraj* its older meaning while retaining its newer sense to interpret the term *Swadeshi* and considerably extended its application. He restored the close connection between *swaraj* and *Swadeshi*, between individual self-rule and individual self-reliance, between self-government and national self-dependence. Instead of assimilating the concept of freedom to that of community by merging the individual into an organic conception of society, he derived the very notion of communal self-reliance from his doctrine of individual self-rule and showed how the pursuit of *swaraj* must necessarily involve the acceptance of *Swadeshi*.

The concept of *swaraj*, or self-rule, was developed during the Indian freedom struggle. In his book *Hind Swaraj* (1909), Gandhi was emphatic that *swaraj* "much more than simply wanted [systems of] English rule without the Englishman; the tiger's nature but not the tiger."[3] His argument centered on the belief that the socio-spiritual underpinnings of British political, economic, bureaucratic, legal, military, and educational institutions were inherently unjust, exploitative and alienating. As Pinto explicates, "The principal theme of Hind Swaraj is the moral inadequacy of western civilization, especially its industrialism, as the model for free India." Gandhi was particularly critical of the deeply embedded principles of might is right and survival of the fittest.

On another level, the call for *swaraj* represents a genuine attempt to regain control of the self-our self-respect, self-responsibility, and capacities for self-realization - from institutions of dehumanization. As Gandhi states, "It is *swaraj* when we learn to rule ourselves." The real goal of the freedom struggle was not only to secure political *azadi* (independence) from Britain, but rather to gain true *swaraj* (liberation and self-rule). Self-rule is the term used to describe a people or group being able to exercise all of the necessary functions of power without intervention from any authority which they cannot themselves alter. Self-rule is associated then in contexts where there is the end of colonial rule, absolute government or monarchy, as well as demands for autonomy by religious, ethnic or geographic regions which perceive themselves as being un- or under-represented in a national government. Self rule is therefore a fundamental tenet of republican government and democracy as well as nationalism.[4]

Gandhi, it may be noted at the outset, employed the term *Swaraj* in its specific and generic sense, to borrow an expression of Green. While he organized the Indian masses for *Swaraj* conceived as a constitutional, democratic political order,[5] he at the same time stressed on its economic, mass 'organic' content. Swaraj which first acquired its political meaning (of independence) through its use in that sense by Naoroji[6] and later through its popularization by Tilak is closely allied with the meaning of tapas or renunciation. Svaraj literally means 'self-rule' and in its original connotation meant autonomy of the moral self (as in the *Brhasaranayaka Upanisad*) where strict control is exercised over the senses. In another words, it means self-rule and self restraint, and not freedom from all restraint which 'independence' often means.[7]

In 1924 Gandhi wrote "freedom for the meanest of our countrymen.... I am not interested in freeing India merely from the English yoke. I am bent upon freeing India from any yoke whatsoever. I have no desire to exchange 'king log for king stork'.[8]

While discussing the more concrete question of Political Power and its organization, Gandhi wrote in 1925: "By *Swaraj* he meant the government of India by the consent of the people as ascertained by the largest number of the adult population, male or female, native born or domiciled, who have contributed by manual labour to the service of the State and who have taken the trouble of having their names registered as voters...real *Swaraj* will come, not by the acquisition of authority by a few, but by the acquisition of the capacity by all to resist authority when it is abused. In other words, *Swaraj* is to be attained by educating the masses to a sense of their capacity to regulate and control authority."[9] Self-government means continuous effort to be independent of government control, whether it is foreign government or whether it is national.[10]

Gandhi wrote in *Young India*, "The *Swaraj* of my our dream recognizes no race or religious distinctions. Nor is it to be the monopoly of the lettered persons or yet of moneyed men. *Swaraj* is to before all, including the former, but emphatically including the maimed, the blind, and the starving, toiling millions."[11]

Similarly, he wrote on another occasion, "The *Swaraj* of my dream is the poor man's *Swaraj*. The necessaries of life should be enjoyed by you in common with those enjoyed by the princes and the moneyed men. But that does not mean that they should have palaces like theirs. They are not necessary for happiness. You or I would be lost in them. But you ought to get all the ordinary amenities of life that a rich man enjoys. I have not the slightest doubt that *Swaraj* is not *Poorna Swaraj* until these amenities are guaranteed to you under it."[12]

"... What we mean and want through *Poorna Swaraj* is an awakening among the masses, knowledge among them of their true interest and ability to serve that interest against the whole world, harmony, and freedom from aggression from within or without, and a progressive improvement in the economic condition of the masses. ..."[13]

"Real *Swaraj* must be felt by all man, woman and child. To labour for that consummation is true resolution. India has become a pattern for all exploited races of the earth, because India's has been an open, unarmed, effort which demands sacrifice from all without inflicting injury on the usurper. The millions in India would not have been awakened but for the open, unarmed struggle. Every deviation from the straight path has meant a temporary arrest of the evolutionary revolution."[14]

It has been said that Indian *Swaraj* will be the rule of the majority community, i.e., the Hindus. There could not be a greater mistake than that. If it were to be true, I for one would refuse to call it *Swaraj* and would fight it with all the strength at my command, for to me *Hind Swaraj* is the rule of all people, is the rule of Justice. Whether, under that rule, the ministers were Hindus or Mussalmans or Sikhs and whether legislatures were exclusively filled by the Hindus or Mussalmans or any other community, they would have to do even handed justice.[15]

Today our minds are clouded by delusion. In our ignorance, we quarrel with one another and indulge in rowdyism against our own brethren. For such as these there is neither salvation nor *Swaraj*. Self discipline or rule over self is the first condition of self-rule or *Swaraj*.[16]

In a vast country like this, there must be room for all schools of honest thought. And the least, therefore, that we owe to ourselves, as to others, is to try to understand the opponent's view point and, if we cannot accept it, respect is as fully as we expect him to respect ours. It is one of the indispensable tests of a healthy public life and, therefore, fitness for *Swaraj*.[17]

Freedom of speech and pen is the foundation of *Swaraj*. If the foundation stone is in danger, you have to exert the whole of your might in order to defend that single stone.[18]

Gandhi's scheme of comprehensive freedom as elucidated in the *Hind Swaraj* can thus represented:

1. True *Swaraj* = Kingdom of the soul (Spiritual and Moral Freedom).
2. *Satyagraha* as the key to it (Political Freedom).
   (*Satyagraha* = Dayabala or Atmabala)
3. *Swadeshi* = (Economic Freedom)
   (Necessary for putting *Satyagraha* into practice).

1. *Moral and Spiritual Freedom*: According to Gandhi, moral and spiritual freedom depends on the effective cultivation of the ancient virtues of truth and non-violence. Moral freedom means the conquest of the demands of the senses and the appetites, for the realization of the higher self. Thus the self-subsistence of the particular will has to be purified by the devoted adherence to truth and non-violence.[19] Self indulgence eventually leads to destruction. The conquest of empirical desires alone is the path to immortality. Hence Gandhi stressed the rigid adherence to the Code of Mahavrata (the eleven great vows) in his Ashrama. The daily repetition of the vows was a deliberate attempt to strengthen one's moral resolve. Gandhi firmly believed that immature persons subject to the fluctuations of temporary emotions and arbitrary fancies and passions could not enjoy moral freedom. He wrote: "Freedom is a fruit of suffering, license is born of violence. What we are all pining for freedom that imposes restraints upon itself for the sake of society. License imposes suffering upon society so that it may enjoy exclusive privileges."[20]

Hence he never accepted the view of freedom as arbitrariness or license. Genuine freedom results in self denial for the sake of society. Thus genuine *Swaraj* is a function of tile development of the moral sources of power.

Spiritual freedom for Gandhi lay not in the self centered assumptions of the claims of the individual ego but in identification with the Supreme Being. He went to the extent of stating at the Belgaum Congress in 1924 that *Swaraj* is part of Truth. This view amounts almost to a sanctification and spiritualization even of the work of national emancipation or freedom. Freedom is the essence of man's spiritual personality. Like Rousseau in the Social Contract, Gandhi also considers freedom as the essence of man. If freedom is renounced, Man becomes an "automaton." Any attempt to build a society by the denial of liberty is "contrary to the very nature of man."[21] The renunciation of freedom would be the repudiation of human conscience. If Truth is God, and if the Constructive Programme and *Satyagraha* which are the bases and technics for the realization of *Swaraj*, are also, by implication, part of Truth, then it implies a conception of God as concrete real unity, an organic universal manifold including different entities[22] and not an undifferentiated abstract universal absolutely removed from human struggles. He said: "On the principle that the greater includes the less, national independence or material freedom is included in the spiritual."

Gandhi laid down two stringent prerequisites for the enshrinement of moral and spiritual freedom. First, his conception of moral and spiritual freedom postulates the cultivation of *Anasakti*, or disinterestedness. As a follower of the *Bhagavad Gita*, he stressed absolute disinterestedness, complete imperturbability and a resignation to the will of God as the essence of *Karmayoga*. Disinterestedness (*Anasakti*) is linked up with spontaneous devotion to the cause of the good of all living beings. The essence of the *Karmayoga of Gita* is the subjective disposition to will the good of all and to work according to what is inherently right without being attached to results. Disinterestedness or desirelessness results in the concentration of energy. In place of the misuse of mental and moral resources in imagining about future consequences, *Karmayoga* stresses concentration of efforts in the path of dedication to duty. Hence non-attachment as stressed in the theory of *Karmayoga* accepted by Gandhi is completely removed from the charge of passivity sometimes leveled against it.

Besides disinterestedness, the second necessary requirement for moral and spiritual freedom is fearlessness. Fearlessness can be acquired by making surrender to God whose implication and consequence is the absolute refusal to be bound by mundane temptations and threats. A man who realizes his spiritual humanity is not afraid of any law except the law of God. In a speech at the anniversary of the Gurukul Kangri, he said: "In my humble opinion, fearlessness is the first thing indispensable before we could achieve anything permanent and real. This quality is unattainable without religious consciousness. Let us fear God and we shall cease to fear man. If we grasp the fact that there is a divinity within us who witnessed everything we think or do and which protects us and guides us along the true path, it is clear that we shall cease to have any other fear on the face of the earth save the fear of God. Loyalty to the Governor of governors supersedes all other loyalty and gives an intelligent basis to the latter."[23]

Being a spiritual and ethical idealist, Gandhi was an optimist. Although critical of the mechanical and technological aspects of modern western civilization, he had abiding faith in the realization of freedom in the future. He is hence, more optimistic than Max Weber, according to whom there are slender prospects of genuine human freedom because of the accentuated technological rationality of the modern age. According to Gandhi, on the other hand, it is possible to have freedom in the modern age if there is a moral renaissance of man. Hence, against the immense and engulfing power of the technological and political structure, he stood for the purification of motives and conduct as the sure way to freedom. There genuine freedom without the practice of moral obedience the laws of the Spirit. The perfection of the value of liberty, equality, social justice and fearlessness will act as foundations for the kingdom of God on earth. Gandhi's life was dedicated to this end this is his message.

2. *Political Freedom* : Gandhi's devotion to the concept of individual rights made him a fighter for democratic freedoms. In South Africa, as earlier pointed out, he launched the *Satyagraha* movement for safeguarding the civil rights of Indians. He stood up for the rights of the poor suppressed indigo planters in Champaran in 1917. He effectively sponsored the cause of the labourers in the spinning factories in Ahmedabad in February- March, 1918. He also championed the rights of the peasants of the Khaira district in Gujarat in March-May 1918. He advised the peasants of Khaira not to pay rent because crops had failed and the government reluctantly acceded to the demands of the peasants.

Gandhi accepted the truth of the famous Mantra given by

Tilak that *Swaraj* is the birthright of Indians. In an article entitled "Tampering with Loyalty" he wrote that spreading disaffection against the British Government in India was the *Dharma* of Indians? He condemned British imperialism because it resulted in the political and economic prostration of India. In his famous Trial Speech on March 19, 1922, he had said:

> "I came reluctantly to the conclusion that the British connection had made India more helpless than she ever was before, politically and economically. A disarmed India has no power of resistance against any aggressor if she wanted to engage in an armed conflict with him. So much is this the case that some of our best men consider that India must take generations before she can achieve the Dominion Status. She has become so poor that she has little power of resisting famines."

Hence he had dedicated his life from 1920 onwards to secure the freedom of India from imperialistic bondage.[24] He wrote "We are challenging the might of this Government because we consider its activity to be wholly full. We want to overthrow the Government. We want to compel its submission to the people's will. We desire to show that the government exists to serve the people, not the people the Government. Free life under the Government has become intolerable, for the price exacted for the retention of freedom is unconsciously great. Whether we are one or many, we must refuse to purchase freedom at the cost of our self-respect or our cherished convictions."

Gandhi prescribed rigorous self control, discipline, moral exercise and patient suffering for the winning of *Swaraj*. Even in his early writings, for example, he categorically states that freedom does not mean license. One may enjoy what is his but should never attempt to rob others of what is theirs. He says: "Humility, earnestness, thoughtfulness these are the foundations of *Swarajya*."[25] He also wrote: "Voluntary discipline was the first requisite of corporate freedom. If the people were well behaved, the Government officials would become their, true servants." Only a *Swaraj* won by patient suffering and sacrifice could be lasting and stable. Political freedom or *Swaraj* could be obtained only by intense suffering and struggle. It would be chimerical to believe that it could come as a gift. In 1929, Gandhi said: "A man who is made for freedom has got to take tremendous risks and stake everything." He said at the Second Round Table Conference in 1931: "...the page of history is soiled red with the blood of those who have fought for freedom." He believed that Indians were entitled to freedom, because of the immense sufferings they had undergone for it.

Political freedom also postulated social cohesiveness besides disciplined suffering. It is essential to combine the quest for political individuality with the voluntary acceptance of social and political discipline which is the basis of social solidarity and cohesiveness. A divided and disrupted social structure could not wage successful political struggles. Only a community constituted by persons imbued with a sense of deep social cohesiveness can attain the benefits of *Swaraj*. Hence Gandhi stressed communal unity and the absolute elimination of unsociability among the foundations of political freedom.

3. *Economic Freedom*: Gandhi stressed the economic pre-requisites and foundations of freedom since he would accept that economic resources act as an effective apparatus for the realization of man's will. He felt that freedom was bound to remain a mere philosophical abstraction unless the vast masses had some gainful employment. Unemployment snatches the morsel from the mouth of the poor villagers and completely damages the personality of the victims. Hence Gandhi wrote: "Political freedom has no meaning for the millions if they do not know how to employ their enforced idleness.

As a moral prophet of Ram Rajya, Gandhi accepted the doctrine of equal distribution. A fundamental item in actualizing genuine equality, as discussed earlier, will be the revolutionary step of the acceptance and practice of equality of wages for the lawyer, the doctor or the teacher who are entitled to no more than the *Bhangi*. This would provide the key to true civilization and be the basis of the reconstruction of an ideal humanity.

Thus Gandhi pleaded that all useful labour should bring the same and adequate wages to the worker. But until that rather remote ideal of equal distribution was realized, he prescribed a more realistic formula of equitable distribution for the immediate present. The proposal was that every labourer should get enough remuneration to feed and clothe himself and his family. It was the imperative duty of the government to ensure this much to all. "A government that does not ensure this much is no government. It is anarchy. Such a State should be resisted peacefully."[26]

Certain essential characteristics of *swaraj* by Bandhopadhaya are summarized as follows:

(i) *Swaraj is based on inward Freedom.* Since freedom of action comes through acquired virtue, it follows that *swaraj* or the external freedom enjoyed by an individual would depict directly on the degree of his self perfection through acquired virtue. His external *swaraj* cannot exceed his internal moral evolution. "The outward freedom that we shall attain," says Gandhi, "will only be in exact proportion to the inward freedom to which we may have grown at a given moment. And if this is the correct view of freedom, our chief energy must be concentrated upon achieving reform from within."

*Swaraj* is thus fearlessness born out of self perfection as in the case of Socrates or Jesus Christ a fearlessness that defies not only all external authority, including the authority of the mightiest sate or empire, but even death itself. As Gandhi observes: "If *Swaraj* is delayed (in the case of India), it is because we are not prepared calmly to meet death and inconveniences less than death." And this applies not only to the individual, but also to the nation. "That nation is great," he says, "which rests its head upon death as it pillow. Those who defy death are "free from all fear." An individual of a nation that that has developed this inner Freedom cannot be controlled by any external authority. Tolstoy says, Gandhi, had understood the nature of such inward Freedom. What Tolstoy preached, like all world-teachers, he says, is that ever man has to "obey the voice or his own conscience, and be his own master, and seek the Kingdom of God from within". For him there is no government that controls him without his sanction.

(ii) *Swaraj belongs to the individual alone*: A corollary of the inwardness of Freedom and of personal moral responsibility is that *swaraj* is essentially a matter of individual attainment. Gandhi challenges the very basis of all totalitarian political thought by his insistence that Freedom necessarily belongs only to the individual, and Freedom can, according to Gandhi, exist only as a corollary of individual Freedom, not in opposition to it. "The individual is the one supreme consideration", he declares. Therefore, any conception of Freedom must begin with the individual. As Gandhi observes: "The first step to *swaraj* lies in the individual. The truth: 'As with the individual, so with the universe, is applicable here as el sewhere."[27] Hence, Freedom for a society or a nation only is the result of the Freedom of all the individuals comprising it. He insists that "*Swaraj* of a people means the sum total of the *swaraj* of the individuals". "Political self-government of the people, therefore, cannot be external, but can only be the result of the inward moral Freedom of all the individuals as explained by Gandhi in the following words: "I have, therefore, endeavoured to show both in word and deed that political self-government that is self-government for it large number or men and women, is no better than individual self-government, and, therefore, it is to be attained by precisely the same means that are required for individual self government or self rule."[28]

(iii) *Swaraj means Freedom for all or Sarvodaya*: An essential concomitant of such absolutist individualism is the rejection of the utilitarian view of democracy as representing the greatest good of the greatest number. Fundamental to the Gandhian social and political thought is the contention that true Freedom can be ensured in human society only by the greatest good of all. Freedom is not a numerical phenomenon and cannot be quantitatively expressed. Every individual represents an end-in-itself, and the curtailment of the Freedom of a minority of individuals leads to a qualitative deterioration of the Freedom of the whole society. To such a concept of Universal freedom Gandhi gives the name of Sarvodaya (the equal development of all), a Sanskrit word used by Gandhi also as the title for his Gujarati translation of Ruskin's *Unto The Laṣt* (done by him when he was in South Africa).

In a Sarvodaya society, naturally, Freedom would mean simply majority rule: "Unlike democracy," says Gandhi, "Individual liberty of opinion and action is jealously guarded. I, therefore, believe that the minority has a perfect right to act differently from the majority..." In matters of conscience, moreover, he argues, "the law of majority has no place."[29]

But such universal Freedom would also necessarily limit the Freedom of each individual in such a way that it does not interfere with the Freedom of others. In other words, by his own value commitments the individual is also committing the whole society, and it is therefore, his moral responsibility to see it that his actions do not interfere with the values of other individuals. "There is not a single virtue," says Gandhi, "which aims at, or is consistent with, the welfare of the individual alone. Conversely, there is not a single offence which does not, directly or indirectly, affect many others besides the actual offender. Hence, whether an individual is good or bad is not merely his own concern, but really the concern of the whole community, nay, of the whole world.

(iv) *Swaraj is eternal vigilance on the part of the individual*: Freedom of this kind would naturally transient the mere political independence of a country from foreign rule. Although Gandhiji immediate objective was the ending of the British rule in India. He never regarded India's freedom as identical with the achievement of political independence. On the other hand, he regarded independence from foreign rule as a mere prelude achievement of freedom by the Indian people. To him there was no distinction, as he said many times in his life between British Tyranny and actual or potential Indian Tyranny. Nor was there any distinction between an American Rockefeller and a potential Indian Rockefeller, as he said in Hind Swaraj. Where there is no freedom, there is no Freedom, whether the country is ruled by its own people or by foreigners. And so Gandhi declared: "I am not interested in freeing India merely from the English yoke. I am bent upon freeing India from any yoke what soever."

It follows that the kind of Freedom envisaged by Gandhi exists only in a society in which the people do not depend heavily on the State for protection of their rights. "Self-government means", he says, '...continuous effort to be independent of government control, whether it is foreign government or whether it is national. *Swaraj* government will be a sorry affair if people look up to it for the regulation if every detail of life.

As a matter of fact, fundamental to the Gandhian concept of Political Freedom is the idea, as there is a basic contradiction between the Freedom of individual and the authority of state. The free society visualized by Gandhi is, therefore, "an exploitation-free society in which the supreme instrument of defending just rights lay within the grasp of the unarmed individual." Awakening a consciousness of this fact in Indian society and even outside was regarded by Gandhi as one of his primary tasks in life. "My work will be finished." He said, three-and-a-half years before his death, "If I succeed in carrying conviction to the human family, that every man or woman, however weak in body, is the guardian of his or her self-respect and liberty. This defence avails, though the whole world may be against the individual register."

(v) *Swaraj involves equality*: 'The Freedom' of the individual cannot obviously be regarded as fundamental to the concept of Freedom unless there is a prior acceptance of the hypothesis that all men are equal. The Gandhian conception of Freedom, therefore, necessarily includes the notion of equality Freedom and the equal development of all, which Gandhi calls Sarvodaya, are, interchangeable terms. Without Equality, therefore, social, political and economic, there can be no true Freedom. Inequality in any sphere vitiates *ab initio* the possibility of universal Freedom. Economic Equality, he says, is the master-key to *swaraj*. Without the elimination of the disparities between the rich and the poor, between labour and capital, there can be no real Freedom for anyone in society. The contrast between the palaces of India's major cities and the hovels of the poorer classes which existed in India, if India was ever to achieve Freedom in the real sense. He demanded that in an India that was truly free sweepers, doctors, lawyers, teachers and merchants must all get the same wages for an honest day's work.

(vi) *Swaraj involves non-violence*: The Sarvodaya society representing universal Freedom must be necessarily based on non-violence, for non-violence alone, Gandhi insists, can preserve and promote Freedom. The violent way would inevitably lead to dictatorship, he argues, the non-violent way to democracy. The reason is obvious to him: "true democracy or the *Swaraj* of the masses can never come through untruthful and violent means, for the simple reason that the natural corollary to their use would be to remove all opposition through the suppression or extermination of the antagonists. That does not make for individual Freedom. Individual Freedom can have the fullest play only under a regime of unadulterated *ahimsa*." Moreover, it is necessary for the growth of this universal Freedom that every individual, including women and children, should participate actively in it, for the very participation in the process of Freedom widens the horizons of individual Freedom. Such a universal development of Freedom would not be possible, argues Gandhi, in a society where Freedom is protected by the violent power of the state; it would emerge inevitably only in a non-violent society. As he puts it: "Granted that India produced sufficient arms and ammunition and men who know the art of war, what part or lot will those who cannot bear arms have in the attainment of *swaraj*? I want *swaraj* in the winning of which even women and children would contribute an equal share with physically the strongest. That can be under *ahimsa* only."[29]

## Notes

1. B. A. Saletore, *Ancient Indian Political Thought,* Bomaby, Asia Publishing House, 1968, p p. 74-75.
2. N. Ragahavan Iyer, *The Moral and Political Thought of Mahatma Gandhi,* Delhi, Oxford University Press, 1973, p. 347.
3. M. K. Gandhi, *Hind Swaraj*, Ahmedabad, Navajivan Publishing House, 1929, pp. 49-55.
4. *http://en.wikipedia.org/wifi/self rule.*
5. *Young India*, 8-12-1920, pp. 884-85.
6. Tendulkar, D. G., Mahatma, New Delhi, Publications Division, Government of India, 1961, Vol. 2, p. 326.
7. *Young India*, 19-3-1931, p. 38.
8. *Ibid.*, 12-6-1924, p. 195.
9. *Ibid.*, 29-1-1925, p. 41.
10. *Ibid.*, 6-8-1925, p. 276.
11. *Ibid.*, 1-5-1930, p. 149.
12. *Ibid.*, 26-3-1931, p. 46.
13. *Ibid.*, 18-6-1931, p. 147.
14. *Harijan*, 3-3-1946, p. 31.
15. *Young India*, 16-4-1931, p. 78.
16. *Harijan*, 28-4-1946, p. 111.
17. *Young India*, 17-4-1924, p. 170.

18. *Harijan*, 29-9-1940, p. 306.
19. *Ibid.*, 1940.
20. *Young India*, 1-5-1930.
21. M. K. Gandhi, *In Search of the Supreme*, Vol. 1, p. 267.
22. *Young India*, 3-4-1924, p. 109.
23. M. K. Gandhi, *To The Students*, Hingorani ed., Ahmedabad, Navajivan Publishng House, 1953 pp. 47-48
24. *Harijan* , 1939.
25. The Indian Opinion of 1909, Collected Works of Mahatma Gandhi, New Delhi: The Publications Division, Ministry of Information and Broadcasting, Vol. IX, p. 451.
26. *Harijan*, 9-6-1946.
27. *Speeches and Wrirings of Mahatama Gandhi,* Madras, G. Natesan & Co., p. 409.
28. Mahadev Desai, *With Gandhiji in Ceylon,* Madra, S. Gansesan, Triplicane, 1928, p. 98.
29. *Harijan*, 3-3-1945.

## 13

# The Concept of Non-Violence

*– Ashu Pasricha*

It has more or less become a dogma, among students of Gandhian Thought, to assume that violence and non-violence are opposites which cancel each other out. They have tended to look the world of reality in terms of black and white, forgetful of the infinite nuances of grey that confront u s at every turn. Life is not what these well meaning people have assumed it to be a clear cut progression from the infra red of brute violence to the ultra violet of ethereal non-violence. Life is rather like a close knit web, in which violence and non-violence interpenetrate one another, not as contradictory elements but as complementaries. This interpenetration of seeming opposites good and evil, light and darkness, life and death, violence and non-violence—is the essence of reality. We ignore it at our own peril.

Gandhi, being the 'practical idealist' that he was, always spoke of truth and non-violence, never of non-violence alone. Within the meaning of his 'practical idealism', the practice of non-violence became, in other words, an exercise in the art of the possible.

Non-violence and truth were one interpenetrated whole a mosaic in which each patch of colour lent meaning to the other. Gandhi never spoke of non-violence in the abstract but only as it related to some concrete situation. Of course, like all human beings, he did at times, especially in his later years, indulge in the luxury of generalizing from particular events. But as a rule his awareness of reality, painfully acute at all times, tended to overmaster the natural human gravitation towards romanticism.

Gandhi was never tired of saying that his whole life has been a series of compromises. Though he undoubtedly regretted this as who wouldn't? nevertheless it was not his way to let himself be consumed with remorse and frustration on that account. All life is a compromise. Human perceptions, no less than human sensations, are subjected to the law of *dvandva* or what may be called the hot cold, good bad, syndrome. Violence and non-violence are no exception to this rule. Pure non-violence, as much as pure violence, is an impossible stance for human beings and human institutions. Neither would exist for a second on such a diet. The kind of permanent, enduring peace that man has been seeking since the dawn of creation is a will or the wisp. War and peace, conflict and reconciliation, are two aspects of the on-going human process of social, political and psychological evolution. The evolution is not, as it is commonly misperceived, from war towards peace, but rather from one kind of war and peace towards another kind of war and peace. It is a relative, not an absolute evolution.

Perhaps this point needs to be amplified somewhat, to fore-stall any suspicion of casuistry on our part. That forms of war-fare 'evolve' (in the primary sense of that word) is nowhere more apparent than in the nature of modern nuclear war itself. No nation, unless it is quite mad, prepares for a nuclear war in order to fight it. But rather in order to ensure that such a war will never take place. This is the essence of the modern concept of nuclear deterrence which, whether we like it or not, continues to preserve the world, despite endless provocations, from the horrors of a third World War. While our ancestors sharpened their swords in order to use them at the first opportunity, whether for defence or depredation, we pile up our bombs in order never to have to use them. The evolution is from secrecy to openness on the one hand, and from the Janus faced concept of defence and attack to that of deterrence on the other.

Gandhi lived well into the dawn of the nuclear age. He also lived through the Nazi Tyranny. But faced with these, bizarre happenings he fell into the generalizations that all great men resort to at times of stress and dismay. For once he let go of his hold on truth and unconvincingly argued that non-violence still was the answer both to Auschwitz and Hiroshima. It is more than probable that Gandhi, had he lived long into our nightmare age of the Chinese Red Guard, the Viet Cong and the genocidal American bombing of Vietnam, would have characteristically owned his error and shown us where and how our doctrinal moorings had to be readjusted.

But in his absence, it devolves on us who claim to be working towards the revolution he left unfinished, to make those necessary readjustments.

If, on the other hand, we continue to look upon non-violence as an absolute concept, not subject to the exigencies of history or to the evolutionary, trial and error nature of all human ideas, we thereby achieve only what each one of the great religions has achieved in the past a progressive fossilization. Doctrinal purity is a meaningless obsession when our aim is to achieve certain well defined social and political goals. In this the followers of Gandhi at any rate most of them are different from Gandhi in a very vital sense, though few dare to admit the difference. With Gandhi a saint to the manner born the achievement of the secular goals of political freedom and social justice was always subservient to the religious goal of *moksha*, or self-realization. If the former had come in the way of the latter and had proved an obstacle in the path of his well set spiritual journey (which they fortunately did not), Gandhi would have had little hesitation in discarding them. For him, therefore, non-violence became in consonance with Hindu tradition both the means as well as the end. This can hardly be said to be the case with the bulk of present day Gandhian.

The spiritual overtone in Gandhian non-violence, exceedingly though it is when non-violence is practiced primarily spiritual ends and only secondarily for the achievement of the secular goal of social change, nevertheless has led to certain inner compulsions which have reduced its acceptability to modern societies. This is unfortunate, for the importance of the Gandhian orientation lies precisely in the successful manner in which he showed how the heavenly Ganga of non-violence can be brought down to earth and tamed for worldly ends. Among these inner compulsions, probably the most serious was the need he felt (no doubt genuinely) to make sweeping generalizations about non-violence and, in the process, to ignore the essentially finite nature of all human instruments.

Gandhi's greatness as a leader and thinker lay in his transformation of the individualistic message of non-violence into a success technique for direct mass action. Mahavira, Buddha, Nagesena and Santideva have conceived of *Ahimsa* as a tenet of personal action and motivation. But Gandhi transformed it also into a social and political technique. He, thus, attempted to apply the theory of *himsa* enunciated by the old Indian teachers and prophets on a social and political plane. The supreme concept, according to him, which is necessary for the reformation of politics, is non-violence.

Violence is a comprehensive category and is manifested both at the personal and the institutional levels. Evil thoughts, sentiments of revenge and brutality, verbal pugnacity, and even accumulation of unnecessary things represent examples of personal violence. Falsehood, trickery, intrigues, chicanery and deceitfulness are also forms of violence, according to the comprehensive connotation given to the term by Gandhi. Physical punishments, imprisonment, capital punishment and wars represent examples of violence committed by government. Economic exploitation and strangulation of others are also manifestations of violence. Even excess of emulation and competition can become species of violence. Non-violence or *Ahimsa* is, hence, necessarily, equally comprehensive and represents the total neutralization of violence in all forms.

*Ahimsa* is not merely the negative act of refraining from doing offence, injury and harm to others but really it represents the ancient law of positive self-sacrifice and constructive suffering. Gandhi interpreted it as signifying utter selflessness and universal love. The ultimate aim of *Ahimsa* is even to love the so called enemies or opponents. In 1930, Gandhi said that he would suck the poison out of a dying enemy of his if he was a victim of snake bite. *Ahimsa,* thus, is equivalent to positive compassion and love."[1] It even implies the cultivation of gladness and felicity involved in suffering for others. *Ahimsa* is implicitly latent in all human beings because all are sharers in the divine spiritual reality and its culmination is the negation of self subsistent particularity and a realization of the feeling of love and substantive unity with the whole of creation.[2] it is the substitution of arrogance, antagonism and alienation by love. Hence Gandhi wrote in his *Autobiography,* "I must reduce myself to zero. *Ahimsa* is the farthest limit of humility."[3] The supreme vocation or man is the purposive evolution, of *Ahimsa* as universal positive love. *Ahimsa,* as thus conceived by Gandhi, is a profound social import. Aristotle had said that friendship is the cohesive bond of communities. Gandhi also pleaded for brotherly ethic and believed that *Ahimsa* has, almost an obligatory and compelling power to bring peace and unity to the world.

He also interpreted human history in terms of the slow evolution of *Ahimsa*. Like some of the western anthropologists he says that "our remote ancestors were cannibals." That was succeeded by stage of chase the life of wandering hunters. The third stage was of agriculture which marked the growth of civilized stable life. Man "founded villages and towns, and from member of a family he became member of a community and a nation. All these are signs of progressive *ahimsa* and diminishing *himsa*. Had it been otherwise, the human species should have been extinct by now, even as many of the lower species have disappeared."[4]

It may appear surprising to several students of Gandhism to find speaking here as an adherent of the school of evolutionary anthropology rather than one deriving his theory of social origins from the *Purusha Sukta* or the *Puranas*. He regarded the process of human evolution as a vindication of the superiority of *Ahimsa as love*. "It is my firm faith that man is by nature going higher," he wrote.

The social application of *Ahimsa*, according to Gandhi, is upon the acceptance of spiritual metaphysics and the necessity of the growth of social charity. He stressed *Ahimsa* the universe is permeated with a divine spirit and all life is sacred. *Ahimsa* is vitally integrated with Truth or God. All men, according to Gandhi, are children of God. Hence to slight a single being is really to inflict injury upon the divine spirit in man and thus it amounts to an injury upon the whole world. "The Bible rightly taught that vengeance belonged to God."[5]

The tyrannical group leaders and governments which are the repositories of violence are to be firmly resisted by the *Satyagrahi* are proved to be in the wrong. Non-violence is only the replacement of retaliation and is no surrender to wickedness. But resistance does not imply hatred for the adversary. Gandhi holds that it is possible and advisable to resist a perverse system but "to resist and attack its author is tantamount to resisting and attacking oneself." Hence Ahimsa is the attitude of harmlessness even to the wrong doer. Gandhi goes a step further and says that it implies positive love even to the wrong doer. But this does not mean rendering any help to the wrong doer in the prolongation of his wrong.

The practice of Ahimsa requires faith in the reality and compassion of God and deep self introspection, the votary of non-violence has to cultivate the acquisition of freedom from envy, hatred, malice, lust, cupidity and uncharitableness." This leads to the acceptance of an elevated standard of virtues. The code of vows or Vrata has to be followed by the non-violent *Satyagrahi* and has to become the standard for cultivation by others. The acceptance of the norm of non-violence would thus almost amount to a moral transvaluation of values. The law of love, if courageously practiced, is bound to lead to the elevation of the accent, quality and character of politics and civilization.

As a Vedantist and a Vaishnava, Gandhi regarded all life as sacred and precious. Hence he had deep faith in the sanctity of the right to life. He would not kill even a snake. He said: "God alone can take life, because He gives it." The believer in Ahimsa would regard even the lives of the opponents as worthy of reverence. In an article in the Harijan Gandhi wrote: "You are no *Satyagrahi* if you remain silent or passive spectators while your enemy is being done to death. You must protect him even at the cost of your life."[6] He accepted the supremacy of the right to life merely because man as an individual is the subject of social and political rights but because in his inmost essence man is a soul. Hence like Tolstoy, Gandhi accepted the immutability and obligatory character of the law of love. For himself, he regarded the law of Ahimsa as absolute, although he had acquired it after a long struggle. He considered it an infallible weapon, mightier than the force of arms, and believed in it as a categorical imperative.

Like Rousseau, Gandhi thinks that the growth of the military art and the display of the military livery by the soldiers is a sign of decadence and not of progress. The cult of armament and preparedness is the indirect testimony to the wide prevalence of fear distrust and suspicion. Hence Gandhi wanted the freedom to preach non-violence as a "substitute" for war. He condemned war as an absolute evil and would not accept even the plea of a defensive war or a just war. He would have absolutely repudiated the notion of anticipatory war. He felt that there is always some party which is guilty of initiating a war. It is not correct and adequate to state that war is the mechanism of devil or of uncontrollable forces. He said that behind the hand that hurls the sword, there is always the brain and the mind that prescribes the use of the sword. He wrote: "When two nations are fighting, the duty of a votary of Ahimsa is to stop the war."[7] Leo Tolstoy also recognized the clamouring contradiction between the profession of Christianity and the simultaneous acknowledgement of the necessity of armaments for national security. Gandhi taught the absoluteness of peace and had even visualized universal disarmament. His Ahimsa provides an ultimate vision of universal fraternity and he hoped that in world politics there would be the increasing resort to consultation and arbitration in place of armed conflicts.

Although, according to Gandhi, all war is unjust from the standpoint of Ahimsa, still the aspirant after freedom would distinguish between the aggressor and the defender and render all moral support to the latter.

Sometimes a contradiction has been felt to exist between Gandhi's non-violence and his participation in some forms in wars. During the time of the Boer War in 1899, he raised a Volunteer Ambulance Corps. In 1906, he raised a stretcher bearing party of twenty Indians at the time of Zulu Rebellion. In 1914, he raised a Volunteer Ambulance Corps in London consisting chiefly of Indian students residing in London. In 1918, he nearly killed himself by strenuous activity for the recruitment of Indian soldiers for the war on the British side. While Tilak wanted to help the allies through recruitment only on certain conditions being fulfilled, Gandhi was for unconditional military support. Hence it is asked that if Gandhi was a votary of absolute *Ahimsa* why did he participate in any way in a war. When he was helping recruitment in 1918, was he not aiding in planning the killing of German soldiers? But Gandhi had defended his action on the ground that so long as he was subject of the British Empire it was his duty to help it in times of crisis. He says in his *Autobiography:*

"When two nations are fighting, the duty of a votary of *ahimsa* is to stop the war. He who is not equal to that eg. duty, he who has no power of resisting war, he who is not qualified to resist war, may take part in war, and yet whole-heartedly try to free himself, his nation and the world from war. I had hoped to improve my status and that of my people through the British Empire. Whilst in England I was enjoying the protection of the British Fleet, and taking shelter as I did under its armed might, I was directly participating in its potential violence. Therefore, if I desired to retain my connection with the Empire and to live under its banner, one of the three courses was open to me: I could declare open resistance to the war and, in accordance with the law of *Satyagraha,* boycott the Empire until it changed its military policy; or I could seek imprisonment by civil disobedience of such of its laws as were fit to be disobeyed; or I could participate in the war on the side of the Empire and thereby acquire the capacity and fitness for resisting the violence of war. I lacked this capacity and fitness, so I thought there was nothing for it but to serve in the war. I make no distinction, from the point of view of *ahimsa,* between combatants and non-combatants. He, who volunteers to serve a band of dacoits, by working as their carrier, or their watchman while they are about their business or their nurse when they are wounded, is as much guilty of dacoity as the dacoits themselves. In the same way those who confine themselves to attending to the wounded in battle cannot be absolved from the guilt of war."[8]

But it may also be pointed out that in the course of the Second World War, he categorically refused to adopt a position similar to the one adopted in 1918.

Although opposed to militarism, power politics, violence and imperialistic vandalism, Gandhi was not a believer in peace at any price. He said that he did not want the peace of the stone or the grave. Peace is not to be equated with feebleness, inertia and exhaustion. An individual or a nation can only want peace with honour. Peace does not mean appeasement of the aggressor or acquiescence in his imperialistic adventures. Gandhi's comment on the Munich Pact of 1938, as being a settlement for "peace without honour", is significant. A genuine peace must be founded on the rectification of the forces that threaten peace. Hence it must accept the conception of justice as the apportionment of due claims and rights and is thoroughly antithetical to the imposition of the will of the aggressor on the weak. Addressing a prayer meeting at Sodepur on November 1, 1946, Gandhi said that any peace to be substantial must be honourable, never at the cost of honour. He, therefore, pointed out that he could never agree to any settlement which amounted to the humiliation or loss of self respect for any one.

But, on the other hand, the Gandhian theory of peace did not mean the elimination of the antagonist. Resistance has to be offered to the oppression but for the wrong doer there is to be no hatred. A comprehensive theory of Ahimsa ultimately postulates positive love even for the opponent. Gandhi even pleaded for the cultivation of good feelings towards the opponents because, like Buddha, he felt that enmity or *Vaira* leads to more enmity and thus a vicious circle is created because the antagonists ever remains disgruntled and hungers for a chance of revenge. Thus the best way conversion" of the opponents. *Ahimsa*, thus, wants to replace the ferocious character of politics of power by the righteousness of universal moral will.[9] This authority of moral inducement and persuasion for the conversion of the opponents can be built up by adherence to the great vows (Ekadasa Mahavrata) which produce the moral fervour and strength necessary for the life of a fighter for the cause of right. Thus the basis of the Gandhian philosophy of politics consists in stressing the persistent, overpowering and, resolute power of love as a significant factor which can solve group and national tensions and antagonisms through non-constrained conversion.

Gandhi believed in the thorough practice of the ideal of *Abhayam* or fearlessness along with non-violence. He was always stressing for practicing Ahimsa it is essential to shed all fear. The votary of Ahimsa only has one fear of God. As he pursues the Godourney he realises the eternal Atman and feels absolute indifference towards the temporary pleasures of the world. He sheds the attachment for the mortal physical frame. "Violence is needed for the protection of things external; non-violence is needed for the protection of the *Atman*."[10] *Ahimsa* or positive creative love can be practiced only on the basis of fearlessness and it may even be said that perfect Ahimsa means absolute fearlessness. It is the path of the brave. He pleaded only for the heroic non-violent action of the brave and was never attached to the non-resistance offered by the weak. He wanted the cultivation of courage as a preparation for life, but he wanted this courage to be expressed non-violently and not violently. He insisted on the development of that moral courage and strength which proceed from an indomitable will. He Noakhali on November 27, 1946: "The only real guarantee is to be sought in the personal courage of individuals. Everything else depends on it."[11] The operation of *Ahimsa* is the exercise of soul-force and it is a gospel of strength, according to Gandhi. It proceeds from moral and spiritual strength. It is the strongest force known and it is a force of the subtlest kind, according to Gandhi. It is a demonstration of the resolute strength of the heroic soul which refuses to hurt any body because every living creature is essentially a spirit and fundamentally one with himself. Ahimsa is the farthest removed from a false masquerade for one's weakness.

There is a solid concern for the actual and the concrete in Gandhi's saying that the sword is not the sign of strength but the symbol of fear and weakness. Fear generates suspicion and sometimes even arrogance. The accumulation of fear results in the formation of complexes. Sometimes it may produce aggressiveness. A greatly disturbing situation of our times is the growth of perverted and maladjusted personalities who are prone to being exploited by demagogues who raise bogeys and scares of different kinds and play upon the fear of the people. Gandhi teaches the psychological efficacy of fearlessness based on spiritual faith as the way to counteract the blighting influences of political coercion, group jealousies and rivalries and individual appetites.

Fearlessness is acquired by perfection of personal character and by deep faith in the existence of God. A believer in the reality and kindness of God cares only for truth, faith in the creative and beneficent power of the Spirit provides to man a firm determination to fight all factors of injustice even at the cost of the sacrifice of one's life.

Gandhi was a perfect devotee of civility and humility, but he explicitly, unconditionally and categorically stated that if the only actives were cowardice and violence he would choose the latter. He was not tired of repeating that fear or cowardice should have no place in the national dictionary. He wrote:

"The truth is that cowardice itself is violence of a subtle and, therefore, dangerous type, and far more difficult to eradicate than the habit of physical violence. A coward never risks his life. A man who would kill often risks it. A non-violent person's life is always at the disposal of him who would take it. For he knows that the soul within never dies. The encasing body is ever perishing. The more a man gives his life, the more he saves it. Thus non-violence requires more than the courage of the soldier of war. The *Gita* definition of a soldier is one who does not know what it is to run away from danger."[12]

Non-violence, hence, is to be regarded as, the summit of bravery Gandhi pointed out that he could no more preach non violence to a cowardly man than be could tempt a blind man to enjoy healthy scenes.

Gandhi wanted India to follow the doctrine of non-violence not because she was prostrate due to political subjection. He affirmed that India had an imperishable "soul" which could rise above all weaknesses. But after Independence, nevertheless, Gandhi, a little pessimistically and with some amount of mortification, said that India had adopted only the non-violence of the weak because once the British power was out of the picture, the people engaged in unrestrained and intensely violent slaughter and internecine struggles. He confessed, "I have to hang down my head in shame." Gandhi wrote: "I have already said that the non- violence that was offered during the past thirty years was that of the weak . . . . India has no experience of the non-violence of the strong."[13] He stuck, however, to his faith in the moralization and spiritualization of politics and remained thoroughly devoted to the principle that increasing adherence to Ahimsa alone would emancipate mankind from all kinds of conflict and evil.

Gandhi preached the gospel of *Ahimsa* both for the East and the West. But in their different situational contexts *Ahimsa* implied somewhat different things for them. For India, *Ahimsa* as a social and political technic meant a pooling together of the energies of the people for the work of national liberation. It implied the elimination of petty local jealousies and group, caste and communal discriminations and persecutions and notions of regional superiority. It also signified the notion of the realization of a national community based on suffering, tolerance, self abnegation and the neutralizations of fissiparous trends. For the western world, the Gandhian philosophy of *Ahimsa* mainly appeared as a gospel of renunciation. In 1947, Gandhi wrote that if Europe was to save itself from suicide something along the lines of non violence had to be adopted. Non-violence applied to international politics signified a spiritual substitute for struggle and war and the consequent repudiation of "blood and iron" and "the mailed fist." It, thus, meant the negation of the cults of power, stratagems, exploitation, enslavement, economic imperialism, and war. But it was to be only a moral substitute for war and not the tame acceptance of *status quo*. In face of the advancements in nuclear energy, Gandhi, stood for the resort to techniques of love because he was deeply concerned with the survival of man.

As a spiritual and ethical idealist, he believed in the moralization of public administration to make it patterned, more and more, on the basis of non-violence. He wanted to reform the structure of modern political life. If *swaraj* could be achieved by non-violence then, the *swaraj* polity had to be increasingly based on the principle of Ahimsa. Hence he emphasized the application of honesty, integrity and beneficent purpose in public administration.[14]

The world is swept by the wind of violence. This storm which ravages the harvest of our civilization did not break out from a clear sky. Centuries of brutal national pride, whetted by the idolatrous ideology of several religions and crowned by a century of inhuman industrialism, rapacious plutocracy and a materialistic system of economics where the soul perishes, stifled to death, were bound to culminate in these dark struggles where the treasures of the West succumbed. It is not enough to say all this was inevitable. Each people kill the other in the name of same principles, which hid the same covetousness and Cainish instincts. All be they Nationalists, Fascists, Communists, members of the oppressed to use the force, while refusing this right to others. In the past might dominate right.

The peace of the world is far off. We have no illusions. We have seen, abundantly, during the course of the last century, the hypocrisy, the cowardice, and the cruelty of mankind. "But this does not prevent us from loving mankind." Asserts Romain Rolland a French biographer of Mahatma Gandhi, "For even among the worst there is a nescio quid Dei. We know the material ties that weigh on the world today, the crushing determinism of economic conditions which hem it in; we know that centuries of passion and systematized terror have built a crust about our souls which the light cannot pierce. But we also know what miracles the spirit can work."[15]

The true characteristic of faith is not to deny the hostility of the world, but to recognize it and to believe in spite of it! Faith is a battle. And our non-violence is the most desperate battle. The way to peace is not through weakness. We do not fight violence so much as weakness. Nothing is worthwhile unless it is strong, neither good nor evil. Absolute evil is better than emasculated goodness. Moaning pacifism is the death-knell of peace; it is cowardice and lack of faith. Let those who do not believe, who fear, withdraw. The way to peace leads through self-sacrifice.

One thing is certain: either Gandhi's spirit will triumph, or it will manifest itself again, as were manifested, centuries before, the *Messiah* and Buddha, till there finally is manifested. In a mortal half god, the perfect incarnation of the principle of life which will lead a new humanity on to a new path.

## Notes

1. *Harijan*, 17-8-1934.
2. *Ibid.*, 29-6-1940.
3. M. K. Gandhi, *An Autobiography or The Story of My Experiments with Truth*, Ahmedabad, Navajivan Publications, 1975
4. *Harijan*, 21-7-1940.
5. *Ibid.*, 27-4-1947.
6. *Ibid.*, 18-8-1940.
7. *Ibid.*, 22-8-1940
8. M. K. Gandhi, *An Autobiography or The Story of My Experiments with Truth, op. cit.*
9. *Harijan*, 12-10-1935.
10. *Ibid.*, 18-8-1940.
11. *Ibid.*, 27-11-1946.

12. *Young India*, 18-12-1924.

13. *Harijan*, 29-6-1947

14. V. P. Varma, *The Political Philosophy of Mahatma Gandhi and Sarvodaya,* Agra, Lakshmi Narayan Agarwal, 1959

15. Jai Narain Sharma, "Gandhi's Non-Violence How Relevant is it Today?", The Tribune, Chandigarh, 2-10-2000.

# 14
# Gandhi on Religion

– *Anju Jhamb*

## Meaning

Religion is a universal phenomenon, found in all human societies and communities. It is defined as a belief in an unseen and mysterious power which has control over the living and non-living and all that exists and man owes his obedience and reverence to it. It is also seen as propitiation and reconciliation of powers superior to man which are believed to direct or control the course of nature or human life. It is the worship of supernatural beings. Man has an inherent religious element in him. So, it is distinctively human activity.

The word religion has no one accepted definition. Philosophers, Sociologists, Psychologists and many others defined religion in their own ways and for their own purposes. Some Philosophers have called it 'a superstitious structure of incoherent metaphysical notions'; some Sociologists refer it to religion as the 'collective expression of human values'; and some Psychologists call it the 'mythical complex surrounding a projected super ego'.[1]

The Oxford Dictionary defines religion as "Human recognition of super human controlling power and especially of a personal god entitled to obedience and worship, effect of such recognition on conduct and mental attitude".[2] Religion is a belief in the ultimate values which are in harmony with the enduring structure of the universe. Whitehead says, "Religion is the vision of something which stands beyond, behind, and within, the passing flux of immediate things; something which is real, and yet waiting to be realized, something which is a remote possibility and yet the greatest of present facts; something which gives meaning to all that passes and yet eludes apprehension, something whose possession is the good and yet is beyond all reach, something which is the ultimate ideal and the hopeless quest".[3]

The Dictionary of Political Thought defines religion as "the belief in, worship of and attempt to obey transcendent beings, usually on the assumption that they possess the power to regulate affairs in the world, and to distribute rewards and punishments in another".[4]

Swami Vivekanand says, "Temples and churches, books and forms are simply the kindergarten of religion, to make the spiritual child strong enough to make steps. Religion is not in doctrines or in dogmas, nor in intellectual argumentation: it is being and becoming, and it is realization".[5]

According to Mohammed Neguib: "Religion is a candle inside a multi-coloured lantern. Every one looks through a particular colour, but the candle is always there."[6] It is the means for purification of the soul. It is a binding force to save humanity from catastrophe. Ogburn and Nimkoff rightly said, "If religion brings peace to the soul, expands the soul to infinite proportions, makes life bearable and arouses us to noble aims, then there is a great need for it."[7]

Religion is not merely the knowledge of dogmas or rituals. It is a dynamic process, a renewed effort of the creative impulse working through exceptional individuals, and seeking to uplift mankind to a new level. Religion awakens the reality in man. Radhakrishnan says that the religion is an insight into reality, and though inaccessible to reason, is consistent with it.[8] The path of religion is the path of happiness and peace to humanity.

## Gandhi on Religion

Religion was central to Gandhi's life, thought and work. Romain Rolland once remarked "To understand Gandhi's philosophy, it should be realized that his doctrine is like a huge edifice composed of two different floors or grades. Below is the solid ground work, the basic foundation of religion. On this vast and unshakable foundation is based his political and social philosophy".[9] So, Gandhi's political philosophy and political techniques are only two corollaries of his religious and moral principles. However, his religious ideas were complex and varied according to the occasion. He himself said that his views on religion were subject to change. Gandhiji regarded religion as purely a personal matter. There can be as many religions as there were minds, as each mind has a different conception of God from that of the other.

Gandhi brought down religion from the cloistered seclusion of yogic contemplation to man's socio-economic and political plane. The well-being of man is the touchstone of every religion. "If religion is an awakening it must embrace humanity. If religion is a positive force of inner awakening, it must be divine and must embrace truth, beauty and goodness". For Gandhi religion was another name for truth and righteousness. All the great religions of the World are practically laid on the basis of conduct and morality. "True religion is identical with morality. There is no religion higher than truth and Righteousness".[10] For Gandhi religion and morality are convertible terms. "For me, morals, ethics and religion are convertible terms. A moral life without reference to religion is like a house built upon sand. And religion divorced from morality is like 'sounding brass' good only for making a noise and breaking heads".[11]

Gandhi believed, "No man can live without religion. There are some who in the egotism of their reason declare that they have nothing to do with religion. But it is like a man saying that he breathes but that he has no nose. Whether by reason, or by instinct, or by superstition, man acknowledges some sort of relationship with the divine."[12] He again said, "By religion, I do not mean formal religion or customary religion, but that religion which underlies all religions, which brings us face-to-face with our maker."[13]

Gandhi defined religion as "a belief in the ordered and the moral government of the Universe".[14] Religion is not a refuge from the world but a great source of inspiration to act in this world. Gandhi's concept of religion had little in common with what generally passes for organised religion: dogmas, rituals, superstition and bigotry. Indeed, shorn of these accretions, Gandhian religion was simply an ethical framework for the conduct of daily life. "Religion which takes no account of practical affairs and does not help to solve them, is no religion."[15]

## Sources of Gandhi's Religious Thought

Although Gandhi grew up in a devout and educated Vaishnavite family, in a religious atmosphere, his knowledge of religion was extremely limited. His autobiography reveals that he had learnt little Sanskrit, was innocent of Hindu philosophy and had not even read the *Gita* until persuaded to do so in England by two theosophists. "They were reading Sir Edwin Arnold's translation—*The song celestial* and they invited me to read. I felt ashamed, as I had read the divine poem neither in Sanskrit nor in Gujrati. I was constrained to tell them that I had not read the Gita".[16] Gandhi himself said that I am a Hindu by birth. And yet I don't have much knowledge of where I stand and what I do or should believe and intend to make a careful study of my own religion.

Gandhi's interest in religion was awakened. It was in England Gandhi was introduced to the Bible. The *New Testament*, particularly "The sermon on the mount", went straight to his heart. In his autobiography, he said that "the idea of returning love for hatred and good for evil captivated me".[17] He said that three 'moderns' had influenced him most–Tolstoy, Ruskin and Rajchandra. Tolstoy's *'The Kingdom of God is within You'* overwhelmed him. Before the independent thinking, profound morality and the truthfulness of this book all the books seemed to pale into insignificance. This book give him a good idea of what he looked for in a religion. Gandhi said "when I was passing through a severe crisis of skepticism and doubt, Tolstoy's book deeply impressed me. He practiced what he preached and reckoned no cost too great in his pursuit of truth. He said, "The kingdom of God would come if all men – (a) Live in peace with all men, (b) Be pure, (c) Never resist evil".[18]

John Ruskin also influenced Gandhi. Gandhi's friend Mr. Polak gave him a book to read during journey '*Unto The Last*'. It became impossible for Gandhi to lay aside the book when once he started reading it grippled him. Gandhi determined to change his way of life in accordance with the ideals presented in the book. He learnt value of a life of simplicity and the dignity of manual labour from this book. Later on he translated this book into Gujrati as "*Sarvodaya*" (The welfare of all). But it was Rajchandra who had given a sense of direction to Gandhi's religious quest. He was a Gujrati Jain, Bombay Jeweller. Gandhi was in close touch with him and admired him for his '*vairagya*' (renunciation) "I never saw him tempted by objects of pleasure or luxury in the world... He disapproved the prevalent idea that a man who is wise in the sphere of '*dharma*' will not be wise in the affairs of practical life. A student of philosophy of religion, he tried to practice what he believed".[19] Rajchandra taught him that it is the way a man lived, not the recital of a verse or the form of a prayer which made him a good Hindu, a good Muslim or a good Christian. Though, he was a Jain but he restored 'Gandhi's faith in Hinduism. Gandhi said, "In my moments of spritual crisis he was my refuge".[20] In a state of confusion, Gandhi once asked Rajchandra *'27 questions'*[21] on soul, God, Liberation, the *Vedas*, the *Gita*, the *Bible*, incarnation, *Brahma*, *Vishnoo*, *Mahesh*, devotion, etc. Rajchandra tried to answer these questions in detail[22]. He also explained "the doctrine of the many sidedness of religious truth". He regarded different faiths 'like many walled enclosures in which men and women confined themselves. On the meaning of religion (*dharma*) Rajchandra said "*Dharma* does not mean any particular creed or dogma. Nor does it mean reading or learning by rote books known as *shastras* (sacred texts) or even believing all that they say"[23] rather *Dharma* is the quality of the soul present in every human being. "*Dharma* is the mean by which we can know ourselves. No organised religion is a special repository of *dharma*. We may accept this means from wherever we get it whether from India or Europe or Arabia".[24] So, Rajchandra enabled Gandhi to find the answer to the question he had been struggling with since his childhood. "Which was the one true religion that he could adopt and reject the other as false".[25] To answer this Rajchandra said "Religion is not an 'ism' and it is not merely intellectual knowledge or belief in any set of doctrines, but an inmate attribute of the soul. It enables to define the human duties in life and establish correct relationship with the fellow beings. Religion is the means of the self realization or realization of the true nature of self".[26] Rajchandra used to say that the real test of spiritual progress was the extent to which one could translate one's belief in day to day life. Gandhi himself came to the conclusion "what cannot be followed in day-to-day practice cannot be called religion". Altough Gandhi never accepted Rajchandra his spiritual Guru but his idea of a "religion which underlies all religions"[27] has its source in Rajchandra.

The greatest influence of a book, *The Bhagvad Gita* can be seen on Gandhi's religious thought. *Gita* became an infallible guide of conduct and dictionary of daily reference just as one refers to English dictionary for the meanings of the difficult English words, Gandhi referred to this dictionary (*Gita*) of conduct for the ready solution for all his troubles and travails. Two words in the *Gita* '*aparigraha*' (non-possession) and '*sambhava*' (equability) opened to Gandhi limitless vistas. The real object of the *Gita* was to point to a goal of self realization and to show that '*Nishkam Karma*' (detached activity) was the way to achieve the goal. Gandhi's life was more in accord with the description of a *Karmayogi*. As he meditated on the *Gita* and the ideal of *aparigraha* (non possession) grew upon him, Gandhi began to reduce his needs. He made sure that even his wife Kasturba accepted *aparigraha* along with him; and prevailed upon her to give up the valuable Gold Necklace which the Indian followers of Gandhi has given her on the eve of their departure for India in 1901. Gandhi also felt that the central teaching of the *Gita* is bounded by truth and non-violence.

*Ramayana* also left a deep impression on Gandhi. During his father's illness (1885) a friend of his father, Ladhe Maharaj, used to visit their house and recite the *Ramayana* to him in Tulsidas's version. Gandhi was present during these recitations. He later on described '*Ramayana*' of Tulsidas as the greatest book in all devotional literature. He see it as embodying the idea that truth is the foundation of all merit and virtue and Ramnam is a door of purification even for the illiterate. Rama as an ideal man, with heroic qualities, is regarded as God like. (see personal god).

Vivekanand also exerted profound influence on Gandhi. His conception that 'service to the poor is service to God' impressed him. In Vivekanand the combination of two ideals – the individual salvation and the universal well-being could be found. Vivekanand brought social context to religion to make it meaningful and purposive. Gandhi humanized religion by making the individual supreme. He could not find God apart from rest of the human activity. He made religion, the religion of service and he held that God could be realized only through service.

All these concepts viz. truth, non-violence, service, renunciation, morality are commonly found in all religions. They are of greater significance and bear perennial relevance. Gandhi gave utmost importance to the purity of means and ends in recognition of the significance of the moral law binding on man.

## Gandhi on Religion and Politics

Gandhi was an ardent supporter and practitioner of religion in politics. It was under the profound influence of Gopal Krishna Gokhle, Gandhi's political Guru, he learnt to spiritualize politics. Gokhale gave to India the mantra, 'Politics must be spiritualized and brought politics and religion together. Gandhi said, "Gokhale taught me that the dream of every Indian who claims to love his country should be not to glorify in language but to spiritualize the political life of the country. He inspired my life so I wish to purify myself and spiritualize myself. I have dedicated myself to that ideal."[28]

Politics divorced from religion, has absolutely no meaning. "...those who say that religion has nothing to do with politics do not know what religion means".[29] Gandhi does not look upon politics as a game of deception, exploitation, coercion and suppression. Instead, he regards it as an art of doing what is morally right and way of serving humanity on a mass scale. Both religion and politics have the same object. For what a religion stands for? Gandhiji's answer was, "I believe in the fundamental truth of all great religions of the world... They were at the bottom all one and were all helpful to one another. Each religion desires upliftment of man's life and gives it a purpose." The object of politics too was serving the cause of the people. It is here that the religious activity and political activity, for Gandhiji, intermingle with each other. It is here that he thought of religion as 'participating in politics'. Much damage has been done to humanity throughout the world by separating religion from politics. Ordinarily people think that religion is a matter of private concern whereas politics is concerned with public affairs. But Gandhi said that this divorce between private and public conduct is baseless. Politics is as essential as religion for the good and welfare of humanity. Politics divorced from morality or religion is like a corpse which soon begins to stink. Thus Gandhi tried to revolutionize politics by ethics.

Lord Irwin, the viceroy of India, was quite confused when he wrote after his first meeting with Gandhi. "Mr. Gandhi's religious and moral views are admirable, but I confess that I find it difficult to understand the practice of them in politics".[30] Actually, those who think that why Gandhi mixed religion with politics, don't know what he meant by religion. "Let me explain what I mean by religion. It is not the Hindu religion which I certainly prize above all other religions, but the religion, which transcends Hinduism, which changes one's very nature, which binds one indissolubly to the truth within. It is the permanent element in human nature... leaves the soul restless until it has found itself."[31] Gandhi accepted that he cannot conceive of politics without religion. Indeed "religion should pervate every one of our actions. Here religion does not mean sectarianism. It means a belief in ordered moral government of the universe. It is not less real because it is unseen. This religion transcends Hinduism, Islam, Christianity etc. It does not supersede them. It harmonizes them and gives then reality."[32]

Gandhi held that religion should pervade every texture of the human life. For him, human life is an undivided whole and life can be never drawn between different compartments social, political and religious, nor between ethics and politics. All act and react upon another. Religion does not mean exclusion of politics from its domain. Politics apart from religion is a dirt. He categorically wanted to bring religion into politics as for him the road to salvation lies through incessant toil in the service of his country and of humanity. "I want to identify myself with everything that lives. I want to live at peace with both friend and foe. Thus, for me, there is no politics devoid of religion. Politics without religion is a death trap as it kill the soul".[33]

Gandhi was compelled to enter into political field as he felt that he could not do the minimum social service without entering into politics "for me politics bereft of religion is absolute dirt ever to be shunned. Politics concerns nations and that which concerns the welfare of nations must be one of the concern of a man who is religiously inclined... Therefore, in politics also we have to establish the Kingdom of heaven. The core of Gandhi's position lies in his belief that while "politics today encircles us like the coils of a snake from which one cannot get out no matter how one tries", the only way of wrestling with the snake is to introduce religion into politics. Religion means a spiritual commitment which is total.

Religion binds man to God and man to man. Gandhi declared that religions are not for separating men from one to another, but they are meant to bind them. The religion based politics of Gandhi has laid utmost stress on the moral values to set his politics on right action with an object to keep politics apart from the evils such as corruption, injustice and expediency away. Gandhi said that all fundamental religions and ethical values which are common to all great religions, have to be incorporated in the political philosophy. The religious basis of Gandhian politics means the supremacy of the concept of the moral right of conscience. Gandhi felt that the religious ethics of piety, forgiveness, meekness, humility and universal tolerance should guide all human actions.

Religion and politics must alike embrace all walks of life. Gandhiji was for religion, but he was not in favour of a particular religion. He was for politics, but he was not in favour of politics that forced man to live the lives of the slaves. His religion was the religion that binds man with truth and his politics was to make man help seek the truth and serve humanity. That is why he made no case for separation of either politics from religion or religion from politics.

## Gandhi and Tilak: A Dichotomy

Politics has generally been regarded as an aspect of human life where the moral values do not apply. It is considered as a game in which expediency must take precedence over morality. Here, the main controversy was between Tilak and Gandhi. Tilak was of the opinion that politics could not be regarded solely from a religious standpoint. In January 1920 Tilak wrote to Gandhi, "Politics is a game of worldly people, and not of *sadhus*, and instead of maxim "*akkhodhenajine kkhodham*" (conquer anger by non-anger) as preached by Buddha, I prefer to rely on the maxim of Shri Krishna, "*ye gatthaa nam parapadyamthe thaamasthatthaiva bhajaamyaham*" (in whatever way men resort to me, even so do I render to them).. Both methods are equally honest and righteous but the one is more suited to this world than the other."[34]

Gandhi replied, "for me there is no conflict between the two texts... The Buddhist text lays down an eternal principle. The text from the *Bhagwad Gita* shows to me how the principle of conquering hate by love, untruth by truth, can and must be applied. If it be true that God metes out the same measure to us that we mete out to others, it follows that, if we would escape condign punishment, we may not return anger for anger but gentleness even against anger. And this is the law not for unworldly but essentially for the worldly. The epitome of religions is to promote '*Purushartha*', and '*Purushartha*' is nothing but a desperate attempt to become a '*sadhu*', i.e. to become a gentleman in every sense of term".[35]

So, if they differed in their conception of politics, this was because they also diverged in their views of religion. Tilak believed that a religious ideal may be very high guide but there must be a practical ideal in our political activities. A mere high religious ideal does not prove very useful in practical politics. So Tilak and Gandhi both disagree with each other. Gandhi's full reliance on moral power both in personal and public life and his strict observance of non-violence, fasting etc. made Tilak quiet confused. He (Tilak) was greatly surprised when he knew that Gandhi was a devout *Vaishnav*. He remarked, "It is strange that up to now I did not know Gandhi's religion. People will laugh at my ignorance about such a great man. I was under the impression that Gandhi was a Jain, because all his opinions and teachings favour of the Jain teachings than the Hindu religion. But these means are of no use in politics, which is required to change its attitude from time- to-time. Exalted religious principles or abstract doctrines about truth are not of much value in the present political game. I don't think that *Satyagraha* and fasting will have any effect upon the mind of our rulers who are adepts in political warfare. We must use against them the same means as they used against us as their tactics change, so must ours".[36]

This remark clearly indicates the difference between the attitudes of Tilak and Gandhi. Gandhi certainly believed in soul force rather than the power of brute force. He humbly submits,

I have nothing new to teach the world 'Truth and non-violence are as old as the hills". Gandhi tried to appeal to one's heart, i.e. one's inner sense of goodness rather than to mere reason. This is because he was fully convinced that a human being is essentially moral or righteous. "Men and beasts are alike in matters of eating, sleeping and fearing. '*Dharma*' alone is the additional prerogative of man and those who are devoid of '*Dharma*' are like beasts". Politics certainly can be dangerous and easily corruptible, but it is not beyond redemption and it can serve a great purpose, if its corrupting nature is duly diagnosed and continually countered through an effective process of moral and spiritual purification.

## Gandhi on God: The Personal and Impersonal

Religion represents the way man conceives and relates himself to God. Gandhi postulates both personal and impersonal God. The 'formal', customary' 'organised' or 'historical' religions centre on the personal God and the 'pure', 'true' or 'eternal' religion around the impersonal god. For Gandhi Hinduism, Islam, Christianity and the other religions are all based on specific conceptions of a personal God. They involve district forms of prayer, worship, rituals and beliefs. The 'pure' and the 'true' religion lies beyond them. It has nothing to do with rituals, beliefs and organization. It recognizes that the universe is pervaded and governed by a cosmic power and represents the purest form of spirituality. Gandhi said "There is an indefinable mysterious power that pervades everything. I feel it, thought I don't see it. It is this unseen power which makes itself felt. It transcends the senses. But it is possible to reason out the existence of God to a limited extent. Even in ordinary affairs we know that people do not know who rules or why, and how he rules. And yet they know that there is a power that certainly rules."[37] Later on, he preferred to call it *Satya* or Truth and thought that this was the "only correct and fully significant"[38] description of god. For a long time, Gandhi believed, that 'God is truth' but later on he reversed the proposition and said that 'Truth is God'.

Gandhi's personal image of God was 'Ram'. In his autobiography, Gandhi said that he recite *Ramayana* Mantra 'Ramnam' to overcome a fear of ghosts and spirits[39] This Ramnam mantra is the unfailing panacea for all ills. He continued to worship God in person of Ram even to the point of dedicating his last words to him at the moment of death 'Hey Ram'. When he explained what the India of his dreams would be like, he often used the image of '*Ram Rajya*', where there would be 'rights alike of prime and pauper', sovereignty of the people based on pure moral authority, rule over self', 'the kingdom of righteousness on earth'.[40]

Gandhi's impersonal God was 'Truth' or 'Satya'. His auto-biography reveals the early roots of his concern for seeking truth. He was inspired by Raja Harishchandra to follow truth. "Why should not all be truthful like Harishchandra"? Was the question he asked himself day and night. Through numerous experiences Gandhi found that morality is the basis of all things and that truth is the substance of all morality'. After reading Tolstoy in 1905 Gandhi considered, *ahimsa* to be the only means of attaining truth. Even his concept of '*Satyagraha*' may be literally translated as 'holding firm to '*Sat*' (Truth). In the *Mahabharta*, it has been said that "Put a thousand *Yajnas* (sacrifices) in one pan of a balance and truth in the other. Truth will be found to weigh heavier".[41] Gandhi's Ram Rajya is often referred to as '*Satyuga*', the golden age of truth. Gandhi sees the whole Hindu tradition as a 'relentless' pursuit after truth.

Gandhi held that the world truth or *Satya* is derived from '*Sat*' which implies 'being'. It is only truth that exists in reality and nothing else. That is the reason why '*Sat*' or 'truth' is attributed to god. "To me God is truth and love; God is ethics and morality. God is fearlessness. God is the source of light and life and yet above and beyond all these God is conscience".[42] Truth is the knowledge acquired by identity or it is an integral experience of reality when truth is experienced, all doubts and differences are removed, all discords and discrepancies are vanished and the human life is transformed by the realization of truth to experience bliss. So, there is no true knowledge in the absence of truth.

Radhakrishnan said that the real quality of religion is brought out by man's incessant search and unending quest to know the truth of things. There is a need to keep up the pursuit of the truth until man is able to experience it.[43] The pursuit of truth makes man dignified and a really civilized human being. Truth resides in every human heart and every one has to be guided by truth. Gandhi in his search of truth found non-violence as a means to reach the truth, which is the end. Gandhi said that the definition 'Truth is God' gives me the greatest satisfaction. And when you want to find truth as god, the only inevitable means is love, that is, non-violence and since I believe that ultimately the means and ends are convertible terms, I should not hesitate to say that God is love"[44]. When we say 'truth is God' it means that truth should be the object of worship. It enables us to see God face-to-face. Truth is something which alone is real for nothing is or exists in reality except truth. Truth is the sovereign principle which includes numerous other principles. Truth is not only truthfulness in words but truthfulness in thought. "For me the voice of God or conscience of truth or the inner voice mean one and the same thing. The only way for the realization of truth is through Ahimsa. I am prepared to sacrifice the things dearest to me in pursuit of this quest".[45] So, truth is the only correct and fully significant name for god.

## Equal Respect for all Religions

Gandhi earnestly studied the sacred writings of Christianity, Islam, Sikhism, Buddhism as well as Hinduism. He found examples of truth and non-violence in all the religions. So, equal respect for all religions was central principle in Gandhian thought. He said that "all the great religions of the world stand on a level of equality because they stem from the same God and converge towards the same point. All of them embody truth because they are all divinely inspired; there is divine inspiration in the holy books of the Hindus as in those of the Christians, the Muslims and the Parsees. There is as much divinity in Krishna as in Jesus and Mohammad".[46] Gandhi again said, "God is one whether we call him *Ishwara* or *Khuda*, and that his commands are same for all. We should not harm others for what we regard as truth or right. We should be prepared to die for truth. This is my view is the essence of all religions."[47]

All religions are essentially identical because (a) it is one truth/god that inspires all religions; (b) all seek truth; they are different paths to the same goal; (c) all believe in moral order/a universe governed by moral law; this law is God/truth; (d) all affirm the same fundamental morality; and religion is essentially morality (non-violence, truth, love); (e) all respect a higher power; (f) all religions have served in embellishing mankind, all have produced great saints–i.e. self sacrificing persons. The Budha, Christ, Mohammad, Guru Nanak all lived lives of self sacrifice and renunciation. So, there was an underlying unity in all religions. 'The time has passed when the followers of one religion could stand and say, ours is the only true religion and all others are false. According to Gandhi "God, *Allah, Rama, Narayan*, *Ishwar, Khuda* were descriptions of the same being" "God's grace and revelation were not the monopoly of any race or nation".[48] My approach to other religions is never a fault finding critic but as a devotee hoping to find the like beauties in other religions and wishing to incorporate in my own the good. I may find in them and miss in mine.

Gandhi was quite confused and un-persuaded when he wrote, "I could not swallow the belief that Jesus Christ alone was the son of God and only those believing in him could attain salvation. If God could have sons then we are all his sons."[49] Even on Hinduism he said "I could not make up my mind either about Hinduism being the perfect or greatest religion. It's limitations were clearly evident to me. If untouchability was really a part of Hinduism then it was certainly an excrescence and a corruption. I could not make sense of the multiplicity of sects and caste".[50] Gandhi rejected everything that was against reason and against humanity. "God did not create men with the badge of superiority or inferiority; no scripture which labels a human being as inferior or untouchable because of his or her birth can command our allegiance. It is denial of God and truth".[51] Since God creates and loves all human beings, a true religion must be based on the twin principles of the unity of all men and of all life. The greater the scope for compassion in a way of life, the more religion it has. So, believing in all fundamental moral values is common to all great religions of the world.

Gandhi said, "I don't believe in the exclusive divinity of the Vedas. I believe the *Bible*, the *Koran* and the Zend Avesta to be as much divinely inspired as the *Vedas*. My belief in the Hindu

Scriptures does not require me to accept every word and every verse as divinely inspired... I declined to be bound by any interpretation if it is repugnant to reason of moral sense."[52]

Though Gandhi believed that all religions were true, he did not consider them infallible. As they were the creation of human beings therefore they can have something of imperfection in them. After long study and experience Gandhi came to the conclusion – (a) all religions are true, (b) all religion can have errors in them. A true religion binds man to god and man to man. "Does Islam bind Muslims only to Muslims and antagonize the Hindu? Was the message of the Prophet peace only for and between Muslims and war against Hindus or Non-Muslims? Are eight crores of Muslims to be fed with this which I can only describe as poison? Those who are instilling this poison into the Muslim mind are rendering the greatest disservice to Islam. I know that it is not Islam. I have lived with and among Muslims not for one day but closely and almost uninterruptedly for twenty years. Not one Muslim taught me that Islam was an anti-Hindu religion".[53]

In the modern context, religion has divided people instead of binding them together. These religious conflicts have been generated because of the misunderstanding of religious teachings. We should understand the fundamental truth of all great religions of the world. They are all God given. At bottom they are all one and helpful to one another. There will be no lasting peace on earth unless we learn not merely to tolerate but even to respect the other faiths as our own. A reverent study of the sayings of different teachers of humanity is a step in the direction of such mutual respect. "I do not share the belief that there can or will be on earth one religion. I am striving to find a common factor and to induce mutual tolerance. Tolerance gives us spiritual insight, which is as far from fanaticism as the North Pole from the South".[54]

## Conclusion

J.J. Doke summed up Gandhi's religious thought well, "I few days ago, I was told that 'he is a Buddhist'. Not long since a Christian newspaper described him as 'a Christian Mohammaden', an extra ordinary mixture indeed. His views are too closely allied to

Christianity to be entirely Hindu, and his sympathies are so wide and catholic that one would imagine he has reached a point where the formulae of sects are meaningless".[55]

Gandhi did not envision one religion but mutual respect and tolerance of the different religions. "I don't except the India of my dreams to develop one religion, i.e. to be wholly Hindu, or wholly Christian, or wholly Muslims. But I want it to be wholly tolerant, with its religions working side by side with one another." True religion breaks down the barriers between one faith and other faith. Where such tolerance becomes a law of life, conflict between different faiths becomes impossible. As all religions are one at source, we have to synthesize them. What we need today is not a religion which promotes separatism and fundamentalism or a religion which results in bloodshed but a religion which contributes to the national integration, progress, mutual cooperation, peace and uphold moral values and keeps politics at the service of mankind.

## Notes

1. *Encyclopedia Americana* (1976), Vol.23, p.342.
2. *The New Oxford Illustrated Dictionary* (1978), Vol.2, p.1427.
3. Veerraju Sharma, *Gandhian Philosophy – Its Relevance Today*, New Delhi, Decent Books, 1999 p.32.
4. Roger Scrution, *A Dictionary of Political Thought* (1982), p.399.
5. S.M. Tiwari, "Four Questions of Gandhi's Philosophy: An Attempt at their Answers" *Gandhi Marg*, Vol.51, July 1969, p.208.
6. Justice S. Mohan, "Equality of Faith," *The Hindustan Times*, 16th April 1993.
7. Ogburn and Nimkoff, *A Hand book of Sociology*, p.488.
8. S. Radhakrishnan, *Religion in a Changing World*, London, George Allen and Unwin Ltd.; 1967 p.102.
9. D. Nesy, "Ethical Religíon of Truth, Love and Suffering" in A.D. Mishra (ed), *Gandhian Approach to Contemporary Problems*, New Delhi, Mittal Publications, 1996 p.35.
10. M. K. Gandhi, Ethical Religion, Ahmedabad, Nawajivan, 1968, p.19.
11. *Harijan*, October 3, 1936, p.268.
12. M.K. Gandhi, *My Religion*, Ahmedabad, Navajivan, 2002, p.3.
13. *Ibid.*, p.3.
14. *Harijan*, 10th February 1940, p.445.
15. M.K. Gandhi, *My Religion*, p.4
16. M.K. Gandhi, *Autobiography, the Story of My Experiments with Truth*, Ahmedabad, Navajivan Publishing House, 2000, p.57.

17. *Ibid.*, p.58.
18. *Young India* 20th Sep. 1928, p.319.
19. Raghvan Iyer, *The Moral and Political Writings of Mahatma Gandhi*, Vol.I, New Delhi, Oxford, pp.145-146.
20. M.K. Gandhi, *Autobiography*, p. 75.
21. *C.W.M.G.*, Vol., pp.90-91.
22. *C.W.M.G.*, Vol.32, pp.593-602.
23. *C.W.M.G.*, Vol.32, p.11.
24. *Ibid.*, p.11.
25. Gummadi Veerraju, *Gandhian Philosophy—Its Relevance Today*, *op.cit.* p.16.
26. *Ibid.*, p.16.
27. M.K. Gandhi, *Hind Swaraj*, or Indian Home Pub., Ahmedabad, Navajivan Publishing House, 1975, p.36.
28. M.K. Gandhi, *In Search of Supreme*, Ahmadabad, Navajivan, 2002, Vol.II, p.3.
29. Raghvan Iyer, *The Moral and Political thought of Mahatma Gandhi*, London, Oxford University Press, 1973, p.41.
30. B.R. Nanda, *Gandhi and Religion*, Gandhi memorial Lecturi Gandhi Smriti and Darshan Samiti, 1990. p.1.
31. Raghvan Iyer, *Moral and Political Thought of Mahatma Gandhi, op. cit.*, p. 42.
32. *C.W.M.G.*, Vol.71, p.177.
33. *Young India*, 3rd April 1924, p.112.
34. Raghvan Iyer, *The Moral and Political Thought of Mahatma Gandhi, op. cit.*, pp. 50-51.
35. *Ibid.*, p.51.
36. *Ibid*, p.52.
37. M.K. Gandhi, *My God*, Ahmedabad, Navajivan, 2004, p.3.
38. Bhiku Parekh, *Gandhi's Political Philosophy*, London, Macmillian Press, 1989, p.70.
39. M.K. Gandhi, *Autobiography*, p.27.
40. Margaret Chatterjee, *Gandhi's Religious Thought*, London, Macmillan Press, 1983, p.17.
41. *Ibid.*, p.60.
42. *Young India*, 5th March 1925, pp.80-81.
43. S. Radhakrishnan, *In Search for Truth*, New Delhi, Hind Pocket Book 1989, p.9.
44. M.K. Gandhi, *All Men are Brothers*, p.64.
45. M.K. Gandhi, *Autobiography*, p.XI.
46. In Anil Dutta Mishra, (Ed.) *Gandhian Approach to Contemporary Problems*, New Delhi, Mittal Publications, 1996 p.46.
47. Raghvan Iyer, *The Moral and Political Writings of Mahatma Gandhi*,Vol.I, p.520.
48. B.R. Nanda, *Gandhi and Religion*, pp.12-13.

49. M.K. Gandhi, *Autobiography*, p.13.
50. *Ibid.*, p.14.
51. J.B. Kriplani, *Gandhi His Life and Thought*, New Delhi, Publications Division, 1970, p.337.
52. *Ibid.*, pp.339-340.
53. *C.W.M.G.*, Vol.72, pp.27-28.
54. M.K. Gandhi, *My Religion*, pp.19-20.
55. J.J. Doke, *M.K. Gandhi – An Indian Patriot*, New Delhi, Publications Division, 1992, p.12.

# 15

# Gandhi's View of Politics

*– Jai Narain Sharma*

Gandhi is known to the world as the one man more than any other who is mainly responsible for the mighty upheaval of the Indian nation, which has shaken and loosened its chains. Politicians are not generally reputed to take religion seriously, for the values to which they are committed, such as the political control of one people by another, the economic exploitation of the poorer and weaker human beings, are so clearly inconsistent with the values of religion that the latter could not be taken too seriously or interpreted too accurately. But for Gandhi, all is of one piece. "To see the universal and all pervading Spirit of Truth face-to-face one must be able to love the meanest of creation as oneself. And a man who aspires after that cannot afford to keep out of any field of life. That is why my devotion to Truth has drawn me into the field of politics; and I can say without the slightest hesitation and yet in all humility, that those who say that religion has nothing to do with politics do not know what religion means!"[1] Again, "I have no desire for the perishable kingdom of earth, I am striving for the kingdom of heaven, which is spiritual deliverance. For me the road to salvation lies through incessant toil in the service of my country and of humanity. I want to identify myself with everything that lives. In the language of the *Gita*, I want to live at peace with both friend and foe. So my patriotism is for me a stage on my journey to the land of eternal freedom and peace. Thus it will be seen that for me there are no politics devoid of religion. They subserve religion. Politics bereft of religion are a death trap because they kill the soul."[2] If man as a political being has not been much of a success, it is because he has kept religion and politics apart, thus misunderstanding both. For Gandhi, there is no religion apart from human activity. Though in the present circumstances of India, Gandhi happens to be a political revolutionary, who refuses to accept tyranny or acquiesce in slavery, he is far from the uncompromising type of revolutionary whose abstraction forces men into unnatural and inhuman shapes. In the acid test of experience he remains, not a politician or a reformer, not a philosopher or a moralist, but someone composed of them all, an essentially religious person endowed with the highest and most human qualities and made more lovable by the consciousness of his own limitations and by an unfailing sense of humour.

Gandhi said of himself "I am not a man who sits down and thinks out problems syllogistically, I am a man of action. I react to a situation intuitively. Logic comes afterwards, it does not precede the event."[3] As is well known, he was a "political actionist and a practical philosopher; he was not a theorist."[4] To quote Professor Nirmal Kumar Bose "in the traditional language of ancient India, he is a Ksatriya, not a Brahmana. But his greatness lies in the fact that he has accepted and advocated, the law of love as the supreme law of our being and has lived his life accordingly; he can be regarded as a warrior Brahmana, but he cannot be said to be a sage philosopher Brahmana." How mistaken was Montagu's judgement about Gandhi "He lives practically on air and is a pure visionary".[5]

Gandhi did not set himself to the task of a systematic presentation of his views about the nature of political activity. The construction of a system of political philosophy did never interest or bother him. His ideas were thrown off as comments on given, concrete realities and were intended to give a new shape to events and for the remaking of man as a moral person. It was in the nature of the circumstances that Gandhi did nor could he possibly, evolve a definite and clear cut political theory. For him "theory is all grey-evergreen is life (Goethe). The place of theory was subordinate to that of organic unity, i.e., life. It would be an unrewarding task to look for a consistent, systematized body of thought in Gandhi's writings for he owed absolute allegiance to none of the prevailing schools Anarchist, Marxist, Liberal, Democratic, etc. And construction of any rigid, fixed'ism' was alien to his nature such a continually evolving personality he was. One may, on close examination of Gandhi's writings, come to the conclusion that his political philosophy is indeed elusive. But that does not make any the less significant the basic core of his thought. As has been pointed out by Dr. Bondurant, the contribution of Gandhian political theory "has been not alone to the development of a social and political method. It extends further into the realm of political thought and challenges the substantial presuppositions of the mainstream of political theory."[6] It is in this challenge to the current political theories that its significance lies. The study of Gandhi's political theory is relevant from that point of view.

From the standpoint of methodology. Gandhi's approach was deductive, empirical and pragmatic. He deduced certain conclusions from his basic assumptions metaphysical and ethical. Metaphysics, Ethics, Economics, Sociology and Politics were intertwined. He was for, in Toynbee's language, 'etherialization', that is, spiritualization, of politics. Spiritualizing meant for Gandhi moralizing. But he was no moral fadist. Any student of Gandhi's political thought and his eventful life will readily see for himself that he developed a keen empirical outlook towards life in general and political and social events in particular. He observed, experienced and, suggested the way out. His plea for the removal of untouchability, his crusading mission for communal amity, his solutions for the economic regeneration of poverty stricken India, bear testimony to his rich experience of life based upon empirical investigation. This note of pragmatism is evident in his, political thought. But so, who can help without being a pragmatist in this pragmatic world? And pragmatic approach necessarily leads one to eclecticism. He was eclectic enough to draw from different sources and schools what fitted in with his basic outlook of truth and non-violence. The 'eclectic alchemy' of Gandhi's political philosophy evolved an amalgam out of heteregenous founts of his fundamental faith and inspiration.

His approach to politics was indeed moral. And that lends a special significance to his theory in this age of amoral politics. It is true that he did not care much for the historical and quantitative methods of politics as has been noted by V. P. Varma, but the deficiencies that follow therefrom have been more than compensated in the form of giving a moral direction to politcs. This moral orientation is evident in his analysis of the concepts of political theory, viz. state, democracy, freedom, rights, etc. It is from a normative or valuational standpoint norms or values as he understood and accepted to be fundamental that he elaborated his concepts of political theory.

One may tend to infer that in such an approach of Gandhi's there is more of ethics than of politics. Benoy Sarkar rebutted this point of view. To quote him: "Such a criticism can come only from those who by politics understand solely or chiefly the constitution making, programme planning or party bossing. But in this kind of ethics of politics Gandhi is in very good company with Fichte, as author of the Baden an die Deutsche Nation, and Sukracarya as author of the Nitisara, nay, with Plato, as author of the Republic."[8]

Since he was not committed to any exclusive school of political thought, and since his writings had been responses to particular situations, though within a basic conceptual framework, it is indeed a problem to categorize his thought. His concern was more in the substance of things than in attributing labels to what he thought and for the realization of which he worked. For a western student of Gandhian political theory it is rather difficult to comprehend the indigenous terms like Rama Raj, etc., which he used on different occasions in defining his political ideal. But Gandhi was no traditionalist to cling to the age old meanings of those terms. It was quite characteristic of him to add new meanings to them, so that in quality they became quite different from what they popularly stood for. As has been noted by Nirmal Kumar Bose "Perhaps this was one of the mechanisms by means of which Gandhi kept himself rooted in the past, and yet tried to carry India forward in directions radically different from ancient tradition."[9] The French historian and sociologist, Louis Massignon, has aptly remarked "He was a genius in investing common words with unique meanings."[10] Hence, one must try to understand terms employed by him in the sense he did so and in the connotation he attributed to those terms. One faces another difficulty in a theoretical analysis of his concept of state. Gandhi being "built of tremendous opposites" a unique combination of a prophet and a politician of genius sometimes spoke and wrote in terms of the ultimate ideal and sometimes in terms of the immediately realizable objective. And there emerged two Gandhis one philosophical and the other practical politician eager to come to grip with the realities, with a keen sense of the objective. The citizen leader Gandhi moved with the times and his theory underwent a continuous process of evolution. This evolution, is a distinctive note of the Gandhian theory. Gandhi would have been marked as a political leader of least significance if he could not have moved with the times and reflected the historical urges and aspirations of the Indian masses. There was, indeed, a gap between the ideal political order he envisaged and the national democratic state for the creation of which he led the Indian nation. This hiatus between the ideal and the actual was not of his making; it was implicit in the given objective situation in Gandhi's India. This was not a case of political opportunism as has been sometimes alleged, but a clear expression of astute realism which speaks of his sagacity and political maturity.

For Gandhi the modern age was the age of politics par excellence. Almost all aspects of individual and social life were directly or indirectly organised and administered by the state. Its presence was ubiquitous, and all human relationships were politically mediated. He thought this was particularly true of India and all other colonies.[11] Since politics was so pervasive, Gandhi advanced the fascinating thesis that it was the central terrain of action in the modern age. In a politically dominated age it was impossible to serve ones fellow men and eliminate, social and economic ills without active political involvement. Gandhi thought that if political life could be spiritualized, it would have a profoundly transformative effect on the rest of society. In every age a specific area of life was the unique testing ground of religion and morality and offered them a unique opportunity to revitalise themselves. In the modern age it was politics, and no religion could be taken seriously that failed to address itself to its political challenges. In the modern age and especially in India, political action was therefore the only available path to *moksha*, a truly revolutionary view in the Indian context.[12] The fundamental principles of Hinduism were being weighed in the political scale, and its only chance of regenerating itself lay in reaffirming them on the political plane. As Gandhi put it:

"Every age is known to have its predominant mode of spiritual effort best suited for the attainment of *moksha*. Whenever the religious spirit is on the decline, it is revived through such an effort in tune with the times. In this age, our degradation reveals itself through our political condition ... Gokhale not only perceived this right at the beginning of his public life but also followed the principle in action. Everyone had realised that popular awakening could be brought about only through political activity. If such activity was spiritualised, it could show the path of *moksha.*

"... In this age, only political *sannyasis* can fulfill and adorn the ideal of *sannyasa*; others will more likely than not disgrace the *sannyasi's* saffron garb. No Indian who aspires to follow the way of true religion can afford: to remain aloof from politics. In other words, one who aspires to a truly religious life cannot fail to undertake public service as his mission, and we are today so much caught up in the political machine that service of the people is impossible without taking part in politics. In olden days, our peasants, though ignorant of who ruled them, led their simple lives free from fear; they can no longer afford to be so unconcerned. In the circumstances that obtain today, in following the path of religion they must take into account the political conditions. If our *sadhus*, *rishis*, *munis*, *maulvis* and priests realised the truth of this, we would have a Servants of India Society in every village, the spirit of religion would come to prevail all over India, the political system which has become odious would reform itself."[13]

For Gandhi then every Indian had a duty in the modem age to become politically involved. The purpose of political engagement was to regenerate India along the lines discussed earlier. Political involvement therefore took a number of forms and occurred at a variety of levels. Although participation in the struggle for independence was obviously important, it was not the most important and could itself take different forms. Since independence was merely formal and had no meaning without national regeneration. Politics' in Gandhi's view consisted in revitalizing Indian society, culture and character by working in the villages, fighting against local injustices, helping people acquire courage and self-respect, building up their organised strength and in general devoting oneself to any of the 18 items of the Constructive Programme. Every activity that contributed to India's regeneration and made it just and cohesive was political in nature. Politics was not necessarily connected with, let alone exhausted in the state. Indeed, the fact that it should be so understood showed the extent of degeneration both in India and elsewhere. The state had become the sole arena of political activity because modern man had surrendered all his moral and social powers to it. His regeneration consisted in regaining his powers and running his life himself in co-operation with others. Since 'true politics' was primarily concerned with and spiritual development, it involved removing his 'addiction' to the state and necessarily occurred outside it.

To be sure, Gandhi's conclusion that politics was a spiritual activity was not novel and had been advanced by a large number of his predecessors such as Gokhale, Tilak, Ranade, B.C. Pal and Aurobindo. Indeed, the phrase 'spiritualistion of politics' seems to have been first used by Gokhale, and Gandhi himself acknowledged that he had borrowed it from his 'political guru'. Several important differences, however, separated them from Gandhi. First, unlike them he offered well-considered reasons for regarding politics as a spiritual activity. Second, while many of them separated politics and spirituality and talked of spiritualising politics, for Gandhi the two were identical. Politics as he defined it was itself a spiritual ativity, and all true spirituality culminated in politics. Third, for most of them spirituality largely meant morality, and politics was spiritual in the sense of being a moral activity. Hardly any of them saw it as a vehicle of *moksha*. Indeed, they would have been horrified by such a view. Finally, many of them generally defined morality in social terms and equated politics with social reform. Gandhi was one of the first to define morality in political terms, and politics in terms of active struggle against injustices and oppression.

Gandhi's political theory cuts across several moral, religious and philosophical traditions and rests on an unusually broad philosophical foundation, showing both the rich harvest that can be garnered from and the problems involved in a cross cultural dialogue. Enjoying access to several cultures, he is overwhelmed by none of them and is able to chisel out an autonomous space from which to evaluate them. Like a multilingual novelist skilfully playing with words and images drawn from different languages, he borrows ideas from different traditions, all of which he regards as part of his common human heritage, and produces ingenious combinations, some unstable, some beautifully integrated, but all fascinating.

On the basis of his theory of man Gandhi proposes that a well considered philosophy of politics must find ways of reconciling the claims of the individual, the political community and mankind, the three fundamental axes of moral life for him. Every human being is necessarily an individual, a uniquely constituted, self determining agent coming to terms with himself and the world in his own way and at his own pace. He is the architect and centre of a unique world of relationships structuring and organising it in his own distinct manner. To take over his life and run it for him is to violate his integrity, destroy his wholeness and perpetrate a most unacceptable form of moral violence.

As Gandhi rightly argues, an individual is not an abstract atom but a member of a specific community which profoundly shapes and moulds his deepest instincts, aspirations, unconscious memories habits and ways of life and thought. Since it constitutes and structures him as a self determining agent, it is the necessary basis and presupposition of his existence. It is his spiritual home; he belongs to and feels at ease in it and becomes rootless and dries up outside it. His self respect and love of himself are inseparable from his respect and love of it. As Gandhi argues, the deepest ties of affection, love and loyalty by which he is bound to it are by definition not a matter of conscious choice. They are pre rational and pre-moral and set the limits of his moral choices. Since he derives so much benefit from his community, knows it better than any other and is bound to its members by ties of mutual expectations, rational reflection confirms and reinforces the pre- moral ties.

For Gandhi mankind is the third fundamental unit of moral life. Since all men are moral beings, they enjoy ontological equality and make both negative and positive claims on one another whose strength and urgency cannot be diminished by the contingent factor of physical distance. If a man claimed that as a moral agent his integrity should be considered inviolate and his freedom and self determination not be interfered with, he could not consistently refuse to acknowledge the similar claims of others, let alone interfere with them himself. Unlike many an egalitarian thinker Gandhi grounds moral equality in the unity of all human beings, thereby giving it a philosophical and moral depth. Since humanity is indivisible, men are responsible to and for one another, and it ought to matter to each how others live.

Since the individual, his political community and mankind are: ontologically and morally inseparable, they are all equally important and none can be ignored or treated as a mere means to the other two. As Gandhi observes, a community that treats its members as mere 'resources' or means to its so called collective well-being is guilty of the deepest form of violence and not a moral community at all. And similarly an individual who treats his community as a mere means to his self interest contradicts the basic conditions of his existence and does violence both to it and himself. While this is generally appreciated by most political philosophers, a similar relationship between the community and man kind that Gandhi establishes is not. He rightly maintains that no political community can ignore the claims of those 'outside' its boundaries and still call itself moral. Although territorially outside it, they are very much inside it by virtue of a shared moral nature and ontological and cultural interdependence. As a member of a subject country and race Gandhi was unusually sensitive to this, and knew well that equating the territorial with moral boundaries led to some of the worst and most insidious forms of violence. He rightly insists that every community must recognise the equally legitimate moral claims of others and define and pursue its national interests accordingly. Not to do so is to forfeit the claim, to be a moral community.

Gandhi's spiritual perspective also enables him to notice and highlight some of the morally problematic aspects of the modern state. If man's integrity is inviolate, then the prisons, the domestic use of terror and wars obviously raise disturbing questions. It would not do to say that some men are 'really' brutes and deserve to be locked away, for to give up on them, to put them outside the moral pale and even positively to brutalise them is hardly a form of behaviour consistent with belief in human dignity. A similar problem arises with respect to the poor, the weak and the underprivileged both in other communities and especially in one's own. They are often caught up in a vicious cycle not of their own making and their degradation is often the product of a social order upheld and protected by the state. As Gandhi argues, the modern state is a highly complex institution. Much of its violence is institutionalized, structured, exported abroad, perpetrated behind the backs of its members and cleverly rationalized. It does not cease to exist simply because one does not see it on the streets; indeed what occurs there may be only a reaction to it. Gandhi rightly remarks that it is morally arbitrary to be exercised about one form of violence but turn a blind eye to the others. All forms of violence, those of the state as well as the rioters on the streets, raise questions of justification. The former cannot be justified in terms of the inherently vague ideas of law and order or public interest, for one needs to ask why the maintenance of order and the public interest requires such violence and whether a social order that can only be preserved by massive violence does not need to be radically reconstituted.

Gandhi also raises the important question of the citizen's responsibility for the actions of his government. As he points out, the state is ultimately nothing more than a system of compulsory and institutionalized cooperation, and each of its citizens is a party to its actions and partly responsible for their consequences. Unless he opts out of it altogether, which obviously he cannot, he is implicated in its decisions. Whether he acknowledges it or not, everything he does has a political dimension. He can never be apolitical, and apathy is really a form of moral irresponsibility. A citizen cannot hide behind the facade of collective responsibility for it is composed of and does not replace individual responsibility. As a moral being he has a duty to be concerned about what is done in, his name to this fellowmen both inside and outside his community. As Gandhi points out, the government has a tendency to use the sheer complexity of political life and its monopoly of information to morally overwhelm and paralyse its citizens and foster a culture of moral inertia. Since the entire weight of the state is used to put their consciences to sleep, they have a duty to remain especially alert lest they should be morally seduced or blackmailed into unacceptable compromises.

It is impertinent for any man to set about reforming the universe. He must take up the work that lies nearest to hand. When, on his return from South Africa, he found the people of India suffering from mortified pride, want, pain and degradation, he took up the task of their emancipation as a challenge and an opportunity. It is wrong for the weak to submit to oppression and wrong for the strong to be allowed to oppress. No improvement, he felt, was possible without political freedom. Freedom from subjection be won not by the usual methods of secret societies, armed rebellion, arson and assassination. The way to freedom is neither by abject entreaty nor by revolutionary violence. Freedom does not descend upon a people from above but they have to raise themselves to it by their own effort. The Buddha said "Ye, who suffer, know ye from yourselves; none else compels."[14] In self-purification lies the path to freedom. Force is no remedy. The use of force in such circumstances is foul play. The force of spirit is invisible. Gandhi said "The British want us to put the struggle on the plane of machine-guns. They have weapons and we have not. Our only assurance of beating them is to keep it on the plance where we have the weapons and they have not."[15] If we could combine perfect courage to endure wrong, while resisting it with the perfect charity which abstains from hurting or hating the oppressor, our appeal to the human in our oppressor would become irresistible. To a people oppressed for centuries by outsiders, he gave a new self-respect, a new confidence in themselves, a new assurance of strength. He took hold of ordinary men and women, men and women who were an in credible mixture of heroism and conceit, magnificence and meanness, made heroes out of them and organized an unarmed revolt against British rule. He weaned the country from anarchy and terrorism and saved the political struggle from losing its soul. There were occasions in India's struggle for freedom when he adopted measure which were unintelligible to the mere politician. There are great leaders who know how to bend and flatter in order to draw other men unto them. While they keep their eyes fixed upon the goal, they do not scruple about the means to reach the goal. Not so Gandhi, "If India takes up the doctrine of the sword she may gain a momentary victory, then India will cease to be the pride of my heart. I believe absolutely that India has a mission for the world; however India's acceptance of the doctrine of the sword will be the hour of my trial. My life is dedicated to the service of India through the relilgion of non-violence, which I believe to be the root of Hindusism."[16] He ordered the suspension the movement of non-co-operation when he saw that his people were not able to conform to his high standards. By his withdrawal, he exposed himself to the derision of opponents. "Let the opponent glory in our humiliation and so-called defear. It is better to be charged with cowardice than to be guilty of denial of our oath and sin against God. It is a million times better that I should be the laughingstock of the world than that I should act in sincerely towards myself. I know that the drastic reversal of practically the whole of the aggressive programme may be politically unsound and unwise, but there is no doubt that it religiously sound." What is morally wrong cannot be politically right, On the evening of August 8, 1942, when what is known as the "Quit India" resolution was passed the All-India Congress Committee, Gandhi said: "We must look the world in the face with calm and clear eyes, even though the eyes of the world are bloodshot to-day."[17] When the naval disturbances started in Bombay, he scolded those who organized it: "Hatred is in the air and impatient lovers of the country will gladly take advantage if they can, through violence, to further the cause of independence. I suggest that is wrong at any time and everywhere. But is more wrong and unbecoming in a try whose fighters for freedom have declared to the world that their policy is truth and non-violence."[18] He had faith that the spirit of violence "is a survivial which kill itself in time. It is so contrary to the spirit of India." "I have striven all my life for the liberation of India. But if I can get it only by violence, I would not want it." The means by which freedom is attained are as important end itself. An India made free through immorality be really free. He conducted the struggle with the established government in India as in South Africa, withoutt any trace of racial feeling, with civilized dignity. The transfer of power on August 15, 1947, marked the end of struggle, it has ended in a settlement reached in a spirit of temper and friendliness.

Freedom for Gandhi was not a mere political fact, it was a social realty. He struggled not only to free India from foreign rule but free her from social corruption and communal strife. "I shall work for an India in which the poorest shall feel that it is their country in whose making they have an effective voice; an India in which there shall be no high class and low class of people; an India in which all communities live in perfect harmony. There can be no room in such an India for the curse of untouchability or the curse of intoxicating drinks and drugs. Women will enjoy the same rights as men. Since we shall be at peace with all the rest of the world, neither exploiting nor being exploited, we shall have the smallest army imaginable. All interests, not in conflict with the interests of dumb millions, will be scrupulously respected. Personally, I hate the distinction between foreign and indigenous. This is the India of my dreams."[19]

In the preface to his autobiography, Gandhi wrote that his devotion to truth had drawn him into poloitics, that his power in the political field was derived from the spiritual experiments with himself. He was very much concerned with spiritualization of political life and political institutions. He repeatedly insisted that politics could not be isolated from the deepest things of life. He said that when he found himself drawn into the political coil, he asked himself what was necessary to remain untouched by immortality, untruth and political gains, and decided that a servant of the people must discard all wealth and private possessions. In his own words, 'the ministers and the legislators have to be watchful of their personal and public conduct. They have to be, like Caesar's wife, above suspicion in everything. They may not make private gains for themselves or for their relatives or their friends. If the relatives or friends get any appointment, it must be only because they are the best among the candidates, and their market value is always greater than what they get under the Government. The ministers and legislators have to be fearless in the performance of their duty. They must always be ready to risk the loss of their seat or office".[20]

Gandhi missed no opportunity to expose corruption, just posing the extravagent ways of the rulers with the poverty of the mass of the people. He used to cite corruption as one of the main causes of India's backwardness. He waged a relentless battle against this evil, infact the system which it was heir to, but he was not slow to realize that transfer of power from British to Indian hands would not automatically exercise the evil, especially when the old administrative system continued to prevail. He was aware that after assuming office his own followers might fall into the ways of their British predecessors. He made himself the watchdog of public behaviour of his followers even at the risk of offending many of them.

There is an intersting example of the Mahatma objecting to the Andhra leader, the late T. Parkasam becoming Chief Minister of Madras in 1946 because he had appropriated to himself a purse of Rs. 30,000 given to him by the people of Andhra. Gandhi contended that the money was given to Prakasam not for his personal use, but in capacity as a public man. He, therefore, argued that it should have been made over to the party. When Prakasam ultimately offered to do so, Gandhi pertinently asked him how he proposed to receive it. Prakasam could have no doubt obtained the sum from any of his rich friends, but in Gandhi's eyes it was tantamount to corruption, because in return for the money they would expect some favour from him when he because Chief Minister. The Mahatma took this stand in spite of the fact that T. Prakasam had thrown away a roaring practice at the bar when he plunged into the national struggle and had also given away to the party his entire property worth some hundred of thousands of rupees.[21]

This slide down started almost from the first taste of power in 1937 when Congress Ministerie were formed. The vunerable Mahatma was seriously concerned about growing corruption in Congress ranks and lashed out at it in the columns of '*Harijan*'. In May 1939, he told the Gandhi Seva Sangh workers, "I would go to the length of giving the whole Congress Organization a decent burial, rather than put up with the corruption that is rampat".[22] Nehru felt more or less the same way. In a letter to Gandhi on April 28, 1938 he lamnted, "What is far worse is that we are losing the high position that we have built up with so much labour in the hearts of the people. We are sinking to the level of ordinary politicians who have no principles to standby and where work is governed by a day-to-day opportunism".[23] Gandhi was much relieved when the Congress ministers resigned in October 1939 on political issues arising out of Britain's entry in World War II.

Gandhi's objection to political power was not minimized with establishment of National Government in 1947. He was singularly alone in this respect of declining power even in a free state. Architects of other nations were absorbed in power soon after they were victorious. This is true of those leaders who led a successful revolution and established powerful regimes in their countries, But Gandhi was unique amongst all builders of nations. In his last test amount on January 29, 1948, Gandhi warned Congress about the danger of political corruption and solemnly recommended its dissolution as a political party.[24]

Deviations from the standards set by such an omnibus personality as Gandhi are inevitable. But in no sphere of political life deviation from the Gandhian legacy is as sharp and glaring as in the personal conduct and integrity of politicians. It is not really a deviation but a right reversal of the legacy.

## Notes

1. M. K. Gandhi, *An Autobiography or The Story of My Experiments with Truth*, Ahmedabad, Navajivan Publishing House, 1975, pp. 370-71.
2. *Young India*, 18 6 1925, p. 214.
3. Pyarelal, *Mahatma Gandhi, The Last Phase*, Ahmedabad, Navajivan Publishing House, 1956, Vol. 1, p. 120.
4. Joan V. Bondurant, *Conquest of Violence: The Gandhian Philosophy of Conflict*, Bombay, Oxford University Press, 1959, p. 7.
5. N. K. Bose, *Swaraj or Gandhibad* (a Bengali Publication) Calcutta, I.A.P. Co. Ltd., 1954, p. 19.
6. Joan V. Bondurant, *op. cit.*, p. 189.
7. V. P. Varma, *The Philosophy of Mahatma Gandhi and Sarvodaya*, Agra, Laxmi Narain Agarwal, 1959, p. 168.
8. Benoy Kumar Sarkar, *Creative India*, Lahore, Motilal Banarsi Dass, 1937, p.570.
9. N. K Bose, *Cultural Anthropology*, London, Ara Publishing House, 1961, p. 84.
10. *Gandhian Outlook and Techniques*, New Delhi, Ministry of Education, Government of India, 1953, p. 37.
11. *Young India*, 2-3-1922, p. 135.
12. *Harijan*, 12-9-1936, p. 242.
13. Raghavan N. Iyer, *The Moral and Political Writings of Mahatma Gandhi*, Oxford, Clarendon Press, 1987, Vol. 1, p. 137.
14. S. Radhakrishnan (Ed.), *Mahatma Gandhis Essays and Reflections*, Mumbai, Jaico Publishing House, 2001, p. 343.
15. *Ibid.*

16. *Young India*, 11-8-1920, p. 4.
17. *The Collected Works of Mahatma Gandhi*, New Delhi, Publications Division, Ministry of Information and Broadcasting, Government of India, 1979, Vol. 76, pp. 384-401.
18. *Ibid.*
19. *Young India*, 10-9-1931, p. 253.
20. *Harijan*, September 1947.
21. Surendra Nath Dwivedy and G.S Bhargava, *Political Corruption in India*, New Delhi, Popular Book Service, 1967, p. 7.
22. *Harijan*, May, 1939.
23. *Ibid.*, April, 1939.
24. Jai Narain, *Gandhi's View of Political Power*, New Delhi, Deep and Deep, 1987, p. 119.

# 16

# The Relevance of Gandhism

*– Jita Mishra*

Gandhi neither wished nor willed an 'ism' in his glorified name, but the evolution of Gandhism becomes a global necessity for peace, prosperity, freedom, harmony and survival of the whole human race. Gandhism provides a new hope, new force and above all a new blueprint to solve the challenge of modern world. Gandhism is reminder of something's which the modern world has forgotten, i.e. its basic culture of truth and non-violence.

Mahatma Gandhi was a multifaceted genius who wrote mere not for the pleasure of writing, but always with a purpose and as a guide to action. He applied his mind to a large number of human concerns and left an indelible impact on the social, economic and political forces of the day. He left an everlasting impact on the world at a large because he always spoke and understated the language of the masses and downtrodden. He made the people fearless to fight against injustice and exploitation. He was a man far ahead of his times. Voices all over the world today are re-echoing what Gandhi said about industrialization, mechanization, development, economic growth, empowering women, environmental protection, social justice, communal harmony etc.

New millennium is only six years old, even then human beings, under severe strain are compelled to sit up and reassess their own nature, culture and future. Due to technological development the world is changing fast and we want to keep ourselves in a better position we have to change according to the need of the hour. The change should be for better and with human face, where even the poorest can live in peace and harmony. There should not be any alienation. The technological developments have its own price and we have to pay it. Therefore, the Gandhism become important.

Since the thought process begins in the minds of men. It is the minds of men that need to be molded on Gandhian lines.

Humanity is undergoing almost a phase of moral collapse and ethical nihilism. Service is being given in quest of personal aggrandizement. In the era of the mad rush for power and material gain, the significance of Gandhian principle lies in stressing the permanent value of self-abnegation and to enshrine the primacy of goodness and character in place of the skill of manipulation and self-assertion.[1] Gandhism provides an alternative to solve the problems of unemployment, unequal distribution of wealth, violation of human right, terrorism and poverty.

The whole world is in search of an alternative. Gandhism provides an answer and an alternative. Gandhi's relevance is eternal. His political philosophy possesses a variety of meanings ranging from religious purity to political expediency. Politics was, to Gandhi, not a profession but a vocation. He sought to apply moral values to the difficult domain of politics. He was a 'Karma Yogi' in the true sense of Indian tradition. His moral and political thought is intrinsically linked with his religious and ethical beliefs. Such a thought needs serious study always and more so when the world is so much corrupt and inhuman as the one in which we are living. The ultimate goal, for Gandhi, was the greatest good of all people. Good, to him, means the self-realization and not the material well-being of the individuals or the society. The Gandhian principles are capable of meeting the greatest challenge of the age. The most urgent need of today is the abolition of human suffering as well as of war. Even sarvodaya will be very important in 21st century due to complexity of human behaviour. His philosophy of Sarvodaya, by laying stress on the goodness of human nature, unity of mankind, service of man, application of moral principles considered valid for individuals to group life and inter-state relations, the non-violent process of change, social and economic equality, economic and political decentralization, tries to resolve the various kinds of tensions that disturb domestic and international harmony. It is capable of strengthening the forces of love, creativeness and joy of life. It takes a whole view of man and emphasizes his spiritual nature. In modern context, the concept of sarvodaya can be interpreted as the "awakening of one and all".

Thus, in addition to the awakening of everyone, it refers to the awakening of the total human spirit and personality. Savrodaya is also related to achieving the highest level of self-realization in which one sees one's manifestation in all others.[2]

Thus the tragedy of modern India is that the ruling elite could never understand the crux of Gandhian philosophy. Our quest for social justice and sustainability will remain a dream until we realize what Gandhi meant when he said: that economics is untrue which ignores and disregards moral values. He was also convinced that without democratic decentralization and rural development freedom would not mean anything to the masses of India. He continuously emphasized this through his speeches and writings throughout the freedom struggle. He maintained that the country's prosperity and progress depends upon the villages and if the village perishes, India will perish too. The Swaraj of Gandhi was intrinsically linked with rural development.[3] We would like to remind what Gandhi wrote in the 22nd July 1946 issue of Harijan "Independence must begin at the bottom."[4] Till Indian politics and politicians learn to practice it, the interpretations of Gandhian thought and perspective will need to be reiterated again and again.

Gandhi's social ideas constitute a challenge to the main currents of present civilisation. He advocated abolishment of untouchability. Gandhi tried to abolish the social system through non-violent mean.

Mahatma's ideas about the dangers of Western civilization have assumed significances in the context of several issues concerning the survival of the humanity and evolution of a just and viable world order. Gandhi saw clearly the moral degradation and cultural decay long back. The *Hind Swaraj* of Mahatma Gandhi published in 1909, long before the negative consequences of industrial civilization were exposed to the common experience, must have appeared to the generation of his times, a book of reaction and retreat from modernity and civilization.[5] The fact is that long before the people in the new millennium will be awakened to the peril and limits of unrestrained economic growth and technological innovations, Gandhiji pointed out the pitfalls of industrialism and the damage to nature and man and he strongly criticised the emerging trends of consumer culture in future in all spheres of life and emphasized austerity and the moral principle in development, which is essential for new millennium.

Schumacher, Henderson and Capra were among the earliest to appreciate Gandhi's view on Indian economic system. Henderson's and Schumacher's concern of modern man's mad rush for amassing wealth, his utter disregard for values. In his "Small is beautiful", Schumacher focuses on the reorientation of Science and Technology. As Gandhi said the poor of the world couldn't be helped by mass production, based on sophisticated highly Capital-intensive technology high energy dependent on human labour. The technology of mass production is inherently violent and ecologically damaging, self-defeating in terms of non-renewable resources. The technology of production by the masses is conducive to decentralization compatible with the laws of ecology. The non-violent world order that Gandhi envisioned would ensure the widest possible dispersal of means of employment and job.[6]

Twentieth century is undoubtedly a century of unprecedented economy growth. The optimum production was the key to peace and prosperity. Nature become commodity and society is only of the human beings. It is our primary duty to sublimate nature with the help of science and technology so that she does not lose her capacity to sustain all life on the earth. The basic needs of all beings should be fulfilled from their surroundings with least efforts. The present system, which relies more and more upon the use of non-renewable resources like metals and minerals, cannot survive because the supplies of these are limited. The ancient cultures survived, because they sustained on renewable resources. Edward Goldsmith, on the basis of his study conducted for 32 years, has reached the conclusion, when he says, "Inspiration must come from the world-view of vernacular societies, in particular the Chatholic world-view of the earliest period when people everywhere lived in harmony with the natural world."[7]

Modern life has become so complex and complicated that we cannot do without certain things. So the next step should be to find out the Alternatives. The real development will take the society from *Vikriti* (perversion) to *Sanskriti* (culture). It is not going back, but going in the right direction. Equity and justice are the *sin qua non* of sustainable development. It is four dimensional : (1) Equity among nations—rich nations, poor nations, developed nations, developing nations; (2) Equity with countries between regions, social classes, genders, sectors of activities; (3) Equity between generations; and (4) Equity between economics and ecology and science and spirituality.[8]

Sustainable development demands a change in our attitude towards nature. There is an urgent need, to move away from the Cartesian world-view and post ourselves in the ecological world—view. The idea is not to go back to the past, but to create a new future out of the present, the present as it is. The past can help in the shaping of the new future.

The present crisis is consequence of follies, of greed, exploitation and domination. Therefore present exigency demands that one acquires the basic wisdom of nature, that is to follow its laws and learn to manage according to its principles. Therefore, the present developmental crisis demands a different world-view that is give up the present lifestyle and reduction in consumerism. Gandhiji's choice was clear. He was for the poorest of the poor. In fact his advice to everyone was that, before embarking on any project or programme, he or she must use a simple talisman–recall the face of the poorest and weakest man you may have seen and ask yourself if the step you contemplate to take is going to be of any use to him. Will be gain anything by it ? Even in this present era of globalization this has to be the acid-test of all development.

Gandhi opposed the orthrodoxical traditions of Hinduism based on untouchability, superstitions, worship of stock and stones and animal sacrifice. He was concerned about the degeneration of Indian civilization to an orthodox decadent traditionalism.

The intensity and form of conflicts vary from society to society and period to period. But one can make a proposition that the structural violence is increasing day by day. Society in this new millennium cannot hold the human groups in peace and harmony when structural violence is increasing. Today, both at National and international level, the situation is grim. At the national level, economic exploitation, social inequality, religions intolerant, caste-conflicts, inhuman treatment to the women, unscrupulous race for political power and linguistic fanaticism and chauvinism, are playing havoc with the lives of innocent people, compelling every one to live in the grip of insecurity and threatening the very integrity of the nation. At the international level the situation is not better. The threat of nuclear warfare is hanging like a Damocles sword. Near about 424 nuclear reactors are operating worldwide and more planed for future, which are neither safe nor friendly with environment. The principal factor behind these maladies have been the need of the poor, greed of the rich and careless application of technology in each and every field of economic activities. In this context Mahatma's ideas about the dangers of Western civilization have assumed significances.

The challenges of new millennium require total newness on all fronts. The holistic analysis, churning of knowledge, ruthless codification of lessons of past, total transparency, viability and replicability are some issues are for clear accelerated plan of action. As the time passes the need to look at Mahatma Gandhi from practical utility with reference to action becomes important.[9] What gamut of synergisation of truth, non-violence, simplicity, characteristics, mission and on the whole a personification of action.

Swadeshi will be the greatest tool for solving the economic problems of the new millennium. Swadeshi means self-reliance in every filled. In other words, Swadeshi is service and if we understand it, we will simultaneously benefit ourselves, our families, our country and the world. Gandhi delimited the modus operandi of Swadeshi in terms of limited wants and the capacity of social surroundings and resources to meet the need of the people. In his famous sentence he laid down his dictum: "Nature produces enough to meet the needs of all the people but not enough to satisfy the greed of anyone." Our motto should be simple living and high thinking so that we can stop the evils of the society. Infact, Swadeshi movement may become part of socio-economic movement in new millennium. Because it conveys the idea of returning to one's own country–to its culture and heritage, its own givens and tradition and screen the mud of the next door neighbour. This is the appropriate times for us to understand the concept of *Swadeshi* and implement it in every possible manner and we will be doing this progress by making ourselves self-reliant and self-suffocate in every field and we would be free from moral degradation, economic exploitation and political subjugation.

Satyagraha will be also an important means by which individuals and groups can have and immediate effect on government policy and programmes. Individuals and groups can organises the people and draw the attention of the Government and masses of issues of borrowings, exploitations, deteriorating law and order, pollution, poverty, malnutrition etc. to save society. At a personal level also lot of people can work. To operationalize the 'Satyagraha for better future', it would be desirable to bring like minded people under one umbrella to fight against injustice and wrong governmental policy which is creating social tensions and alienation.

If there is anything that can solve the contemporary problems is Gandhian path, along with the opportunities, which will emerge from modern science and technology. Our approach to development and economic growth must be harmonized with human value. Our aim should be to have worth living place and worth living life, which can be achieved through change of our lifestyle, and controlling our unlimited needs and grids. Gandhi's economy is called a bullock cart economy. Gandhi wanted that development to be centred on the village, manufacture to be labour intensive, economy to be self-reliant and organisations decentralized.The concept of the Village Republic which was self-sufficient with Panchayats excersising power was incorporated into the constitution in article 40 of the Directive Principles of State Policy.

We cannot erect the city of peace on the foundation of violence. If mankind is to live in peace and achieve progress in all spheres, it has to eschew violence and has to develop a way of life anchored in the philosophy of love and cooperation. We should be cautious to these who want to reach heaven by creating a hell on earth. It is high times for the individual to change the chemistry of thought and action by adopting Gandhian values in our daily life.[10] We have to start from somewhere to come to overcome the hurdle coming in the way of promoting world peace. People must translate his ideals into real life.

Today everyone is talking in terms of rural development. Gandhiji did not approve of the Western civilization, which is urban for the entire world. He said that "a big country with a teeming population with an ancient rural tradition which has hitherto answered its purpose, need not, must not copy the western model. What is good for one nation situated in one condition is not necessarily good enough for another differently situated". So he advocated a rural style of life and culture based on neighbourliness and sharing. This need to be analysed and implemented by the government.

Gandhi's picture of the India of his dreams can be realized if our government honestly implement few of the his philosophy of rural development which is on the following values and premises:

1. Real India is found not in its cities, but in its villages.
2. The revival of villages is possible only when the villagers are no more exploited. Exploitation of villagers by city dwellers was 'violence', in Gandhi's opinion.
3. Simple living and high thinking, employing voluntary reduction of materialistic wants, and pursuit of moral and spiritual principles of life.
4. Dignity of labour, everyone must earn his bread by physical labour and one who labours must necessarily get his subsistence.
5. Preference to the use of indigenous (*swadeshi*) products, services and institutions.
6. Balance between the needs and the means—Gandhiji believed that non-violence and truth could not be sustained unless a balance between the needs and the means was maintained.[11]

R.K. Patil tried to summarize how village development was envisaged by Gandhi in the last phase of his life. The cities and towns today are exploiting the countryside. The interests of the town and country and of industry and agriculture are divergent and cannot be reconciled. The only efficient, least expensive and surest way of ensuring a decent standard to the people at large in the immediate present in the system of economy recommended by

Gandhi. The salient features of this system may be summarized as follows:

> (i) intensive small scale, individual and diversified farming supported by a cooperative effort as opposed to mechanized, large-scale or collective farming; (ii) development of cottage industries as ancillary to agriculture; (iii) a cattle-based economy with strict enforcement of the "law of return"; (iv) a proper balance of animal, human and plant life; and (v) voluntary protection of both man and animal against the competition of machinery as the price of social insurance.[12]

## Summing up

Gandhi is unique in political history. He has invented an entirely new and humane technique for liberation struggle of an oppressed people and carried it out with greatest energy and devotion.Though Gandhi had left South Africa in 1914, his ideas of Passive Resistance continued to inspire the liberation struggle in South Africa.Fatima Mir her the work South African Gandhi emphasized that Gandhi's ideas would continue to inspire the challenges of Political integration and economic reconstuction in South Africa.[13]

Gandhi rejected meat eating and embraced Vegetarianism as the result of traditional obligation but as a reasoned contextual choice.[14]

Gandhian alternative are echoed everywhere directly or indirectly. It is high time for both our policy makers and the people, to turn the torch within so that they may be inspired to adopt the Gandhian way, if not for any other consideration, but for its pragmatic strength to solve our present day maladies of India as well as the whole world. There is need to reiterate Gandhian values, and instead of merely garlanding the portraits of Gandhiji, Indians must translate his ideals into real life and make India free from hunger, poverty and exploitation. Only than Indian can become the economic power and model for the other country. And at the same time the policy makers, politicians, intellectuals and scientists must remember in thought and action the Talisman of Mahatma Gandhi:

> I will give you a Talisman. Whenever you are
> In doubt, or when the self becomes too

much with you, apply the following test.
Recall the face of the poorest and the
Weakest man whom you may have seen,
and ask your-self, if the step you contemplate is
going to be of any use to him?
Will he gain anything by it?
Will it restore him to a control over his
own life and destiny?
In other words, will it lead to swaraj for the
Hungry and spiritually starving millions?
Then you will find your doubts and your self
Melting away.

## Notes

1. Anil Dutta Mishra and Sushma Yadav (Eds.), *Socio-Political Thoughts,* Vol.3, *Gandhian Alternative*, R.P. Misra and K.D. Gangrade (Eds), New Delhi, Concept, 2005, pp.v-vi.
2. *Ibid.,* p.v.
3. Anil Dutta Mishra, "The Gandhian Perspective on Rural Development", *Gandhi Marg,* Vol.24, No.4, p. 466.
4. *Harijan*, 28-7-1946.
5. Anil Dutta Mishra (Ed), *Gandhian Approach to Contemporary Problems*, New Delhi, Mittal Publications, 1996, p. 196.
6. Radha Krishnan, "From Gandhi to Schumacher the Stream of Nonviolent Economics" *Kuruskhetra*, October 1994, p.11.
7. Anil Dutta Mishra, "Environmental Ethics-A Dialoque of Culture" in Anil Dutta Mishra and Govind Prasad (Eds), *India and Canada: Past, Present and Future*, New Delhi, Mittal Publications, 2003, p.209.
8. *Ibid.*, p.10.
9. Anil Dutta Mishra, *Challenges of 21st Century*, New Delhi, Mittal, 2003, p. viii.
10. *Ibid.*
11. Kartar Singh, *Rural Development : Principles, Policies, and Management,* New Delhi, Sage, 1999, pp. 85-86.
12. Anil Dutta Mishra, *The Gandhian Perspective on Rural Development*, *op.cit.*, pp.471-72.
13. B.R. Nanda, "Tarring the Mahatma", *Hindustan Times*, November 22.
14. Looyd I. Rudolph and Susanne H. Rudolph, "*Post modern Gandhi and other essays*", "*Gandhi in the world and at home*". Oxford Publishers, 2006, P-10.

# Bibliography

*– Sunita Gulati*

Agarwal, Shriman Narayan, *Gandhian Constitution for Free India,* Allahabad, Kitabistan, 1946.

Alexander, Horace, *Gandhi Through Western Eyes,* Bombay: Asia Publishing House, 1969.

Andrews, C.F., *Mahatma Gandhi's Ideas*, London: George Allen & Unwin Ltd., 1949.

Anjaria, J.J., *An Essay on Gandhian Economics,* Vora and Co., Bombay, 1944.

Appadorai, A., *Documents on Political Thought in Modern India,* Vol. 1, Oxford University Press, New Delhi, 1981.

Ashe, Geoffrey, Gandhi: *A Study in Revolution,* Bombay: Asia Publishing House, 1968.

Bandyopadhyaya, J., *Social and Political Thought of Gandhi,* Allied Publishers, Calcutta, 1969.

Bhattacharyya, Buddhadeva, *Evolution of Political Thought of Gandhi*, Calcutta: Calcutta Book House, 1969.

Birla, G.D., *In the Shadow of the Mahatma*, Bombay: Orient Longmans Ltd., 1953.

Biswas, S.C. (Ed.), *Gandhi : Theory and Practise Social Impact and Contemporary Relwance,* Indian Institute of Advance Study, Shimla, 1969.

Bondurant, Joan, *Conquest of Violence : The Gandhian Philosophy of Conflict,* Bombay, Oxford University Press, 1959.

Bose, Anima, *Dimensions of Peace and Non-violence : The Gandhian Perspective,* Crian Publishing House, New Delhi, 1987.

Bose, N.K., *Studies in Gandhism*, Ahmedabad, Navajivan Publishing House, 1962.

Bose, N.K., *Gandhiji the Man and His Mission*, Bharatiya Vidya Bhawan, Bombay, 1966.

Bose, N.K., *Selections from Gandhi,* Navajivan Publishing House, Ahmedabad, 1972.

Brown, Judith M., *Gandhi and Civil-Disobedience,* London: Cambridge University Press, 1977.

Brown, Judith M., *Gandhi's Rise to Power, Indian Politics,* 1915-22, London: Cambridge University Press, 1972.

Brown, M. Judith, *Gandhi Prisoner of Hope,* Oxford University Press, Delhi, 1992.

Chakrabarty, Bidyut, *Social and Political Thought of Mahatma Gandhi*, London, Routledge, 2006.

Chatterjee, Partha, *Nationalist Thought and the Colonial World,* Oxford University Press, New Delhi, 1986.

Chopra, Pran, *The Sage in Rivolt : A Remembrance*, Gandhi Peace Foundation, New Delhi, 1972.

Choudhuri, Manmohan, *Exploring Gandhi,* Gandhi Peace Foundation, New Delhi, 1987.

Datta, D.M., *The Philosophy of Mahatma Gandhi*, Madison: University of Wisconsin Press, 1953.

Dhawan, Gopi Nath, *The Political Philosophy of Mahatma Gandhi*, Ahmedabad : Navajivan Publishing House, 1962.

Diwakar, R.R., *Saga of Satyagraha*, Gandhi Peace Foundation, New Delhi, 1969.

Doke, J.J., *M.K. Gandhi An Indian Patriot,* Madras: Natesan, 1909.

Erikson, Erik H., *Gandhi's Truth : On the Origins of Militant Non-violence,* Faber and Faber Limited, London, 1970.

Fischer, Louis, *The Essential Gandhi,* George Allen and Union Limited, London, 1962.

Gandhi, M.K., *An Autobiography or the Story of My Experiments With Truth,* Navajivan Publishing House, Ahmedabad, 1988.

Gandhi, M.K., *Hind Swaraj or Indian Home Rule,* Navajivan Publishing House, Ahmedabad, 1975.

Gandhi, M.K., *Satyagraha in South Africa,* Ahmedabad,

Navajivan, Publishing House, 1975.

Gangal, S.C., *Gandhian Thought and Techniques in the Modern World,* Criterion Publications, New Delhi, 1988.

Gangrade, K.D. and Misra R.P., *Conflict Resolution Through Non-violence Role of the Universities*, Concept Publishing Company, New Delhi, 1990.

Ganguli, B.N., *Gandhi's Social Philosophy; Perspective and Relevance,* Delhi: Vikas Publishing House Pvt. Ltd., 1973.

George, S.K. and Ramchandran, G., *The Economics of Peace : The Cause and the Man,* Peace Publishers, New Delhi, 1992.

Gregg, Richard B., *The Power of Non-Violence,* Ahmedabad, Navajivan Publishing House, 1960.

Hardiman, David, *Gandhi in His Time and Ours,* New Delhi, Permanent Black, 2003.

Holmes, J.H.; Bridge, P.C. and James, F.E., *Mahatma Gandhi, World Significance*, Calcutta : C.C. Basik, The Research Home.

Hunter, Doris A. and Mallick Krishna, *Non-violence : A Reader in the Ethics of Action,* Gandhi Peace Foundation, New Delhi, 1990.

Huttenback, Robert A., *Gandhi in South Africa : British Imperialism and the Indian Question, 1860-1914*, Cornell University Press, London, 1971.

Huxley, A., *Ends and Means,* London, Kegan Paul, 1937.

Iyer, Raghavan, *The Moral and Political Thought of Mahatma Gandhi,* Oxford University Press, Chicago, 1973.

Jack, A. Homer (Ed.), *The Gandhi Reader,* Samata Books, Madras, 1984.

Kalelkar, Kaka, *Stray Glimpses of Bapu,* Ahmedabad: Navajivan Publishing House, 1957.

Karunakaran, K.P., *Gandhi-Interpretations,* Gitanjali Publishing House, New Delhi, 1985.

Keer, Dhananjay, *Mahatma Gandhi Political Saint and Unarmed Prophet,* Popular Prakashan, Bombay, 1973.

Khan, Afaque, *Gandhian Approach to Communalism : A Critical*

*Study,* Ajanta Publications, Delhi, 1986.

Kripalani, J.B., *Gandhi: His Life and Thought,* New Delhi, Publications Division, Ministry of Information and Broadcasting, Government of India, 1968.

Lohia, Rammanohar, *Marx, Gandhi and Socialism,* Rammanohar Lohia Samata Vidylaya Nyasa, Hyderabad, 1978.

Mishra, A.D. (Ed.), *Perspectives on Human Rights*, New Delhi, Radha Publications, 2002.

Mishra, Anil Dutta (Ed.), *Gandhian Approach to Contemporary Problems*, Mittal Publications, New Delhi, 1996.

Mishra, Anil Dutta and M.S. Dadage, *Panchayati Raj: Gandhian Perspective,* Mittal Publications, New Delhi, 2000.

Mishra, Anil Dutta, *Challenges* of *21st Century and Gandhian Alternative,* Mittal Publications, New Delhi, 2003.

Mishra, Anil Dutta, *Fundamentals of Gandhism,* Mittal Publications, New Delhi, 1995.

Mishra, Anil Dutta, *Rediscovering Gandhi,* Mittal Publications, New Delhi, 2002.

Mishra, Anil Dutta, *Gandhian Approach to Contemporary Problems*, Mittal Publications, New Delhi, 1996.

Mishra, Anil Dutta, *Gandhism After Gandhi*, Mittal Publications, New Delhi, 1999.

Mishra, R.P., *Gandhian Model of Development and World Peace,* Concept Publishing Company, New Delhi, 1988.

Mishra, Sweta, *Democratic Decentralisation in India,* Mittal Publications, New Delhi, 1994.

Misra, K.P. and Gangal, S.C., *Gandhi and the Contemporary World : Studies in Peace and War*, Chanakya Publications, Delhi, 1981.

Mukerjee, Hiren, *Gandhi: A Study,* New Delhi: People's Publishing House, 1960.

Mukherjee, Subrata and Ramaswamy, Sushila, *Facets of Mahatma Gandhi,* Deep and Deep Publications, New Delhi, 1994.

Namboodiripad, E.M.S., *The Mahatma and the Ism*, New Delhi: People Publishing House, 1959.

Nanda, B.R., *Gandhi Pan-Islamism Imperialism and Nationalism*, Oxford University Press, Bombay, 1989.

Nanda, B.R., *Mahatma Gandhi: A Biography*, London: George Allen and Unwin Ltd., 1959.

Narain, Jai, *Economic Thought of Mahatma Gandhi*, Sehgal, New Delhi, 1991.

Narayan, Shriman, *Selected Works of Mahatma Gandhi*, Navajivan Publishing House, Ahmedabad, 1956.

Nehru, Jawahar Lal, *Mahatma Gandhi*, Calcutta: Signet Press, 1949.

Ostergaord Geoffrey, *Non-violent Revolution in India*, Gandhi Peace Foundation, New Delhi, 1985.

Parekh, Bhikhu, *Colonialism, Tradition and Reform : An Analysis of Gandhi's Political Discourse*, Sage Publications, New Delhi, 1989.

Parel, Anthony J., *Hind Swaraj and other Writings*, Cambridge, Cambridge University Press,1997.

Parel, Anthony J., *Gandhi, Freedom, and Self-Rule*, New Delhi, Vistaar Publications,2000.

Polak, H.S.C., H.N. Brailsford and Lord Pethick, Lawrence, *Mahatma Gandhi*, London, Odham Press Limited, 1949.

Prabhu, R.K., and Rao, U.R., *The Mind of Mahatma*, Ahmedabad: Navajivan Publishing House, 1967.

Prasad, Nageshwar, *Hind Swaraj : A Fresh Look*, Gandhi Peace Foundation, New Delhi, 1985.

Pyare Lal, *Mahatma Gandhi: The Early Phase*, Volume 1, Ahmedabad: Navajivan Publishing House, 1965.

Pyare Lal, *Mahatma Gandhi: The Last Phase, in* 2 volumes, Ahmedabad: Navajivan Publishing House, 1956, 1958.

Pyarelal and Nayar Sushila, *In Gandhiji's Mirror*, Oxford University Press, Delhi, 1991.

Pyarelal, *Mahatma Gandhi, The Last Phase*, Ahmedabad, Navajivan Publishing House, 1958.

Radhakrishnan, S. (Ed.), *Mahatma Gandhi: Essays and Reflections on His Life and Thought*, Allahabad: Kitabistan, 1944.

Radhakrishnan, S. (Ed.), *Mahatma Gandhi 100 Years,* Gandhi Peace Foundation, New Delhi, 1968.

Rajendra Prashad, *At the Feet of Mahatma Gandhi,* Bombay: Asia Publishing House, 1961.

Rao, U.R., *The Way to Communal Harmony,* Ahmedabad, Navajivan Publishing House, 1963.

Rao, U.S. Mohan (Ed.), *The Message of Mahatma Gandhi,* Publication Division, Ministry of Information and Broadcasting, Govt. of India, New Delhi, 1968.

Rolland, Romain, *Mahatma Gandhi, The Man Who Became One with the Universal Being* (Translated by Catherine D. Groth), Agra: Shiva Lal Aggarwala & Co. Ltd.

Roy, Ramashray, *Contemporary Crisis and Gandhi,* Discovery Publishing House, Delhi, 1986.

Roy, Ramashray, *Gandhi : Soundings in Political Philosophy,* Chanakya Publications, Delhi, 1984.

Sethi, J.D., *Gandhi Today,* New Delhi: Vikas Publishing House Pvt. Ltd., 1978.

*Sharma Jai Narain,* Alternative Economics, New Delhi, Deep and Deep, 2003.

Sharp, Gene, *Gandhi Wields the Weapon of Moral Power Three Case Histories*, Ahmedabad: Navajivan Publishing House, 1960.

Sharp, Gene, *The Politics of Non- Violent Action: Power and Struggle, Part 1,* Boston: Porter Sarget Publishers, 1973.

Sheean Vincent, *Mahatma Gandhi : A Great Life in Brief,* Publication Division, New Delhi, 1990.

Shukla, Chandrashanker, *Reminiscences of Gandhiji,* Bombay, Vora and Company, 1951.

Sitaramayya, Pattabhi, *Gandhi and Gandhism.* Allahabad: Kitabistan, 1942, in 2 volumes.

Tendulkar, D.G, *Mahatma,* New Delhi, Publications Division, Ministry of Information and Broadcasting, Government of India, 1952.

*The Collected Works of Mahatma Gandhi*, New Delhi, Publications Division, Ministry of Information and Broadcasting, Government of India, 1965, (Vols. 1-100).

Verma, V.P., *The Political Philosophy of Mahatma Gandhi and Sarvodaya,* Agra: Lakshmi Narain Aggarwal, 1981.

Vinobha, Bhave, *Swaraj Sastra,* Sarva Seva Sangh Prakashan, Varanasi, 1963.

Watson, Francis and Tennyson Hallam, *Talking of Gandhi,* Sangam Books, Bombay, 1957.

Weber, Thomas, *Conflict Resolution and Gandhian Ethics,* The Gandhi Peace Foundation, New Delhi, 1991.

# INDEX